BLOOD FEUD

Also by Lisa Alther:

Nonfiction

Kinfolks: Falling Off the Family Tree—the Search for
My Melungeon Ancestors

Fiction

Kinflicks

Original Sins

Other Women

Bedrock

Birdman and the Dancer

Five Minutes in Heaven

Washed in the Blood

BLOOD FEUD

THE HATFIELDS AND THE McCOYS:
THE EPIC STORY OF MURDER AND VENGEANCE

LISA ALTHER

LYONS PRESS
Guilford, Connecticut
An imprint of Globe Pequot Press

Lyons Press is an imprint of Globe Pequot Press.

Family trees designed by Sally Neale
Maps by Melissa Baker © Morris Book Publishing, LLC
Text design: Sheryl P. Kober
Project editor: Meredith Dias
Layout: Justin Marciano

Library of Congress Cataloging-in-Publication Data is available on file.

ISBN 978-0-7627-7918-5

Printed in the United States of America

10 9 8 7 6 5 4 3

For Ava, who inspired this project and enriches my life

The world is a stage, but the play is badly cast.

—O<small>SCAR</small> W<small>ILDE</small>

See inside the book jacket for a family tree of the Hatfields and McCoys.

❧ CONTENTS ❧

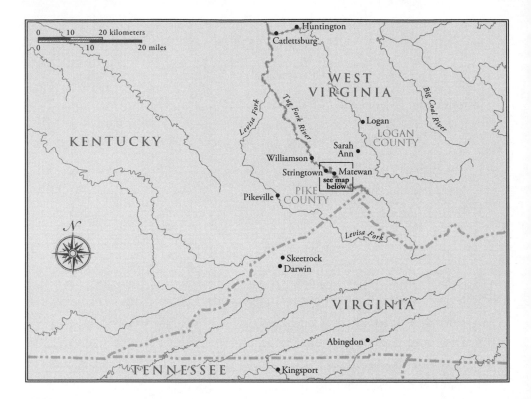

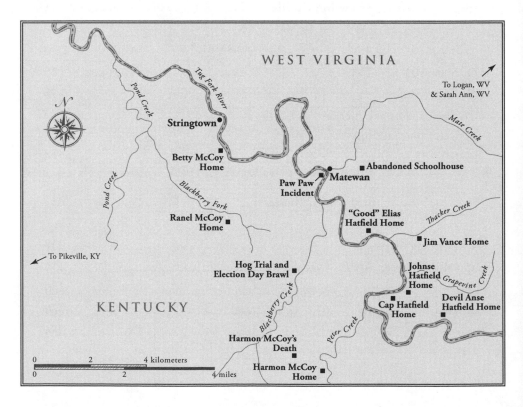

⊰⊱ INTRODUCTION ⊰⊱
Murderland

I DON'T KNOW WHEN I FIRST HEARD ABOUT THE HATFIELD-MCCOY feud; I can't recall ever not knowing about it. Nor can I remember ever being unaware of the stereotype of the hillbilly that the feud spawned: the dullard with bib overalls, messy beard, slouch hat, and bare feet, rifle in one hand and jug of moonshine in the other. This character appeared in the cartoon strips *Snuffy Smith* and *L'il Abner,* at which I chuckled every Sunday in the funny pages in my East Tennessee hometown of Kingsport. Later, once my family owned a television set, this same caricatured creature showed up on *Hee Haw, The Beverly Hillbillies, The Real McCoys,* and *Petticoat Junction.*

The Waltons and *The Andy Griffith Show* provided more sympathetic variations on the theme, portraying Southern mountain people as merely innocent and backward, rather than as stupid, lazy, drunk, and venal—or, as one feud reporter described them: "dull as death when sober and . . . when drunk . . . simply quarrelsome and murderous."[1]

Although we lived in a river valley in the heart of the southern Appalachians, my family, friends, and I didn't think of ourselves as hillbillies. We, too, mocked the panting and the gospel music of the evangelical preachers on the radio. We worked hard to erase our accents and the dialect common to Appalachian people. We ridiculed the grammar "mistakes" (that I have since come to value as remnants of ancient speech patterns). L'il Abner, Snuffy Smith, John Boy, and Jed Clampett weren't us. We were sophisticated, clean, well-dressed, intelligent, peace-loving, polite folks, more like Scarlett O'Hara and Ashley Wilkes than Daisy Mae Yokum and Jethro Bodine.

Hillbillies were the farmers who gathered downtown by the train station on Saturday mornings. They came into town in battered trucks, dressed in suit jackets, overalls, and starched white shirts. They chatted and spat tobacco juice on the sidewalk while their wives and children window-shopped at Woolworth's Five and Dime. Hillbillies inhabited the shacks my family passed when we drove to our farm in the hills outside town on weekends. Hillbillies had chickens on their front porches, petunias growing in bald tires in their front yards, colored glass bottles stuck on the branches of their trees, and fighting cocks chained to blue plastic cages. Their children rolled naked in the dirt, while their menfolk, in tattered T-shirts, tinkered with the carcasses of junked cars.

But when I went to college in Massachusetts during the civil rights years and watched the racial convulsions of the Deep South, I began to realize that the mountain South differed somewhat from the plantation South. There had been slavery in the Southern mountains, but the terrain had been too rough for plantations, so those who had slaves had very few. When I was growing up, only about 7 percent of our town was black.[2]

I began to suspect that I was not a fugitive from Tara after all—I was a hillbilly. This harsh truth had been concealed from me because, according to the stereotypes in circulation, hillbillies were supposed to be quaint and impoverished rural folks. But our town was a booming industrial center where most citizens made living wages, and some did much better than that.

My grandfather and father were physicians, and my grandparents belonged to the local professional set that had sought, welcomed, and befriended industrial entrepreneurs from the North when the town was founded early in the twentieth century. Colonel Palmer from New Hampshire, who ran the Kingsport Press, lived just down the street from us, and his wife played bridge with my grandmother. So did the wife of Max Parker from Boston, who ran a textile mill. John B. Dennis, the Columbia graduate from Maine who had incorporated the town, lived just across the river from my grandparents in a mansion that had survived the Civil War. These Yankees lived large in Kingsport, like the British in India under the Raj, and my grandparents had tried to copy their example.

One summer afternoon in 2007, I attended a reunion of my father's family, the Reeds, held at a Dunkard church in Kentucky some ten miles, as the crow flies, from the Tug Fork Valley, where the Hatfield-McCoy feud took place.* After running away from his sister's farm in Virginia following the deaths of his parents when he was a boy, my grandfather Reed lived first with his older brother, Madison, on Johns Creek, just over a ridge from the Tug Fork, which separates Kentucky from West Virginia. Then he moved to his brother Robert's house, not far from this Dunkard church.

The matriarch of the Reed clan, who has organized our reunion for many years, is Ava Reed McCoy. She is the youngest daughter of my grandfather's brother Robert, a carpenter and a Dunkard preacher. "Dunkard" is a nickname for the Church of the Brethren, originally a German sect that based its beliefs and practices on the New Testament and especially on the Sermon on the Mount. One of the three historic "peace churches," along with Quakers and Mennonites, Dunkards traditionally embrace simplicity, humility, and pacifism.

Ava is a tall, slender, handsome woman with silver hair and high cheekbones. Her father was said to have been seven feet tall, as was her uncle Madison. At just six feet four inches, my father and grandfather were the family shrimps. Ava also has the same distinctive long earlobes as my father and grandfather. My father and Ava, who hadn't known each other as children, became close friends in their later years. Each could talk to the other about long-dead relatives whom no one else still alive knew anything about.

Ava was a McCoy by marriage, but I didn't give it much thought. A couple of years after the reunion, when I was visiting her in her neat, cozy house in Huntington, West Virginia, she asked me, "Did you know that my husband, Homer, was one of the Fighting McCoys?" I said no, and she proceeded to tell me what had been passed down to her from her husband and her family members who were alive at the time of the feud. She said

....

* "As the crow flies" is an important distinction when discussing the Appalachians. The distance required to get somewhere via a road may be two or three times longer than that a crow would fly because the roads twist and meander endlessly in order to cross or to avoid the steep mountainsides.

that everyone she knew talked about the feud all the time, whereas other McCoy descendants to whom I spoke while writing this book said that no one in their households would ever utter a word about it.

Ava spoke of the fear she used to feel while visiting friends on the West Virginia side of the Tug Fork when she heard a band of drunken men gallop by outside at night, shooting their guns into the air. She wasn't born until twenty-five years after the feud ended, but she speculated that she might have absorbed that fear from her elders, who had lived through an era when thundering hoofbeats outside could spell death and disaster.

Ava said that her husband, Homer, wasn't closely related to Randolph "Ranel" McCoy, the feud leader of the McCoy clan. But a look at their family tree revealed that Homer's grandfather, William, was a first cousin to Ranel and a brother of Ranel's wife, Sarah. Neither William's name nor that of his son Johnson, Homer's father, appears in the extensive feud literature. They, like several other McCoy families, left the feud region to escape the hostilities, moving to Catlettsburg, Kentucky, and returning only after the feud had ended. Just to further confuse family loyalties, one of Johnson's sisters married a Hatfield. It was startling to find such a close connection to the feud right within my own family, and it turned out to be the first of several that I later discovered.

I had always regarded the Hatfield-McCoy feud with derision, at what I saw as the drunken antics of dim-witted psychopaths fighting over the ownership of a hog. But as I researched the topic, it soon became clear not only that I myself have more than one dog in this unfortunate fight but also that derision is hardly an appropriate response to a tragedy with such far-reaching consequences.

The Hatfield-McCoy feud took place during the last decades of the nineteenth century along the Tug Fork, which forms the boundary between Kentucky and West Virginia. A newspaper reporter, writing during the feud, christened this region Murderland.[3]

Depending upon which episodes you consider feud related, somewhere between one dozen and two dozen people died. Of course, even one death is too many, but a dozen and a half is not a high casualty rate when compared to the number of victims in other Kentucky feuds during that era. However, these dozen and a half deaths had far-reaching ramifications both for the region and for the nation as a whole.

Attempts to extradite the Hatfields from West Virginia to stand trial in Kentucky for some of these deaths resulted in a US Supreme Court case. Several Hatfield supporters went to prison. An uncle and a younger brother of William Anderson "Devil Anse" Hatfield, the Hatfield feud leader, were killed. His older brother died in prison, and his nephew was hanged. Seven children of Ranel McCoy died as a result of the feud. Ranel's wife, Sarah, was handicapped by a severe beating. Ranel also lost a younger brother, a cousin, and a nephew to the violence.

Many more members of both families suffered emotional scars for life, and the newspaper-hyped stereotypes inspired by the feud have scarred the generations of Appalachian people born after it ended, contributing to the so-called Appalachian Brain Drain, during which any resident who could figure out how to leave the region did so. A reporter who came to the Tug Fork during the feud years uncharitably described the population who didn't flee as "strange, half-civilized natives who live in the blood-stained wilderness."[4]

After the feud ended, railroad, timber, and coal corporations moved into the region to exploit the natural resources and the labor of its remaining inhabitants under the guise of bringing Progress to this race of feuding "white savages."[5] These corporations left in their wake poverty, maimed and diseased workers, and poisoned moonscapes where once towering forests and clear-running, fish-filled streams had thrived.

It is important, therefore, to see the Hatfield-McCoy feud as it really was and to understand why and how relatives, neighbors, and friends who had lived together in peace for half a century could end up wanting to kill one another—and then did so. We have seen this tragic pattern play out repeatedly through human history, most recently in Bosnia, Rwanda, and Sudan. Perhaps the microcosm offered by the Hatfield-McCoy feud can provide some fresh insights.

Not surprisingly, existing accounts of the Hatfield-McCoy feud each reflect the bias or agenda of the teller. Most participants were illiterate and signed official documents with *X*'s. None left a written eyewitness testimony to what actually happened. Quotes taken from them for newspaper articles were often inaccurate or self-serving. Many official documents that could have provided information were destroyed or were never executed during the chaos of the Civil War and Reconstruction. The courthouse at Logan, West Virginia, the county in which the Hatfield feudists lived, was burned during the Civil War, and one researcher calls the courthouse records from the 1880s "abysmal."[6]

So like all oral histories, the various versions of the Hatfield-McCoy feud have been embellished, pruned, and honed, like rocks roiled to smoothness in a creek bed, by generations of tellers, some creating myths, others righting wrongs, most trying to explain or justify the bad behavior of their ancestors or relatives. Chronologies are scrambled. Hearsay appears as evidence, anecdotes as facts. Motives that may never have occurred to participants are sometimes provided for their atrocious acts.

Both the Hatfields and the McCoys have their own official compilations of feud stories as told by family members who were alive at the time. In 1976, the Preservation Council Press of Pike County, Kentucky, published Truda McCoy's *The McCoys: Their Story as Told to the Author by Eye Witnesses and Descendants*. A teacher and poet, she wrote an account that reads like a novel—and is probably about as reliable as one. Often, people who experienced the feud years firsthand wouldn't talk about them to outsiders because they were embarrassed to have had relatives who behaved so badly and because they were afraid that any negative comments might trigger a renewal of the hostilities. But Truda, a McCoy by birth, married one of her distant cousins, a grandson of Ranel McCoy, which gave her privileged access to many McCoys, especially her mother-in-law, Martha, the wife of Ranel's son Sam, himself a feudist. Martha McCoy lived through the feud years with Sam, and she was very close to Ranel's wife, Sarah, and their daughter Roseanna. Both Sarah and Roseanna suffered greatly from feud-related events.

The Hatfield family historian was Coleman A. Hatfield, a West Virginia attorney who recorded much information about the feud in journals and on tape. His primary sources included his grandfather Devil Anse Hatfield and his father, William Anderson "Cap" Hatfield, who was Devil Anse's second son and most trusted deputy during the feud years. Coleman A. Hatfield's son Dr. Coleman C. Hatfield, an optometrist, shaped his father's information and interviews of his own into *The Tale of the Devil: The Biography of Devil Anse Hatfield* with the help of historian and journalist Robert Y. Spence. The Hatfield book reads like a rather dry legal brief when compared to Truda McCoy's more florid prose. At the points where the two versions diverge—and of course there are many—reality probably lies somewhere near the crossroads.

The most concise and coherent secondary source about the feud is Otis K. Rice's *The Hatfields and the McCoys*. Altina Waller's *Feud: Hatfields, McCoys, and Social Change in Appalachia, 1860–1900* is the most thorough and well documented. A history professor, Waller was teaching at West Virginia University when she researched and wrote her book. Coleman C. Hatfield had written, "I honestly believe . . . that the history of this feud has been told for the last two generations in a light more favorable to the McCoy family of Pike County, Kentucky, than to the Hatfields of Southern West Virginia."[7] Waller's book corrects this imbalance and also constructs a plausible chronology from all the confusing and conflicting oral histories and prior books on the subject.

My version of the feud derives from these sources and others. It may be that some anecdotes I deemed implausible and excluded actually happened; it may be that some I did include didn't happen. In the end, it comes down to the judgment of each person who tries to write about this confusing and often upsetting saga.

My goal in writing this book has been to learn what actually happened during the most famous feud in American history, insofar as that is possible, rather than to assign blame at this late date. There is no one overriding Truth about this bloody tragedy, just many private individual truths as experienced by each participant and observer. These personal truths agree sometimes and contradict at others—exactly like the accounts of every other episode in human history.

PART 1:

ORIGINS

1

THE PATH TO PIKEVILLE

HE LAY IN A FOREST CAVE, SHIVERING WITH FEVER AND COUGHING IN THE smoke from the smoldering fire. Snowflakes drifted down the mouth of the cave that overlooked his Peter Creek farm in Pike County, Kentucky. His leg ached at the site of its poorly healed break, but at least he had made it home from Catlettsburg in time for New Year's.

It was January 9, 1865, night would soon fall, and Harmon McCoy's mouth was parched. His water jug lay empty, but he felt too weak to drag himself to the cave's edge to collect some snow. The sweat dampening his black hair made it even curlier than usual. His wife, Patty, loved his curls, but he always tried to slick them down. She also liked him clean shaven, which made him just about the only man he knew who didn't have a beard or at least a mustache. Those curls and bare cheeks made him look younger than his thirty-seven years. So to command respect when serving with his Union regiment, the 45th Kentucky Mounted Infantry, he had let his beard grow out.[1] He would be with his regiment still but for his leg.

When Harmon had mentioned returning to the cabin so that Patty could tend to him, Pete, his former slave, had urged him to stay hidden in the cave. Pete had promised to bring Patty here, leaving his wife, Chloe, with the children. But Harmon could no longer bear the thought of Patty's struggling through the snow in her condition. Their baby was due in a few weeks. He needed to go to her instead.

Harmon shoved his sack of rifle shells into a saddlebag and struggled to his feet. Hanging his saddlebags over one shoulder, he wrapped his wool army blanket around himself like a shawl. Then he grabbed his rifle and lurched across the dirt floor to the mouth of the cave.

Down below he could just pick out his log cabin alongside the silver thread of Peter Creek. Smoke was drifting up from the chimney into the glowering sky. It would be warm inside. Patty would put him to bed and cover him with quilts and bring him water from the well. The tussling of his four rowdy boys would cheer him up. Pete's footprints in the snow far below led from the cabin across the silent pasture to the woods—like stitching on a muslin quilt backing.

Leaning on his rifle, Harmon squatted outside the cave to scoop up a handful of snow. Pete's boots had packed the snow around the cave's entrance. He and Patty were lucky to still have Pete and Chloe to help with the crops and the animals, the housework and the children, especially while Harmon was fighting with his regiment. When Lincoln had emancipated the slaves—over a year ago now—many headed north to escape the wrath of their owners, who had supported the Union in the belief that they would be allowed to keep the slaves they already had, or would at least be compensated for their loss. But Pete and Chloe had wanted to stay even after Harmon told them they were free to leave. They had asked him where he thought they could go instead, as old as they were.

Harmon nibbled the snow, letting it melt in his mouth and soothe his raw throat. By going back home, was he putting Patty and the children at risk—both from this lung disease and also from the Logan Wildcats? On the path to Pikeville, the day after he had arrived home, he ran into "Bad Jim" Vance, tall, muscular, still mean as a snake, and with that droopy black mustache. Vance had a condition that made his eyes bulge and roll. He couldn't focus on you when he talked, but to think he wasn't paying attention was a mistake: He could draw his pistol faster than a copperhead could strike. Jim wore a gold watch chain looped across his vest and a

Harmon McCoy, younger brother of family leader Ranel McCoy and father of four second-generation feudists, was killed by Bad Jim Vance in January 1865, thereby igniting the tensions that helped spark the feud. COURTESY OF WEST VIRGINIA STATE ARCHIVES

Posed for a photo prior to a hunting trip, left to right, Devil Anse Hatfield and Jim Vance. COURTESY OF WEST VIRGINIA STATE ARCHIVES

bowler hat. Harmon had eyed the bulge of Bad Jim's holster beneath his suit jacket and the rifle in its sheath attached to his saddle.[2]

Until his desertion last year, Bad Jim had ridden with Gen. Vincent Witcher's raiders, who had plagued Union supporters all over southeastern Kentucky and southwestern Virginia. They once made a wide sweep across the Tug Fork Valley, flying a black flag as they rode, seizing food and livestock, killing Unionists and burning down their houses and barns. Bad Jim had stolen horses for these raiders, several from his own cousin, some said.

Jim Vance had now become the most ruthless of the Logan Wildcats, a guerrilla group led by his sister Nancy Hatfield's son, Bad Jim's notorious nephew, "Devil Anse" Hatfield. The Wildcats, mostly Confederate deserters, hailed from the West Virginia side of the Tug Fork. Now that West Virginia had seceded from Virginia to rejoin the Union, the Wildcats set themselves the mission of defending Confederate farms and families from avenging Union troops. The Wildcats were furious that the Confederacy was about to lose this wretched war, and they especially hated Harmon for having fought for the Union—though he was far from the only man in the Tug Fork Valley to have done so.

But Devil Anse Hatfield had plenty of other reasons to hate Harmon McCoy. At the start of the war, Harmon had served as a Union Home Guard under "General Bill" France.[3] Devil Anse crossed the Tug Fork with two friends to watch the Home Guards drill. General France decided that they were spying for the Confederates and ordered Harmon to fight Devil Anse. Although Harmon lost the fight, he helped his fellow Home Guards chase Devil Anse and his friends back across the river to Virginia—still undivided then—by throwing rocks at them.[4]

Harmon, Pete, and General France later shot a friend of Devil Anse through the chest while stealing horses from him. Devil Anse tracked down General France and shot him down at dawn as he urinated off his porch. Forty of General France's troops crossed the Tug Fork to arrest Devil Anse for the murder. But Devil Anse's wife, Levicy, somehow sensed that they were coming and pushed Devil Anse out the back door to hide in the forest.[5] A rumor started that Harmon himself was planning to kill

Devil Anse for murdering General France. Though Harmon had denied it, the rumor continued to circulate.

In the meantime, during a skirmish, Harmon had taken a bullet that entered at his collarbone and exited between the ribs on the opposite side of his chest. He lay in bed for months, his wounds oozing pus, lucky to be alive. A passing Confederate cavalry unit searched his cabin and found him. They marched him, weak with fever, a hundred miles to a railhead in Virginia, where they put him in a cattle car and shipped him to a prison in Richmond. When he was released in a prisoner exchange several months later, his wounds still oozing, he returned to his bed in the Peter Creek cabin.[6]

After recovering, Harmon McCoy enlisted in the 45th Kentucky—partly to get out of the area. Devil Anse Hatfield had by now deserted from his Confederate battalion and come back home to head up the Logan Wildcats. Harmon had dared to hope that Devil Anse's fury toward him might have faded while Harmon was away serving in northern Kentucky. But on the road to Pikeville the other day, Bad Jim Vance, eyes rolling, had rested his hand on his rifle butt and warned Harmon that the Wildcats would soon come looking for him.

A few days later, as Harmon was drawing water from the well in his yard, a bullet from the woods zinged past him. He ran inside, stuffed supplies into his saddlebags, grabbed his rifle, and limped up the hill to this cave, where he had been hiding out for several days now.

Standing at the mouth of the cave, his thirst sated, Harmon started coughing. It was a dry hacking cough that didn't let him catch his breath. He was freezing. At least at home he would have a chance of getting well before having to deal with the Wildcats again. He had spent this entire war either sick or injured—first his infected gunshot wounds, then his fractured leg, now pneumonia. What next?

He started down the path toward home, dragging his aching leg. Below him he spotted two men among the bare branches of the winter trees, their features indistinct in the forest gloom. As he threw aside his blanket and raised his rifle, gunshots sounded up the hill, and an explosion bloomed inside his chest.

✟

When Patty learned from Pete how sick Harmon was, she rushed around the cabin packing two baskets with food, blankets, teas, and ointments. Donning her warmest clothes, she left the cabin with Pete. They followed Pete's tracks through the snow across the pasture, pausing often for Patty to rest and catch her breath since she was carrying a nearly full-term baby in her belly and the pack basket on her back. As they reached the wood line and began their ascent to the cave, they heard gunshots farther up the hill. Dropping their provisions, they scrambled up the steep trail as fast as Patty could manage.

They reached a junction at which new boot prints emerged from the woods to join Pete's tracks up the hill toward the cave. Pete pointed them out, suddenly afraid that they themselves were about to be ambushed by whoever had fired the shots. But they kept going, more anxious for Harmon's life than fearful for their own. That his tracks in the snow had likely led the Wildcats to Harmon's hideout made Pete feel sick.

Alongside the trail, just below the cave, they spotted a fallen oak tree. Across its trunk sprawled Harmon McCoy. The snow on the ground around him was stained scarlet. They rushed to him, and Pete turned him over. Harmon's jacket was soaked dark red. His eyes were wide open, his dark curly hair damp with sweat, his lips a bloodless blue. Patty closed his eyelids with her fingertips, bowing her head and closing her own eyes as despair swept over her.

They stood there in silence for a long time, trying to work out what to do next. Finally Pete plunged through the snow to an open area in which a neighboring farmer named Mounts had been cutting and skinning logs for an addition to his cabin. Pete found a large sheet of curled bark and dragged it over. He and Patty pulled Harmon's body off the oak trunk onto a blanket and wrapped him up in it. Then they rolled the blanketed bundle into the bark, laying Harmon's rifle and saddlebags alongside him. Pete went into the cave and emerged with a rope. He and Patty tied the bark casket shut and fashioned handles from loops of the rope. Slowly they pulled Harmon's bloody body back down the trail toward home.

Night was falling when they at last reached the foot of the forest. They picked up their abandoned pack baskets and strapped them on their backs. The Mounts cabin sat nearby. They were Confederate friends of Devil Anse Hatfield, but surely they would take pity on their newly widowed neighbor.

Patty knocked at the door. When Mounts answered, she explained the situation and asked if she and Pete could stay in their cabin overnight and head back home the next morning at first light. Mounts replied that she could sit by the fire, since she was obviously with child and frozen nearly to death, but Pete wasn't welcome. Patty asked if they could bring Harmon's body inside, safe from wolves, so that Pete could go home to sleep, returning in the morning to retrieve the body. Mounts refused.

Pete built a fire on the path, wrapped himself in a blanket, and kept watch over Harmon's body through the long, cold night, a mountain cat screaming in the forest, snow in the pasture sparkling in the moonlight.

The next morning Mounts relented and let Pete and Patty borrow his horse and sled to drag Harmon McCoy's body back home.[7]

2

DARK AND BLOODY GROUND

SEPARATING RANEL McCOY'S FARM IN KENTUCKY FROM DEVIL ANSE Hatfield's land in West Virginia, the Tug Fork flows into the Big Sandy River some 160 miles north of its source in the Cumberland mountains of southwestern West Virginia. The Big Sandy, in turn, joins the Ohio River. Calm and shallow for much of the year, the Tug Fork rises and rages in springtime, which allowed loggers in days gone by to ride bucking rafts of primeval timber to sawmills and lumber markets downriver.

But before the loggers came, this region of steep, heavily forested mountains, intersected by narrow creek-carved valleys, sheltered several hundred generations of Native Americans. The Paleo Indians, who arrived after the last ice age, hunted mammoths, mastodons, and buffalos in a landscape much more open than today. When overhunting and climate warming drove those large game animals to extinction around 6000 BC, the descendants of the nomadic hunters settled down in small villages to a life of hunting, fishing, and gathering, fashioning pottery and tools, and constructing ceremonial mounds.

For the next six thousand years or so, their villages and mounds grew larger, and they eventually added the cultivation of corn, beans, and squashes to their menu of subsistence activities. They also added jewelry to their personal adornment, petroglyphs to their spiritual rituals, and games to their leisure hours.[1]

In the seventeenth century, when European settlers first arrived on the Cumberland Plateau, in which the Tug Fork nestles, they found very few natives living there. As with every episode of human migration, there are several explanations: the difficulty of the terrain, the devastation of the Native population by diseases introduced to the Americas by European explorers and traders, and a deliberate vacating of what became West Virginia and Kentucky by the Iroquoian Five Nations to the north, who wanted control of the area in order to monopolize the fur trade with French outposts along the Mississippi and Ohio Rivers. But some tribes still had villages there—the Lenape and Shawnee, Mingo and Wyandotte—and the Cherokee to the south used the region as a hunting ground.[2]

Toponymist George R. Stewart maintained that the name Tug comes from the Cherokee word *tugulu,* referring to the forks of a stream.[3] An alternative explanation for the name Tug comes from a 1756 incident in which an army of Cherokees and Virginians tried to traverse the Tug Fork Valley from southwestern Virginia in order to attack Shawnee tribes along the Big Sandy and Ohio Rivers, intending to punish them for raids on Virginia settlements. The mountain trails were too scrambled and precipitous for horses, though, and the creeks too rock strewn and fast running to use as paths. When supplies ran out and hunting proved difficult, both men and horses grew exhausted and hungry, the soldiers threatening mutiny. They had managed to kill and eat two buffalos, hanging their hides in a tree. In desperation, they cut the hides into strips, called "tugs," and roasted and ate those as well. Then they disbanded and straggled back home to Virginia.[4]

The Cumberland Plateau opened to European settlement in the wake of the various treaties involved in the British defeat of the French in the French and Indian War and the American defeat of the British in the Revolutionary War. By 1783, what had been a trickle of intrepid settlers had increased to a steady stream, if not yet a flood. Disgruntled bands of displaced natives continued to attack the new forts and settlements, and the settlers formed independent militias to combat them. Dragging Canoe, a Cherokee chief trying to stave off this European invasion, is said to have warned the settlers that their new home was "a dark and bloody ground," referring to prior wars among Native tribes there.[5] His warning was prophetic.

Because of the hardships involved in occupying this wilderness—steep and densely forested mountains, Native raids, and the need to clear first-growth timber before crops could be planted on the scarce level ground—only the most determined or desperate left behind the more settled regions to the east. Those who accepted this challenge often had nothing to lose: former indentured servants, escaped or freed slaves, and criminals, all fleeing westward from the Virginia coast; retired soldiers with land grants on the frontiers; new immigrants in search of unoccupied farmland. Many of these people had faced extreme hardship in their previous lives and were fiercely protective of their independence.

Accidents, crop failures, storms, epidemics, attacks by natives and bandits, and all manner of other disasters could occur daily. In a largely lawless wilderness with few schools, churches, courts, or doctors, people were on their own. As with the natives before them, "justice" for these early settlers usually involved eye-for-an-eye retaliation. A man's reputation for violence was often what protected his family and animals from harm.[6] As one reporter during the feud years dryly put it, "It is a region which develops eccentricity of character and excessive independence of thought."[7]

These settlers lived in small log cabins just above the floors of the narrow but fertile coves that often flooded in springtime and during heavy rains. Their cabins generally had one or two rooms downstairs for cooking, eating, sitting, and sleeping around a stone hearth, with a sleeping loft upstairs. Sometimes a second such cabin joined the first by means of a roofed "dog trot." A mortar of orange clay chinked the spaces between the logs. The floors were either packed dirt or puncheons split from logs and stabilized with pegs. Roofs were clad with wooden shakes.[*]

....

[*] My family owns such a cabin in East Tennessee. It was built by a saddlemaker around 1820, the same period during which the earliest Hatfields and McCoys were settling the Tug Fork Valley. The sons of indentured Irish immigrants to Philadelphia, the saddlemaker and his brothers trekked down the Shenandoah Valley in search of farmland, which was in the process of being wrested from the Cherokee. Our cabin had a floor of packed clay, many layers of ancient newspapers on the walls for insulation, and an outhouse in the backyard. Downstairs were a bedroom and a sitting room with a large stone fireplace. A lean-to kitchen had been added off the sitting room, though originally cooking would have been done in the fireplace. The upstairs was an open sleeping loft. There were windows in only the front and back walls, both to conserve heat and to minimize entry points in the event of native attacks, making the cabin more defensible but very dark inside.

The fields of most Tug Fork farms extended up the steep hillsides. Cattle and hogs, marked with their owners' brands, ranged freely throughout the unfenced forests. Horses provided both labor for plowing and transportation along the steep mountain paths and streambeds. Farm families supplemented the yield from their crops and livestock by hunting wild game, fishing, and gathering nuts, berries, and wild plants. Venison, bear meat, and buffalo meat were important staples. Ginseng, dug in the forest, could be bartered at stores for manufactured goods, as could furs and hides. Farmers distilled corn and apples not needed for human or animal consumption into whiskey and brandy as cash crops for trade or sale, and for family meals and recreation.

Many farmers cut a few of the giant trees, often with diameters of six to eight feet, that grew on their hillsides—especially tulip poplar, red oak, and black walnut—and lashed them into rafts. They branded the cut trunk ends and raced them down the creeks during springtime floods to the timber markets along the Ohio River, guiding them with forty-foot rudders at the back and fifteen-foot oars on the front corners.[8]

Beautifully embossed with scenes of mountains, forests, deer, and town street scenes, the concrete floodwall at Matewan, West Virginia, runs for nearly half a mile along the riverbank. (One panel even portrays the Hatfields and the McCoys, facing one another across a stream.) The wall was built in response to thirty-six floods, some catastrophic, that devastated the town in the last half of the twentieth century.[9] Similar floods have ravaged the area throughout its history. The floodwall towers like a defensive wall around a medieval French village. Just looking at it conveys a sense of the force of the raging waters that carried those rafts of lumber downstream to the sawmills 150 miles away—and a sense of the dangers faced by those riding and steering the rafts, like crickets perched on autumn leaves being swept along by a torrent.

Children provided the labor for these home industries, and families were huge. Ranel and Sarah McCoy produced sixteen children, and Devil Anse and Levicy Hatfield, thirteen. Researchers have made much of the isolation of inhabitants of the southern Appalachians,[10] but clearly these researchers have never tried living in a small cabin with sixteen children—with similar cabins located down the creeks and across the ridges.* Families often gathered for group activities like sewing quilts, hoeing and harvesting crops, shucking corn, slaughtering hogs, and building cabins and barns. Neighbors gathered on Election Days, for militia musters, to hear circuit-riding preachers and judges, to buy from itinerant peddlers, to attend weddings and funerals, to help each other when babies were born or when people fell sick or died. The men and boys rode their log rafts to the large towns along the rivers and returned home, walking or poling flatboats upriver against the current, laden with store goods and news. Isolation wouldn't have concerned these people, though privacy might have.

Such was the world into which the progenitors of both the Hatfields and the McCoys moved early in the nineteenth century.

†

Devil Anse Hatfield's family believed themselves descended from Capt. Andrew Hatfield and Joseph Hatfield, both famous frontier scouts and Indian fighters. The former had built Hatfield Fort prior to 1770 on a tributary of the New River in Virginia as a refuge for settlers during Native attacks.[11]

The first Hatfield to arrive in the Tug Fork Valley was Ephraim, who moved around 1820 from southwestern Virginia to Pike County, Kentucky, with his second wife, Anne Musick, and their ten children. His nickname was "Eph-of-All" because every Tug Fork Hatfield descended from him. His son Valentine moved across the river to what was to become West Virginia during the Civil War. Valentine and his wife produced twelve children, including a son they named Ephraim ("Big Eph"), after Valentine's father.[12] Couples typically named their first son after his paternal grandfather, and they often named later sons after favorite brothers or uncles or maternal grandfathers. This sometimes resulted in half a dozen men of varying ages with the exact same name within an

---

* Fitting our family of six comfortably into our cabin on weekends and during school vacations was a major challenge. Living full time in such a space with two or three times that many people is inconceivable to me.

extended family. As in ancient Rome, nicknames describing physical or behavioral traits helped clarify identities.

A half-brother of Valentine Hatfield remained in Kentucky and spawned a line of Kentucky Hatfields. One of these, "Preacher Anse" Hatfield, played the good angel to Devil Anse's bad boy during the feud, through his usually unsuccessful attempts at mediation. Most Kentucky Hatfields tried to remain neutral, but several ended up testifying on behalf of the McCoys in the trials that finally ended the feud.

Big Eph Hatfield and Nancy Vance married when he was sixteen and she fifteen.[13] Known as the strongman of the Tug Fork Valley, Big Eph, the father of Devil Anse, grew to six feet four inches tall and 260 pounds.[14] Some even maintain that he was seven feet tall and 300 pounds.[15] Men constantly arrived from near and far to wrestle him and thereby establish their reputations as tough guys. Fabled for killing a panther with only a hunting knife, Big Eph was sometimes known as "Old Panther Killer." But he was also a justice of the peace, widely respected by his neighbors for his quiet but firm enforcement of the law.[16]

Nancy Vance Hatfield—whose most striking feature was a prominent nose that Devil Anse and several of her other children inherited—was a midwife, "tall and strong with handsome facial features . . . hawk-faced with a high forehead, a jutting nose, and a squared-off chin."[17] Given the staggering number of offspring that Tug Fork couples produced, she undoubtedly never worried about unemployment, although overwork might have been a concern. Unlike most in the valley, she was said to have been literate and to have owned some medical texts.[18]

The fourth of her ten surviving children (out of eighteen born), William Anderson "Devil Anse" Hatfield was born on September 9, 1839, at the family's home on the Straight Fork of Mate Creek. Stories of Devil Anse's skills in hunting, shooting, and riding abound. In his teens, one tale goes, he killed his first bear by kicking it in the rear until it climbed a chestnut tree to escape him. He then sat beneath the tree to prevent its descent for two days and nights, without food or water, until a search party found him and gave him some bullets so that he could shoot the bear out of the tree. The bear was said to be so huge that it took eight men to carry it home, slung from a pole.[19] Even Paul Bunyan couldn't have topped that.

One theory about the origin of the nickname Devil Anse maintains that after he fought a catamount with his bare hands, his mother exclaimed that he "wasn't afraid of the Devil himself." Another theory goes that he got his nickname after Ranel McCoy said of him, "He's six feet of devil and 180 pounds of hell." Yet another claims that he single-handedly defended a mountain ridge called the Devil's Backbone against an entire platoon of Union soldiers during the Civil War. Some attribute the nickname to his behavior, which stood in such contrast to that of his mild-mannered Kentucky cousin, Preacher Anse Hatfield.[20]

Devil Anse came honorably by his need to perform feats of valor. When he was growing up, his great-grandparents, Eph-of-All Hatfield and Anne Musick Hatfield, lived on Blackberry Creek in Kentucky, through several miles of dense forest and across the Tug Fork from Big Eph's home in Virginia. Devil Anse no doubt heard from the lips of Anne herself the story of her capture by Shawnees in 1792: Two of her sons from her first marriage were gathering firewood near the family's cabin in southwestern Virginia when they spotted an Indian raiding party and rushed back home. Their father, Anne's first husband, David Musick, discovered that his rifle was damaged and wouldn't fire. A native shot him through the thigh. He bled to death as they scalped him and abducted Anne and their five children.

The Shawnees slaughtered a family cow, made a bag of the hide, and filled it with the raw meat. Then they marched the family toward the Shawnees' settlement in Ohio. A redheaded son was allowed to ride the family horse because the natives revered the color of his hair. When the youngest son refused to eat the raw beef from the hide bag, however, they ground his face against the bark of a pine tree until the flesh was shredded badly enough to leave lifetime scars.

That night the raiding party camped on an island, where a posse of settlers caught up with them. Anne grabbed her youngest child and herded her four others toward the posse as a Shawnee hurled a tomahawk at them. She and all her children survived and were saved, and she later took up with Eph-of-All, a widower with several small children of his own. Some say he had been a member of the rescue party.[21]

Several other tales of settlers in Native captivity also circulated during Devil Anse's youth—such as that of Mary Draper Ingles, kidnapped by Shawnees in 1755 along with two of her children. During a raid on their neighborhood alongside the New River in Virginia—not far east from where Anne Musick was kidnapped—four other settlers were killed and two wounded. Mary was taken to a Shawnee town near present-day Cincinnati, where she sewed shirts for French fur traders and made salt in the marshes. Her children were sent to villages farther north.

Mary and an old German woman from Pennsylvania, also a captive, escaped and traveled eight hundred miles south through dense forests for six weeks, eating only what they could scavenge in the woods. Twice the German woman tried to kill Mary to cannibalize her. Mary stumbled out of the bushes at her home settlement, naked, skeletal, and completely white-haired, even though she was only twenty-three years old.[22]

Another captivity tale concerned a woman named Jenny Wiley, kidnapped by a group of eleven natives in 1789 from her home in Virginia while her husband was hauling a load of ginseng to market. Her brother and three of her children died during the raid, and her fourth child was killed soon afterward while she was sleeping. Her captors took her to a camp some twenty-five miles northwest of the Tug Fork Valley and held her there for several months, during which time she gave birth to a baby, whom her captors also killed. She managed to escape and sought refuge at a blockhouse, where an intrepid settler rescued her from a river and fought off pursuing natives. She returned home to her husband, and they had six more children.[23]

Shawnee attacks continued in Kentucky and southwestern Virginia throughout the early years of the nineteenth century and ceased only after Tecumseh's death in 1813.*

....

* A tradition in my own family maintains that my twice great-grandmother, Nancy Scaggs, was kidnapped by Shawnees and rescued by her future husband, George Reed. The story is suspiciously similar to that of Anne Musick, and the locations are almost the same, so this is perhaps an example of the rural equivalent of an urban legend.

In addition to these models of courage and perseverance held up to Devil Anse Hatfield as a boy, he would also have heard the story of his great-grandfather Abner Vance, a Baptist minister who lived near Abingdon, Virginia. Nancy Vance, Devil Anse's mother, was said to be a "woods-colt" child of Abner Vance's daughter Betsy. *Woods-colt* is a poetic regional term meaning "illegitimate" and refers to the frequent result when a domestic mare wanders into the forest and encounters wild stallions. Nancy's younger brother, Bad Jim Vance, widely believed to have murdered Harmon McCoy in an opening episode of the feud, was another woods-colt child of Betsy Vance.[24]

Lewis Horton, the son of a well-to-do local family, took a daughter of Abner Vance to Baltimore while attending medical school there. He brought her back home pregnant and unmarried. He allegedly delivered the young woman to her father, Abner Vance, the Baptist preacher, with the words, "Here's your heifer. You take care of her."[25] Understandably (at least to Appalachians), Abner Vance shot Dr. Horton as he was watering his horse at a river. It is unknown whether the gunshot killed Horton or whether he drowned after plunging into the water.

Following the murder, Abner Vance escaped to western Virginia. Some say that while Vance was a fugitive, he visited the Tug Fork Valley and staked claim to several thousand acres there, later dividing the land among his children.[26] Eventually, Vance's conscience got the better of him, and he returned to Abingdon, hoping his crime had been forgotten or at least forgiven. Unfortunately, it hadn't been.

Abner Vance was convicted of the murder of Dr. Horton and was sentenced to death. While awaiting execution in jail, he composed a long song about his plight, including accusations of false testimony against several witnesses in his trial. He had saved the life of one of his jurors by insisting on the juror's innocence in a previous trial, yet this juror had worked for Vance's conviction. At his hanging in 1800, Abner stood on his coffin and sang this song (see appendix). Then he preached a sermon for an hour and a half. Hatfield family legend maintains that Governor James Monroe, later president of the nation, sent a pardon that arrived just after the hanging. The officials held camphor beneath Abner Vance's nostrils to try to revive him—without success.[27]

This story haunted Devil Anse throughout his life and influenced some of his more unfortunate decisions during the feud. The lesson for him may well have been that when the government gets involved, injustice occurs, and that a man should seek his own justice, unaided and unhindered by legal institutions. As with the Native captivity narratives, the underlying message spoke to the need for total self-reliance in a dangerous and unpredictable world.

At the start of the Civil War, Devil Anse Hatfield married Levicy Chafin. They raised their thirteen subsequent children on the Tug Fork in West Virginia. One writer said of the Hatfields, "An enemy . . . might as well kick over a bee-gum in warm weather, and expect to escape the sting of the insect, as to tramp on the toes of one of these spirited, tall sons of the mountains, and not expect to be knocked down."[28]

From the beginning of European settlement in the region, parents had divided their land among their adult children to provide each of them with farms on which to raise families of their own. Big Eph Hatfield gave land to five of his sons but none to Devil Anse. He also willed the land on which Devil Anse had already built a cabin to Devil Anse's younger brother Ellison.

Devil Anse, for his part, didn't observe the tradition of naming his first-born son after his father. In fact, he named none of his nine sons after his father, suggesting a rift between them.[29] This rift must have predated the birth of Devil Anse's first son (named Johnson instead of Ephraim) in 1862, even though the will that excluded Devil Anse wasn't written until 1866. Alike in their physical prowess and courage, perhaps they felt competitive with one another. Or perhaps Big Eph, widely respected for being calm and fair, detected a ruthless streak in his second-born son, of which he disapproved. Hatfield family tradition maintains that Devil Anse's mother, Nancy Vance, worried about him constantly, though no specific reason is ever given.[30]

A newspaper reporter writing toward the end of the feud said that Devil Anse Hatfield resembled Stonewall Jackson: "He has a powerful frame and is broad-shouldered and deep-chested, but with that curve to his shoulders that goes with all the mountain types that I have seen in this neighborhood. . . . [He] has not a gray line in the brown of his thick hair, mustache, and beard. He has a pair of gray eyes set under the deepest of bushy eyebrows.

A master of public relations after the feud caught the attention of the outside world, Devil Anse Hatfield knew when to appear as a law-abiding citizen of West Virginia, dressed in a suit and tie, and when to appear as a mountain desperado. (See photo on page 200.) COURTESY OF WEST VIRGINIA STATE ARCHIVES

His nose is such an enormous hook as to suggest the lines of a Turkish scimetar [*sic*]." This reporter described him as wearing a brown coat, black hat, blue shirt, and blue jeans tucked into tall boots, with a revolver at his hip and a rifle in his hand.[31] He was said to have a "high-pitched, nasal voice," in which he often told tall tales and jokes.[32]

A photograph of Devil Anse Hatfield taken during the feud years shows him wearing a tie, suspenders, an unbuttoned vest, and a suit jacket with a pin on the lapel. His curly beard hangs partway down his chest, and he wears a peaked hat with a brim. He is frowning slightly, and his eyes look anxious. For all his bluster, Devil Anse often appears wary in his photos. Presumably, a truly self-confident man wouldn't need to drape himself with guns and cartridge belts as Devil Anse often did. But then again, a man's reputation for violence at that time often protected his family and homestead from harm.

In photos, Devil Anse's wife, Levicy Chafin, is a solidly built woman, with her gray hair drawn back into a bun. Her steady gaze through dark eyes appears solemn and not unkind. A reporter said she was the "strongest and most muscular-looking woman I have ever seen [with] intensely black hair, a very broad swarthy face, and a stout, powerful figure."[33]

This same reporter claimed that all the wives and daughters of the feudists were "passive spectators" and "faithful slaves."[34] It is indeed hard to view them as anything other than enablers. Many look older than their actual years because of the great toll the physical demands of their lives took on them. They were constantly pregnant or nursing. Some gave birth yearly, most at least every two or three years. They did all the housework—cleaning, cooking, preserving, sewing, spinning, weaving, and carrying firewood and water. Often they performed the farm work as well while their husbands and sons ran around creating havoc and hiding from their enemies. Judging from the huge numbers of children they bore, the women apparently never employed against their husbands their only available weapon: the withholding of sex.

Imagine butchering a hog while pregnant, and you have a picture of what their lives were like. Then imagine watching your husband and children murdered right in front of you and your house burned down around you on a cold winter night. Yet the wives of the feudists continued to conceive children every year or two, and some of these sons grew up to continue the killing.

✝

William McCoy arrived in Pike County, Kentucky, from southwestern Virginia in 1804, and one of his thirteen children, Daniel, moved across the Tug Fork to what became West Virginia. Daniel raised his thirteen children there with his wife, Margaret "Peggy" Taylor, who was sixteen when they married. Their third son, Randolph "Ranel," born on October 30, 1825, became the McCoy feud leader.[35]

We know much less about Ranel McCoy's upbringing than about that of Devil Anse because Ranel's descendants didn't leave behind appreciative stories concerning him. Possibly he wasn't memorable, or perhaps so many of his children died in the feud that the few left to tell the tale were just trying to forget the multiple tragedies that had blighted their family.

But reading between the lines of a deposition that Ranel McCoy's mother, Peggy, filed when divorcing Daniel McCoy following the Civil War gives the impression that Ranel grew up in an unhappy household. Peggy McCoy spoke of the insults and neglect she had suffered, complaining that Daniel was lazy and pleaded illness to avoid the farm tasks expected of a husband, such as planting and harvesting, clearing land, and splitting fence rails. Peggy had to work late each night spinning, weaving, and sewing, both to clothe her family and also to make extra cloth for sale in order to purchase the necessities they lacked and to hire help for the jobs that Daniel refused to do. Peggy also raised livestock for sale so that they could purchase much-needed land.[36]

When Ranel McCoy grew up, he married his first cousin Sarah McCoy, who already had a baby daughter. (Whether it was his remains unknown.) They moved back across the Tug Fork to the Blackberry Fork of Pond Creek in Kentucky. There they raised their sixteen children among their many McCoy cousins and among the many Kentucky Hatfields as well.

Daniel McCoy, like Big Eph Hatfield in his treatment of Devil Anse, also proved the exception to valley tradition by not giving any of his land

Ranel McCoy, feud patriarch, was said to be "tall, broad-shouldered, with deep-sunken gray eyes and a rugged gray mustache." COURTESY OF PIKE COUNTY TOURISM

to any of his children.[37] Only one of his thirteen children named a son after him. Ranel McCoy acquired his Kentucky farm through Sarah's father, who was of course also Ranel's uncle. Ranel's younger brother Harmon McCoy received his farm on Peter Creek from his wife's father, Rich Jake Cline, who owned several thousand acres on both sides of the Tug Fork.[38] But the brothers of Ranel and Harmon who remained in the Tug Fork Valley were landless, a considerable comedown for descendants of one of the original pioneering families in the region.[39]

Truda McCoy states that the McCoy family was, on the whole, "tall and lithe and handsome," often with an olive complexion and dark or auburn hair.[40] In one photograph of Ranel McCoy, he is a handsome and hopeful-looking young man in a suit jacket and white shirt, with very dark hair, mustache, and eyebrows. In another, he sports a trimmed white mustache and looks like everyone's favorite grandfather. His graying hair is short, combed, and parted. He wears a suit jacket and a dress shirt buttoned to the throat. Unsmiling, he has sad eyes that gaze directly into the camera. About sixty years old at the time, he would have already experienced the deaths of three of his sons at the hands of the Hatfields, the seduction and impregnation of his daughter, and the death of her illegitimate child, his granddaughter. He didn't have much to smile about. A reporter at the end of the feud described him as a "broken-down old man," but one with an impressive physique: "tall, broad-shouldered, with deep-sunken gray eyes and a rugged gray mustache and beard."[41] In a final photo, he lies in an elaborate casket, finally at peace.

The only known likeness of Sarah McCoy comes from a newspaper sketch at the time of the trials that ended the feud in 1890. Her hair is drawn back tightly into a bun, and her eyes look pale and blasted. By this time, she had lost seven children to the feud, had been beaten senseless and burned out of her home, and was handicapped for life, needing a cane to walk. In the image, her mouth forms a lowercase *n*.

She didn't have much to smile about either, and in fact she died just a few years later.

When the Civil War began, Ranel and Sarah McCoy had nine young children living in their small cabin partway up a ridge above a stream in Kentucky. Ranel was thirty-five years old. Many researchers maintain that he served in the Confederate army.[42] But his name doesn't appear on the rolls of any regiment, Confederate or Union, even though those of ten of his relatives do.[43] It's hard to say with any certainty whether Ranel McCoy fought for the Union, the Confederacy, or neither.

After the war ended, Ranel and his father, Daniel, harvested timber in a neighbor's forest and were sued for it. Daniel had to sell off his own farm to pay his fine. His wife, Peggy, having had enough of his decades of fecklessness, filed for divorce. It was an unheard-of occurrence at the time for a man and woman in their seventies who had been married for fifty years. She was granted the divorce and ended up working as a domestic servant in Pike County, Kentucky, to support herself. Daniel moved in with a daughter in West Virginia.[44]

Meanwhile, Ranel McCoy had more problems of his own. He had developed a reputation as a gossip. Pleasant McCoy—Sarah's nephew and Ranel's cousin—brought a court case against them both for spreading a rumor that Pleasant had had intercourse with a cow. The records have been lost, so the outcome of this case is unknown.[45] Presumably, with the outraged cow unable to testify, a mistrial must have been declared.

Apart from spreading hearsay, Ranel McCoy's nature tended toward gloom.[46] People sought reasons to flee when they saw him coming with his litany of complaints. In an even worse record than that of his own father, Daniel, none of Ranel's eight surviving children named a son of theirs after him. Fourteen years older than Devil Anse Hatfield, Ranel apparently lacked Devil Anse's charisma. As the feud progressed, though, his gloom seems an appropriate response to unfolding events. Also unlike Devil Anse, Ranel McCoy resorted only to grumbling and lawsuits when he had a grievance, rather than to physical retaliation.

One researcher describes Ranel McCoy as "a kindly old man, unable to throw off his troubles with jest and jovial raconteuring and, because of advanced age, burdened at times by his sorrows. . . . The fight that came from his side of the Tug was carried on by persons other than himself. His own preference, often spoken, was that the law be allowed to take its course."[47]

Deeply religious, Sarah McCoy appears to have restrained Ranel's impulses toward retaliation in the face of Hatfield aggression—and this restraint may have led to the deaths of some of their children.[48] Watching the feud develop raises the eternal question of the efficacy of nonviolence in the face of fists and boots, knives and guns.

†

A common misconception about the feud has it that the Hatfields lived strictly in West Virginia and the McCoys in Kentucky, with the Tug Fork keeping them apart, except when they invaded each other's territories to murder or arrest one another. However, the Tug Fork, when not in flood, is little more than a large stream strewn with rock shelves and sandbars, and branches of both families lived on both sides of it. The West Virginia Hatfields often rode across the river to attend court sessions and Election Day activities in Kentucky, to visit their numerous relatives, and to sell their moonshine.[49]

The Kentuckians and West Virginians living in the Tug Fork Valley had much more in common with one another than they did with those in the inland portions of their own counties. Similarly, residents of the mountainous sections of Virginia, West Virginia, Kentucky, Tennessee, and the Carolinas—not unlike the Kurds of Iran, Iraq, and Turkey— shared, and still share, more culturally with one another than with those in the lowland sections of their own states.

Just as the Tug Fork boundary between the Hatfields and the McCoys was permeable, so too was family membership. Many Hatfields and McCoys intermarried.[50] For instance, Nancy McCoy Staton, Ranel and Sarah McCoy's first cousin, had two daughters. One married Devil Anse Hatfield's younger brother Ellison, who was later murdered by three of Ranel McCoy's sons. The other daughter married Devil Anse's cousin Floyd Hatfield, accused of stealing one of Ranel McCoy's hogs in a clash that occurred early in the feud.

As another example among many, Sarah McCoy's brother Hiram McCoy (also Ranel McCoy's first cousin) had a son named Johnson McCoy—not to be confused with the Johnson McCoy who fathered Ava Reed McCoy's husband, Homer. Johnson McCoy was a close friend of

Devil Anse Hatfield and served with him during the Civil War. Johnson McCoy married a sister of Devil Anse's wife, Levicy Chafin, and Devil Anse and Levicy named their first son Johnson in his honor.[51] This son, Johnson "Johnse" Hatfield, later seduced and impregnated Ranel McCoy's daughter Roseanna, escalating the fury of the feud.

Struggling to follow these tangled family connections, you can easily imagine how confused the Hatfields and the McCoys themselves must have become when trying to figure out in the heat of a gun battle whom to shoot.

Another misconception about the feud holds that it involved only Hatfields and McCoys, and many men from each family. In reality, most members of both families tried to stay out of the conflict. Only three of Devil Anse's thirteen children participated, along with three of his ten siblings. His younger twin brothers explicitly distanced themselves from feud events. A newspaper article cited one as saying that he was ashamed of some of the Hatfields and that he hadn't been raised to behave as they were behaving.[52]

There were about thirty-five Hatfield feudists in all. Three were a nephew and two great-nephews of Ranel McCoy's wife, Sarah. In addition to Devil Anse's three sons and three brothers, fifteen more participants were relatives. Jim Vance, his uncle, was widely rumored to be the killer of Harmon McCoy in the episode that ignited the feud. Four of Devil Anse's nephews took part. Devil Anse's first cousin Floyd Hatfield joined the feud willy-nilly when Ranel McCoy accused him of having stolen one of his hogs, but Floyd retired to the background after the Hog Trial. The husbands of four of Devil Anse's nieces signed on, as did three of Devil Anse's Chafin brothers-in-law and two remote cousins. Most of the rest of Team Hatfield worked on Devil Anse's timber crew or were otherwise economically beholden to him or his family.[53]

Ranel McCoy had twelve siblings, six of them brothers, but none joined the feud at first, despite the murder of their brother Harmon by Jim Vance. In the early years, the McCoy roster listed only seven adherents apart from Ranel and Harmon: five of Ranel's sons and two of his nephews. Ranel's daughter Roseanna participated inadvertently via her love affair with Johnse Hatfield. By the closing years of the feud, though, Ranel's ranks had swelled to some forty men, two-thirds of them unrelated to him.[54]

Some maintain that the fact that so few of Ranel McCoy's relatives joined him in his vendetta against Devil Anse Hatfield proves that they disapproved of his behavior.[55] But it seems at least as likely that most residents of the Tug Fork Valley wanted to keep their heads down, hoping the violence would pass them by. As a reporter put it toward the end, "The majority of the people here are peaceably inclined, but are overawed and domineered by the bullying element."[56]

It takes a rare and noble person to challenge aggressors on someone else's behalf, especially if you have a family of your own to protect. But as the outrages escalated, some outsiders appear to have become so appalled that the more courageous among them stepped forward to assist Ranel McCoy, who clearly lacked the leadership skills, financial resources, and supporters that Devil Anse Hatfield enjoyed. But other motives, mostly economic ones, also came into play for these newcomers who eventually rallied to the McCoys' defense, helping to bring the Hatfields to trial and the feud to an end.

3

Border States

During the Civil War, the situation in the border states was dire, the population at odds over which side to support. When Tennessee seceded from the Union, East Tennessee tried and failed to secede from Tennessee. Kentucky remained in the Union, but the sympathies of a substantial portion of its citizenry lay with the Confederacy. West Virginia seceded from Virginia in 1863 in order to rejoin the Union. Many West Virginian soldiers who had been fighting for the Confederacy switched sides, while others remained loyal to the South.

Some West Virginians deserted the Confederate army to form guerrilla bands in their home territories in order to protect their families and farms from Union troops and Home Guards intent on punishing Confederate sympathizers—and from roving bands of draft dodgers, deserters, outlaws, and escaped prisoners who plundered for survival and, in the cases of a few psychopaths, for pleasure. Union sympathizers also formed Home Guards, like Gen. Bill France's, for the same reason. No one was safe: neither combatants nor noncombatants, pacifists nor partisans, men nor women, adults nor children. No portable property lay off-limits for seizure, and no house or barn was safe from arson.[1]

Civil War loyalties in the Tug Fork region were, as a result, very complicated. The four Hatfields who fought in the war and later became feudists served the Confederacy. But over a dozen extended Hatfield kinsmen who didn't participate in the feud belonged to Union regiments. Of the three McCoys who definitely fought in the war and were involved in the feud, two served the Union. The third McCoy, who became a Hatfield supporter, served the Confederacy.[2] But eight more nonfeuding McCoys appear on Confederate muster rolls, and six on Union rolls.

No documentary evidence places Ranel McCoy on either side.[3] His name appears on none of the muster rolls for either Confederate or Union regiments. After his death, he was buried in the family cemetery of Col. John Dils in Pikeville, Kentucky, along with his wife, Sarah, and their daughter Roseanna. Later, one of Ranel's sons and his wife were also buried there. Dils, a businessman, led Union forces in southeastern Kentucky and southwestern Virginia. He hired many free blacks to work in his tannery and allowed 130 of them to be buried in his family cemetery. That he allowed Ranel McCoy and some of his family to be buried there as well could suggest that Ranel's sympathies had lain with the Union.

Either way, Ranel McCoy was thirty-five years old at the start of the Civil War, with nine young children living at home. He might have been too old and too overwhelmed with parenthood to enlist in either army. Devil Anse Hatfield, on the other hand, a hale and hearty twenty-one-year-old, had a wife but no children—until his first son, Johnson, arrived two years into the war. Devil Anse's service with the Confederacy forms a part of his enduring legend.

Nancy Vance Hatfield maintained that her son Devil Anse could just as well have joined the Union army, except for an unpleasant incident at the start of the war: the Union Home Guard drill episode in which General France accused Devil Anse and his friends of being Confederate spies. After Harmon McCoy lost his fight with Devil Anse, General France's troops chased Devil Anse and his friends back across the Tug Fork to West Virginia. Devil Anse became a Confederate in a fit of pique, according to his mother. Later in the war he murdered General France, and his uncle Jim Vance killed Harmon McCoy.[4]

This is merely one example of the way in which personal antagonisms rather than abstract principles determined loyalties in the border regions during the Civil War. Devil Anse Hatfield was said to have despised the elitist Tidewater oligarchy of eastern Virginia that had helped launch the war. They regarded small farmers in the outer reaches of their state as uncouth and tried to limit their participation in the state legislature.[5] Devil Anse didn't sign up with the Confederacy in order to defend their plantation system. Only 3 percent of the population of his West Virginia county held slaves when the war began,* and Devil Anse wasn't among them.[6] "We were too poor to own slaves," one Hatfield descendant explained.[7] Devil Anse was fighting, rather, to defend his community from any outside forces that might attempt to curb local autonomy.

According to conflicting accounts, Devil Anse served in three different Confederate units simultaneously[8] and fought in most battles in and around Kentucky and Virginia, as well as at Fort Donelson in Tennessee.[9] These admiring anecdotes make him sound like Zorro or Batman, materializing wherever and whenever needed to save the day.

In reality, Devil Anse Hatfield was a cavalry first lieutenant in a Confederate unit of border guards called the Virginia State Line (VSL) for less than a year. One of their battles concerned some coal barges on the Big Sandy River that the 39th Kentucky Mounted Infantry (Union) was trying to seize. Col. John Dils—the Pikeville businessman who later allowed blacks and Ranel McCoy's family to be buried in his family cemetery—had organized and was commanding the 39th Kentucky Infantry.

Dils had moved to Pikeville in the 1840s from what later became West Virginia. He expected the little town to morph into a regional hub because of its strategic location on a navigable river. Working as a schoolteacher, he met and married the daughter of a wealthy Pikeville family, soon establishing dry goods stores and a tannery. Although he owned slaves, he claimed to be an abolitionist, and he employed freedmen for his businesses. Seized by Confederate troops early in the war, he was held at

* Confusingly, Col. John Dils and Harmon McCoy, who owned slaves, fought for the Union. Rich Jake Cline, the father of Harmon McCoy's wife, Patty, also owned slaves, yet some of his sons joined Colonel Dils's Union regiment. These cases suggest that abolition was not the determining issue for Civil War loyalties in the southern Appalachians.

a prison camp near Richmond for a year.[10] On his return to Pikeville, he organized the 39th Kentucky Mounted Infantry, which included thirteen Hatfields and six McCoys.[11]

A photo of Colonel Dils taken shortly after the war shows a lean and handsome man with dark hair, eyes, and eyebrows. He has an aquiline nose and thin lips, tightly pursed. He is wearing a suit jacket with a patterned vest, a floppy matching tie, and a white starched shirt with a standing collar.[12] His fashionable Victorian attire stands in stark contrast to that of the rugged Tug Fork farmers and lumbermen. His expression looks wary, as though baffled that he has reached a position of such prominence, and worried that it might vanish overnight, like Cinderella's pumpkin carriage.

In the battle over the coal barges, Devil Anse Hatfield's Virginia State Line troops routed Colonel Dils's infantry, killing or wounding twenty. The VSL also looted a quarter of a million Confederate dollars, as well as hundreds of rifles, overcoats, hats, shoes, underwear, and socks.[13] Later, members of the VSL, along with Jim Vance's guerrilla unit, are believed to have ransacked Colonel Dils's store and tannery in Pikeville.[14]

In 1863, when its commander was charged with embezzling government funds intended for supplies and soldiers' pay, the VSL disbanded. Devil Anse Hatfield next joined the 45th Battalion Infantry (Confederate), quickly rising to the rank of first lieutenant, then captain. Ten McCoys were under his command, one later joining his side in the feud. His younger brother Ellison served as his second lieutenant, and fourteen other Hatfields served under them. Their assignment was to guard the salt mines at Saltville, Virginia, from Union attacks, the Confederacy needing the salt to produce gunpowder. At least forty-five men in this battalion hailed from Pikeville and knew their Union nemesis, Colonel Dils, as a popular merchant during more peaceful days.[15]

Meanwhile, back in the Tug Fork Valley, Colonel Dils's troops destroyed the crops and burned down the houses of Devil Anse Hatfield and his superior. Devil Anse's family was also subjected to unspecified "indignities" during this raid. Some of Colonel Dils's troops had served with Devil Anse in the VSL before turning coats to join the Union army, so their ravages may have involved personal grudges. Devil Anse's company, in turn, attacked Colonel Dils's troops in the midst of their assault on his neighborhood, killing six and chasing the rest away.[16]

Devil Anse and fifty-four other soldiers abandoned their Confederate regiment in 1864 and headed home, galloping away on stolen horses reportedly provided by Devil Anse's raider uncle, Jim Vance. Legend has it that Devil Anse was ordered to execute an uncle and one of his uncle's friends, who had taken leave without permission in order to visit the friend's dying wife. Devil Anse deserted rather than carry out this order. Others speculate that he and his men, realizing after the defeat at Gettysburg that the Confederacy was doomed, deserted in order to go back home and protect their families and farms from attacks such as the one Devil Anse's household had recently suffered at the hands of Colonel Dils and his Union soldiers.[17]

Once back home, Devil Anse led a partisan unit called the Logan Wildcats, loosely affiliated with a famous Confederate guerrilla leader, Rebel Bill Smith.[18] Rebel Bill commanded a force of six hundred men in the Tug Fork Valley. Union officers, probably including Colonel Dils, had placed a $9,000 bounty on his head (almost $125,000 in today's currency).[19]

Rebel Bill Smith and Devil Anse Hatfield mounted some round bee gums (sections of hollow logs in which bees had made hives) on carts and painted them black to look like cannons. Threatening a Yankee steamboat captain on the Big Sandy River with destruction, they forced him to moor his boat. They and their fellow guerrillas boarded the boat and looted its supplies. Rebel Bill Smith also gets credit for donning the uniform of a Yankee officer and boarding another steamboat ferrying laborers to a Union saltworks. The boat mysteriously went up in flames as the fake Yankee officer swam to shore amid the chaos.[20] The Logan Wildcats conducted many other less whimsical raids. They seized supplies valued at $700 (close to $10,000 today) from a dry goods store in Peach Orchard, Kentucky, owned by none other than Col. John Dils.[21]

Much more than just lofty ideals concerning the preservation of the Union and the demolition of slavery fueled these skirmishes between Union and Confederate forces on the Cumberland Plateau. Personal vendettas were rife, and several flashpoints ignited between those who eventually became Hatfield or McCoy feudists, setting the stage for the murder of Unionist Harmon McCoy in January 1865.

†

There wasn't enough evidence to charge anyone with Harmon McCoy's murder, but most in the area believed that Bad Jim Vance had committed it. Devil Anse denied involvement, claiming to be sick in bed at the time.[22] Throughout the feud Devil Anse was usually sick in bed whenever his followers committed deeds that might get them murdered by McCoys.

Bad Jim Vance went back home to his farm in Russell County, Virginia, to plow his fields and plant his crops. While he was there, a cousin from whom he had "requisitioned" horses during the war planned a retaliatory ambush. Learning about it, Bad Jim organized a counter-ambush and killed one of his would-be attackers, Harmon Artrip (a distant ancestor of the author). Artrip's friends came after Bad Jim, so he moved permanently to the Tug Fork Valley.[23]

Meanwhile, back in the Tug Fork Valley, residents were frozen with horror over the murder of Harmon McCoy, like a drawing room *tableau vivant*. No one did anything. Some claim that Harmon McCoy had been unpopular because of his Union affiliation, so that no one was inclined to avenge his death.[24] But over a dozen Hatfields and half a dozen other McCoys from his region were also on Union troop rosters, as were many others with different surnames. So it doesn't seem likely that Harmon's relatives and neighbors would have found his choice to support the Union uniquely objectionable. Truda McCoy maintains that Ranel McCoy didn't seek revenge or justice for his brother's death because he was in a Union prison camp farther south at the time,[25] though of course no evidence exists to prove that Ranel was in prison—or even in anyone's army, Confederate or Union.

Ranel McCoy did eventually retaliate, though, however blandly. Fifteen months after Harmon's death, in April 1866, he charged Devil Anse Hatfield with stealing a horse from his farm in 1864. Legend maintains that Devil Anse refuted this charge by claiming that he was stationed in Saltville on the date in question with the 45th Battalion Virginia Infantry. Therefore he couldn't have stolen a horse from Ranel's farm in Kentucky. Devil Anse also claimed that Ranel McCoy was with him. But Ranel's name, as we have already seen, doesn't appear on the roster for that battalion among his ten McCoy relatives. So who was actually where, when, and why remains a mystery.

Ranel McCoy and Devil Anse Hatfield filed several similar civil suits against each other in the years following.[26] Clearly there was no love lost between the two men. Each sought to annoy the other and express his contempt—but peacefully and via existing legal channels.

Many in the Tug Fork Valley—said to be a lawless land of personal vendettas—spent much of their leisure time traveling back and forth to their county courthouses at Pikeville, Kentucky, and Logan, West Virginia, to file suits against one another. Both towns lay twenty-five miles away from the Tug Fork Valley along narrow mountain paths, so these were not simple day trips. After the war, many of these cases concerned livestock and supplies seized without compensation by Union and Confederate troops, Home Guards, and guerrillas. Those charged with such thefts invariably justified their actions as essential for the war effort.

Devil Anse Hatfield's younger brother Ellison and three others were sued in 1863 for hijacking four hogs that belonged to two first cousins of Ranel McCoy. One of Ranel McCoy's brothers and several others "requisitioned" six hogs by force in 1863, and their Hatfield owner demanded compensation after the war. Ranel McCoy's father and several others were accused of stealing leather from Thomas Hatfield at gunpoint in 1864, destroying a bee gum in the process. Ranel McCoy's cousin Pleasant, of bovine love fame, was charged with kidnapping three horses in 1863—for what purpose, one shudders to imagine.[27] Col. John Dils brought a suit against members of the Virginia State Line and Gen. Vincent Witcher's rangers for looting his store and tannery in Pikeville.[28]

So it goes on, an endless litany of litigation—but not the vigilante retaliation that the stereotypes about the region have led us to expect. Many had used the excuse of Civil War hostilities to take whatever they wanted or needed from their neighbors. But the victims sought compensation through the court system, rather than revenge through midnight attacks. The attacks came later.

It seems likely that Ranel McCoy and his family were simply afraid to avenge his brother Harmon's murder more forcefully than with annoyance lawsuits. The Logan Wildcats and Rebel Bill Smith, the guerrilla king, were still policing the district after Harmon's death, administering their own bloody version of justice wherever and however they saw fit. "The law is not enforced, and the courts are powerless to protect the inhabitants," said a reporter of the area.[29]

Thirteen years elapsed before the next major installment of the feud— the infamous Hog Trial in 1878—and some cite this period of apparent peace as evidence that these Civil War clashes had no relation to what came later. Yet most McCoys who eventually joined the feud weren't even teenagers when Harmon McCoy was murdered. Harmon's own sons were twelve, nine, six, and three at the time. Ranel's sons were fourteen, eleven, ten, three, two, and one. Sam McCoy, Harmon's and Ranel's brother, had sons who were ten and four. All these young men later fought in the feud on behalf of the McCoys, and five of them died. Even Harmon's two daughters played a part, albeit in supporting roles. Like cicada nymphs, the bitterness inspired by Harmon McCoy's murder appears to have gone underground for thirteen years, until Harmon's children and nephews had acquired the strength to emerge and avenge it.

In the meantime, another annoyance lawsuit was to influence the entire course of the feud.

†

Descended from German immigrants from the Palatinate, Jacob Cline, known as "Rich Jake," owned six thousand acres in the Tug Fork Valley on both the Kentucky and West Virginia sides of the river, as well as at least three slaves. His nearest West Virginia neighbor was Devil Anse Hatfield. When Rich Jake died in 1858, he willed five thousand acres of West Virginia timberland to his son Perry. Perry was nine years old at the time and continued to live at his father's house in West Virginia with a brother and a sister.

When the Civil War broke out, Perry Cline was too young to fight, but two of his brothers joined Col. John Dils's 39th Kentucky Mounted Infantry.[30] Allowed to choose his own guardian after the war, Perry picked Dils. Dils also acted as guardian to nine other young people whose fathers had been killed fighting for the Union. One of these was Frank Phillips, later an important feud leader for the McCoys.

When Perry Cline was old enough, he worked briefly on Devil Anse Hatfield's timber crew. Then he began logging the land left him by his father. In 1872 Devil Anse accused him of logging across the boundary between their properties and initiated a lawsuit against him.[31]

Rich Jake's will read: "I give to my son Peary [sic] H. Cline a tract of land on Tug River in Logan County and state of Virginia bounded as follows to wit Beginning at two maples standing about 1 quarter of a mile above the south of Grapevine Creek thence running up the river including all the land I hold on the river up to Jackson Mounts line."[32] These terms defining Perry Cline's boundaries are so vague that it's hard to imagine Devil Anse Hatfield *not* excusing him for straying off his own land while timbering. The Cline family, like both the Hatfields and the McCoys, were among the earliest settlers in the Tug Fork Valley. They had been Devil Anse's closest neighbors for many years. Nevertheless, six years later this suit was settled out of court, and Devil Anse received all five thousand of Cline's acres in recompense.[33]

Why was Perry Cline willing to give up all his inherited land without a trial? The reason remains a mystery. In a letter to the West Virginia governor in 1887, nine years later, Cline writes of the Hatfields, "These men has made good citizens leave their homes and forsake all they had, and refuse to let any person tend their lands."[34] Reading between the lines here suggests that some kind of intimidation persuaded Cline to forfeit his land.

There were also rumors that the Logan County courthouse was so in thrall to Devil Anse Hatfield that Perry Cline knew it was pointless to pursue the matter any further. Devil Anse served as deputy sheriff at various times, and his brothers as constables. Some of Devil Anse's friends were county officials. His oldest brother, Wall Hatfield, often sat on the county court, the center for all community decisions in those days.[35] Four respected citizens of the county posted the bond required for Devil Anse's court case against

Perry Cline, and Devil Anse named his fifth child after one of them.[36] Young Cline surely felt all of Logan County's leadership arrayed against him.

Prior to the acquisition of Perry Cline's five thousand acres, Devil Anse Hatfield had owned no land, apart from a small plot given to him by his wife's family. He was living in a cabin on land his father had already willed to his brother Ellison, and he was running a small lumbering operation on leased properties. Once he took possession of Perry Cline's five thousand acres, however, he increased the scale of his operation, hired more workers, and obtained lines of credit for supplies with store owners. He also sold off pieces of Cline's land to friends and family.[37] He had gone, in that one legal settlement, from being virtually landless to being one of the largest landowners in the valley, amassing profits from both lumbering and real estate.

Soon after the lawsuit was filed, Perry Cline accepted defeat and moved with his wife and child to Pikeville, where his guardian, Col. John Dils, lived. Making the best of a bad situation, Cline became deputy sheriff and was elected sheriff the following year. He also became deputy jailer. In 1873 he served in the Kentucky House of Delegates and participated in the state's Democratic convention. By 1884 he had become a lawyer, just in time to champion the McCoys against Devil Anse Hatfield during the closing episodes of the feud.[38]

Cline had ties of kinship to Ranel McCoy. Two of Cline's older brothers had married first cousins of Ranel. One of Cline's sisters had also married a first cousin of Ranel, and Perry's sister Martha (Patty) was the widow of Harmon McCoy, Ranel's younger brother. Which made Harmon McCoy Perry Cline's brother-in-law. (But to further illustrate the complicated ties between the feuding families, another of Cline's sisters married a cousin of Devil Anse Hatfield.)

No doubt for Ranel McCoy, the acquisition of Perry Cline's land by Devil Anse Hatfield salted the wound of Harmon's cold-blooded murder. Ranel McCoy was no doubt looking for a way to register his displeasure with Devil Anse Hatfield's rapacious ways—but in his usual passive-aggressive manner.

He soon found one.

PART 2:

AVENGEMENT

❧

Devil Anse's first cousin Floyd Hatfield joined the feud when Ranel McCoy accused him of stealing one of his hogs, but Floyd retired to the background after the Hog Trial. COURTESY OF WEST VIRGINIA STATE ARCHIVES

4

Hog Trial

Building and maintaining fences is demanding work, even more so in rocky, mountainous terrain, so frontier farmers in the nineteenth century often allowed their livestock to range freely through the woods. The half-wild razorback hogs flourished in this arrangement because they could feast on the rich mast of steep hillside forests—acorns and beechnuts, chestnuts and hazelnuts. Territorial, the hogs didn't often wander far from home, and each farmer made specific notches in the hogs' ears to identify his own.

In autumn, farmers herded their hogs back home for fattening and slaughter, branded the ears of the piglets, and released the latter to the wilds. They butchered the adults, rendered their lard, and cured their meat for winter use. Identification marks sometimes became difficult to discern as the hogs grew to maturity, their ears growing along with their bodies.[1] But, like herders the world over, most farmers could identify their own animals by sight.

Many have snorted at the idea of a stolen hog's triggering a bloody feud, but hogs in the Tug Fork Valley in the nineteenth century were no laughing matter. One hog more or less could make the difference between surviving the winter or starving to death before wild greens sprouted in the spring. Livestock also served as a gauge of a subsistence farmer's wealth. So the accusation of hog theft was deadly serious, and one that Ranel McCoy was about to level at a first cousin of Devil Anse Hatfield.

†

In the autumn of 1878, just six months after the settlement that awarded Perry Cline's five thousand acres to Devil Anse Hatfield, Ranel McCoy and his sons went into the forests to gather in their hogs. It was time to fatten them for the winter slaughter. But one of their sows and her piglets were missing.[2]

Searching for his errant sow, McCoy passed the farm on which Floyd Hatfield was a sharecropper. A first cousin of Devil Anse Hatfield, Floyd worked on Devil Anse's timber crew on Perry Cline's former land across the Tug Fork in West Virginia. He had recently bought some of Cline's land from Devil Anse at the bargain price of fifty cents per acre and was preparing to move to West Virginia.[3] Floyd's wife was a daughter of Ranel McCoy's first cousin, so Floyd Hatfield and Ranel McCoy also had ties of kinship, though not so strong as Floyd's ties to the Hatfields. Ranel thought he recognized his missing hog among Floyd's drove—but Floyd indignantly denied it.

Ranel McCoy carried his charges to Devil Anse Hatfield's cousin Preacher Anse Hatfield,[4] who preached at the Old Pond Creek Baptist Church, attended by both Hatfields and McCoys. Preacher Anse also served as a justice of the peace for Blackberry District, in which Ranel McCoy lived. Preacher Anse and Devil Anse both descended from Eph-of-All Hatfield, but via two different wives. So they were half–first cousins once removed. They were removed from each other in other ways, too: Preacher Anse was mild-mannered and peace-loving, whereas Devil Anse was a wily prankster and guerrilla fighter. Preacher Anse ran a church, whereas Devil Anse told a reporter toward the end of the feud that he himself belonged to "the Devil's church."[5] Preacher Anse assured Ranel McCoy that he would organize a hearing about the contested hog at his log cabin.

On the morning of the hearing, farmers in the Tug Fork Valley slopped their hogs, milked their cows, and scattered grain for their chickens. In their fields, fenced with split rails, stood rows of sheaved cornstalks, like Indian tepees, surrounded by ripe orange pumpkins. They saddled up their horses and rode double, carrying rifles and lunch baskets. Everyone wanted to see whether Ranel McCoy or Floyd Hatfield would be awarded the wayward hog. But most were happy just to have a break from routine and a chance to visit with neighbors. They had put on their best clothes—calico dresses, shawls, and sunbonnets for the women; suit jackets, overalls, starched shirts, boots, and hats for the men.

They crowded into Preacher Anse Hatfield's cabin, sitting on his furniture and his bedsteads and on the steps up to his loft. Men squatted on their haunches along the inside walls and in the yard. From the long front porch, people looked in through open windows. The hog lay in the middle of the room, feet bound, eyes puzzled. Some say there were no marks on the hog's ears,[6] others that Ranel's marks were obvious,[7] still others that the marks were so damaged by the hog's rooting and rutting that they couldn't be identified.[8]

Preacher Anse Hatfield was anxious. He wanted, above all, to avert trouble. Trouble was what he would get if he himself rendered a decision about the rightful owner of this hog. But he hadn't been able to persuade anyone else to join a jury. If Ranel McCoy won the hog, the Hatfields might punish the jurors. If Floyd Hatfield won the hog, the McCoys might do the same. Tug Forkers respected the law enough to submit to hearings and trials, but if a legal decision went against them, they sometimes administered their own personal justice. Preacher Anse had decided to copy Solomon's example: He would appoint a jury of six Hatfields and six McCoys. Each man would vote with his own family, resulting in a hung jury. Then he could dismiss the case with everyone's pride intact.

Preacher Anse first insisted that every man stack his guns, pistols, and knives in the front corner of the room, where no one could easily get at them. Then he announced his plan and picked his jury members, who sat down on benches along one wall.

One by one, Preacher Anse invited his witnesses to sit in a cane-bottomed chair and to tell him and the jury what they knew about the hog in question. To no one's surprise, every McCoy witness claimed the hog belonged to Ranel, and every Hatfield witness claimed it belonged to Floyd.

But then came Bill Staton. A large, powerful man with a swashbuckling manner, Bill Staton was the son of Nancy McCoy Staton, Ranel McCoy's first cousin. But Staton's sister Esther was married to Floyd Hatfield, and Staton's sister Sarah was married to Ellison Hatfield, Devil Anse Hatfield's younger brother. Not only were Floyd and Ellison Bill Staton's brothers-in-law, they were also his best friends. Staton himself lived in West Virginia not far from the various Hatfield households.[9] Like many in the audience, Staton had conflicting loyalties. But he testified that he had watched Floyd Hatfield brand the hog with his own mark and that she belonged to him.

Rumor credited Staton with a grudge against Ranel McCoy's family because several of McCoy's rambunctious sons had shot and broken some fishing poles that Staton had planted on the riverbank.[10] Following Staton's testimony, Paris McCoy, Ranel's nephew, called Staton a "damned liar."[11]

Some say the jurors moved to another room to render their verdict.[12] Others maintain that the jurors had to declare themselves on the spot in front of the assembled crowd.[13] But all report that one McCoy juror, Selkirk McCoy, voted with the Hatfields against Ranel McCoy, stating that Ranel had presented no evidence to disprove Bill Staton's testimony.

Another person with divided loyalties, Selkirk McCoy was a son of Ranel's first cousin and a nephew of Ranel's wife, Sarah. But he had fought under Devil Anse in the Civil War, and he and his two sons were working on Devil Anse's timber crew in West Virginia. Some privately questioned Preacher Anse's claim to have selected a jury equally divided in its loyalties between the Hatfields and the McCoys.[14] With such a Gordian Knot of entangled relationships and alliances, though, how could he have? That said, in the years before the trial, Selkirk McCoy owned no land and lived in Kentucky. In the years after the trial, he lived on 120 acres in West Virginia next door to Devil Anse's brother Ellison.[15] Quite a coincidence of fortune.

As one of Devil Anse Hatfield's descendants suggested years later, the entire feud could have been avoided if only Floyd Hatfield had barbecued that wretched hog and invited everyone to supper.[16] Instead, the cauldron of McCoy bile, simmering since Harmon McCoy's death and Perry Cline's land loss, began to boil in earnest. Ranel McCoy nursed his hard feelings, grumbling and complaining, but he avoided retaliation. A good Christian woman, his wife, Sarah, urged him to accept his lot in life and forgive those who had wronged him.[17]

Ranel McCoy was also a religious man, so he no doubt struggled to accept his wife's counsel to turn the other cheek. Truda McCoy says of him that "he had a standard of right and wrong—a code that he lived by. He believed in God and the Devil. No man in his right mind could doubt the Devil—not after he had lived as close to the Hatfields as he had."[18]

Some of Ranel McCoy's sons and nephews, however, refused to forgive and forget. They insulted and sparred with both Bill Staton and Selkirk McCoy. One day when Staton and his brother were poling a boat upstream along the Tug Fork, another boat passed them, headed downstream, piloted by Calvin and Floyd McCoy. Quiet and reserved, Floyd McCoy, Ranel's second son, had no gift for fighting. One researcher says that his enemies regarded him as "chicken-hearted."[19] He did his best to remain in the shadows whenever feud violence flared.

A studious young man, Calvin McCoy, Ranel's sixth son, was so in love with learning that he supposedly repeated the eighth grade three times, constantly borrowing books from his teachers to read at home. One teacher praised his speaking ability and predicted that he would become a politician one day. But he lived in the wrong place at the wrong time to nurture such ambitions to fruition.[20]

Both boats pulled ashore on opposite banks of the river, and the two groups shot at each other until dark. Then they went home for supper.[21]

✝

One autumn day soon after this skirmish, Squirrel Hunting Sam McCoy, Ranel's nephew, came across Bill Staton and Ellison Hatfield as they hunted

A tall, strong, handsome Confederate war hero, Ellison Hatfield was rumored to have fought at Gettysburg. Here he wears his Confederate uniform while showcasing a pistol. COURTESY OF WEST VIRGINIA STATE ARCHIVES

deer on a creek near their West Virginia homes. Squirrel Hunting Sam, obviously, loved to hunt squirrels. Some days he started on a mountain ridge and followed it twenty-five miles into Pikeville, slaughtering squirrels all along the way. His record was one hundred in one day. He usually donated the dead squirrels for church suppers.[22] His relatives reportedly found him "queer"—pronounced "quair" in the mountains, meaning strange.[23]

When Squirrel Hunting Sam spotted Bill Staton in the woods that day, he bristled like a junkyard dog. Taking careful aim, he shot Staton's gun out of his hand. Then he hurled down his own gun, raced over to Staton, and tackled him. Ellison Hatfield pulled Sam off his friend. As he pushed Sam away from Staton, he insisted that the Hog Trial had been fair and needed to be forgotten.[24]

A tall, strong, handsome Confederate war hero, Ellison Hatfield was rumored to have fought at Gettysburg.[25] A photograph shows him buttoned up in his Confederate uniform, fondling his pistol.[26] He displays the calm self-assurance of people who know they are attractive and have enjoyed many advantages because of it. In contrast to his glamorous younger brother, Devil Anse Hatfield resembled a worried troll.

Ellison was "noted throughout the county as being a peacemaker."[27] He was married to Bill Staton's sister, and they had nine children. He and his family attended a Baptist church on the West Virginia side of the Tug Fork. Had he not been killed soon after this incident, he might have been able to avert some of the senseless violence that followed his death. Then again, had he not been killed, a motive for much of the senseless violence wouldn't have existed in the first place.

┼

On June 18, 1880,[28] after enduring two years of insults and threats over his testimony in the Hog Trial, Bill Staton ambushed Squirrel Hunting Sam McCoy and his brother Paris as they were hunting atop a mountain ridge. Staton shot Paris in the shoulder while aiming for his heart. Squirrel Hunting Sam grabbed Staton's gun and tossed it aside. Staton and Sam grappled along the ridgetop, trampling small bushes underfoot. Finally

Staton got a death grip on Sam's throat. He struggled to push Sam's head far enough backward to break his neck. Before blacking out, Squirrel Hunting Sam managed to pull his pistol from his holster and shoot Bill Staton dead.

Or at least this is Truda McCoy's version of Bill Staton's murder.[29] Coleman A. Hatfield, in contrast, tells a different story. He maintains that Staton was riding down a road in West Virginia, minding his own business—though possibly looking for trouble. Paris and Squirrel Hunting Sam McCoy, working as farm laborers, were hoeing corn in a nearby field. They spotted Bill Staton. Throwing down their hoes, they raced across the field. Sam grabbed the horse's bridle, and Paris wrenched Staton from his saddle. Then Sam shot Staton point-blank.[30]

Another version of this story maintains that Bill Staton was fighting Paris McCoy when he sank his teeth into Paris's jugular vein. Squirrel Hunting Sam then shot Staton to save Paris's life. This same macabre account claims that rigor mortis set in, and Staton's jaws had to be pried from Paris's throat after his death.[31]

⸸

Almost every incident in this feud has several conflicting versions that blame different participants, depending upon whether its source supported the Hatfields or the McCoys. But which conveys what really happened? No one can possibly know except the participants themselves, and they are all long dead, the truth buried with them.

Valentine "Wall" Hatfield, Devil Anse's older brother, was a justice of the peace for the Magnolia District of West Virginia, in which the murder occurred. He issued warrants for the arrests of Squirrel Hunting Sam and Paris McCoy. Paris was apprehended a month later, Sam two years after that. Several McCoy relatives testified against the McCoy brothers in their trials, as did Ellison Hatfield, whose wife was Bill Staton's sister. But both Sam and Paris were acquitted on grounds of self-defense.[32] Ranel McCoy was furious that they had been brought to trial in the first place and was equally furious with Ellison Hatfield for testifying against them.

Oral tradition assigns Devil Anse Hatfield the role of peacemaker in arranging the acquittals of Sam and Paris. It's said that he hoped this reprieve would calm the tensions mounting between the two families.[33] He was also preoccupied with problems of his own concerning his new timber enterprise on Perry Cline's former land.

But an episode had taken place by the time of Paris McCoy's trial in the fall of 1880 that had already escalated those tensions.

5

Montagues and Capulets
of the Cumberlands

THE MEN, DRESSED IN THEIR SUNDAY BEST, RODE DOWN TO THE POLLING places from their mountain farms to race and swap horses, to buy and sell votes, to strut and flirt with the unattached women, to dance to fiddles and banjos, to drink moonshine, and to fight. Officials sat at tables to record the votes, spoken for all to hear.[1]

The women couldn't vote, but they came to Election Days anyway in their best calico dresses, sunbonnets with dangling sashes, and soft woolen shawls dyed in the muted colors extracted from plants and nuts gathered in the mountain forests. They brought and served food, and shared in the merriment with neighbors they seldom saw. Some baked and sold ginger cookies to make pocket money or to signal their support for various candidates. They vied with one another over who had the best recipe and could sell the most cookies.[2] It was the closest they could get to suffrage at that time.

Huge beech trees across a creek from Preacher Anse's cabin, where the Hog Trial had taken place, shadowed Election Day for the Blackberry District of Kentucky in early August 1880. Ranel McCoy's family traveled over the ridge from their farm in the next valley, the women riding behind

In this photograph believed to have been taken in Pikeville, Kentucky, after her romance with Johnse Hatfield and the death of their daughter, Roseanna McCoy's dark, mournful eyes betray her suffering. COURTESY OF WEST VIRGINIA STATE ARCHIVES

the men and boys on their horses. Devil Anse, his sons Johnse and Cap, and various other Hatfields rode across the Tug Fork from their West Virginia homes, as they often did on Blackberry District Election Days, outraging the Kentucky women by eating everyone's ginger cookies, rather than just those from the baskets of candidates they favored.[3]

Sometimes the Hatfields tried to buy votes with their moonshine, even though they themselves couldn't vote in Kentucky.* Some Blackberry District citizens looked on such behavior with annoyance, and there were numerous outstanding warrants against Hatfield supporters regarding concealed weapons, illegal liquor, and civic disturbances. Pike County officials abstained from serving them, however, so the heavily armed Hatfield bands traveled the county with impunity.[4]

....

* Vote buying with liquor and money was still in force when I was growing up in Appalachia in the 1950s.

This particular Election Day of 1880, Johnse Hatfield, Devil Anse's oldest son, took one look at Roseanna McCoy, Ranel's fourth daughter, and lost his mind. Roseanna, then twenty-one years old, has been described by those who knew her as "tall and slender with a beautiful, proportioned body. She had a fair complexion that . . . tanned to a pale golden hue during the summer months. . . . The most noticeable of all was her hair, red-brown, abundant and wavy. . . . The sun turned her hair to a burnished gold."[5] In one photo, she is quite beautiful, with a sensual mouth, though her dark eyes look haunted.[6] By the time of that photo, however, she had already endured the multiple tragedies that resulted from loving the unreliable Johnse Hatfield too much.

Johnse, for his part, was a fair-haired, ruddy-cheeked, blue-eyed eighteen-year-old rake, known for his natty wardrobe and his ways with young women—many young women. He was "tall, broad-shouldered, with a dark complexion set off by a black mustache and a slight beard," with a "dare-devil look" about him.[7] In one photo, he displays the glazed gaze of a hard-core alcoholic. In another, his face resembles the death's head often found on the tombstones of New England Puritans. The day he first met Roseanna McCoy, he was wearing yellow boots, a store-bought suit, and a celluloid collar.[8] Who could resist?

Ranel McCoy, noticing the two talking, called Roseanna to him and explained that Johnse was a Hatfield and needed to be avoided. Roseanna waited until her father was no longer watching and vanished into the woods with Johnse. What happened between them in the cool of the forest no one knows—but most can well imagine.

When Roseanna and Johnse returned to the election grounds near nightfall, the McCoys had already gone home. Terrified of her father's wrath, Roseanna agreed to cross the Tug Fork to Devil Anse's house with Johnse, who claimed he wanted to marry her. She stayed for a few months. When she left, she was still single, but pregnant.

Accounts of Roseanna's reasons for leaving Johnse Hatfield vary. Some say Devil Anse refused to let Johnse marry her in hopes of humiliating Ranel McCoy or because he didn't want his blood mixed with that of his enemy, despite the many other Hatfield and McCoy lines that had already cross-pollinated.[9] Others say that Ranel sent some of Roseanna's sisters,[10] or a Kentucky Hatfield whose mother was a McCoy,[11] to persuade Roseanna to quit Devil Anse's household and that she finally agreed. Some say Ranel threatened violence against her Hatfield hosts if she didn't leave.[12] Yet others say that she finally grew sick of Johnse's womanizing, the targets of which included her cousins Mary Stafford and Nancy McCoy.[13]

Whatever the case, in Appalachia at that time, preachers were scarce and contraception even scarcer. Many couples lived together without benefit of clergy, and young women frequently gave birth to babies out of wedlock. Hence the need for the term *woods-colt.* Often women were pregnant when they married, as was regularly the case in Europe for centuries. Some had a child or children from their future husbands or from other fathers, as Sarah McCoy did. Current DNA testing is uncovering many examples of this folkway. Stringent Victorian morality had not yet invaded the Southern mountains. However socially permissible extramarital births may have been at that time, abandoning a woman once she was pregnant without some type of compensation was not highly regarded. In this case, though, Roseanna had left Johnse.

When Roseanna McCoy returned home, she received such a frigid welcome from her father that she soon moved to her Aunt Betty's house in Stringtown, on the Kentucky bank of the Tug Fork. Her Aunt Betty's house was also a much better location for secret trysts with Johnse, should he decide to cross the river from his father's house in West Virginia. The widow of Sarah McCoy's brother, Betty McCoy was extremely religious, but kindhearted and nonjudgmental. She welcomed the pregnant young woman into her home.[14]

In Truda McCoy's version, the romance assumes Shakespearean proportions. She recounts many intense private conversations between the two lovers, in pitch-perfect dialect. They may have been based on hearsay or speculation, but Truda's primary source was Martha McCoy, wife of one of Ranel's sons, who had been close to Roseanna and had no doubt heard verbatim accounts of her intimate conversations with Johnse.

Johnse Hatfield, already a master moonshiner at age eighteen, had taken heavily to drink in his grief over losing Roseanna. He sneaked across the Tug Fork to visit her at her aunt's house, only then learning of her pregnancy. Insisting he would take her away and finally marry her, they agreed to meet later in the woods to finalize their plan.[15]

Ranel McCoy, learning that Johnse Hatfield had been spotted in the neighborhood, sent some of his sons to spy on Roseanna and to inform him when Johnse turned up. Tolbert, Ranel's third son, got himself deputized and, with the help of his younger brother Bud, arrested Johnse for carrying a concealed weapon during a visit to Roseanna—clearly a fabricated charge since most men, young and old, in the Tug Fork Valley carried guns and knives for hunting and for protection.[16]

As Tolbert and Bud McCoy led Johnse Hatfield off to the Pikeville jail, Roseanna became convinced that they would kill him during the twenty-five-mile journey. Without even grabbing a coat, she ran to a neighbor's field and tore a strip of cloth from her petticoat with which to fashion a hackamore halter for one of his horses. Although several months pregnant, she scrambled bareback onto the horse and guided it along a rutted sledge road that wound up to a high ridge and then plummeted down to the Tug Fork.[17] When she left the path to take a shortcut, briars slashed her arms and legs, and locust thorns ripped her dress. Her horse picked its way along the slippery rock shelves that floored the ford across the Tug Fork. It was autumn, so the water would have been dangerously high and cold, and the current swift.

Reaching the farther shore, Roseanna rode through cornfields that stretched along the bottomland until she arrived at Elias Hatfield's house, where a "working" was under way. Many Hatfields, including Devil Anse, had gathered there to help Elias with farm projects. Roseanna warned Devil Anse that her brothers had arrested Johnse and might kill him.

As the Hatfield women tended Roseanna's lacerations and tried to feed and warm the distraught young woman, Devil Anse, his brother Ellison, his uncle Jim Vance, and several others saddled up. Devil Anse's brother Good Elias Hatfield tried to stay home. "Peace between the clans was the desire of this swarthy and more serious-minded member of the family," says one researcher. But Devil Anse barked at him, "Come with me, or you are no Hatfield." Good Elias grabbed his rifle and mounted his horse, however unenthusiastically.[18]

The Hatfield posse crossed the Tug Fork and accosted Tolbert and Bud McCoy and their prisoner, Johnse Hatfield, on a mountain trail en route to the Pikeville jail. They took the McCoy sons' guns away, freed Johnse, and cursed and ridiculed his former captors.

According to one account, this McCoy posse included Ranel and his sons Jim and Pharmer, as well as Tolbert and Bud. Devil Anse Hatfield demanded that they kneel, say their prayers, and beg for mercy. All promptly did so except for Jim McCoy, who remained standing and challenged the Hatfields to kill him.[19] Impressed by his courage, Devil Anse decided not to kill any of the McCoys. Coleman C. Hatfield claims that this anecdote is "an entertaining fiction"—though it's hard to imagine who would find this rather sadistic episode entertaining.[20]

Jim McCoy, Ranel's oldest son, was perhaps the most impressive McCoy feudist. One researcher says that Jim, "a slim man in his early thirties, was the most likeable of the group, even to the opposing clan. He was married, cool-headed, a hard worker, and steady in his actions, and he did more to placate than to antagonize."[21] Devil Anse Hatfield's grandson refers to Jim McCoy as "the most respected leader of his family."[22] A photo of him in his later years shows a calm, stern, pleasant-looking man with wire-frame glasses, a shirt buttoned to the throat, and a suit jacket.

Like all of Ranel McCoy's sons, Jim owned no land and had to farm on other people's property, humiliating in an agrarian community, particularly since his father and grandfather had owned their own land. Ranel McCoy had nine sons, but only the three hundred acres he had inherited from his wife's father, on which he, his wife, and his unmarried children were still living. So Ranel, like his father, Daniel, before him, gave no land to any of his married sons to help them get a start in life. They all had to work as sharecroppers or laborers on other people's farms.[23]

Jim McCoy and his brothers were what you might call downwardly mobile, which may partially explain the frustration and fury of his more volatile brothers, Tolbert, Pharmer, Bud, and Bill. They had few prospects for the future and saw no way to improve upon their situation. Jim did his best to restrain his brothers' fury during tense situations, playing the same placating role among the McCoys that Ellison played among the Hatfields. He seems to have participated in the feud out of loyalty to his family, but he appears to have wished to be almost anywhere else. While Roseanna was riding to West Virginia to warn Devil Anse Hatfield that her brothers might kill Johnse, Jim McCoy, if of course he was actually on this mission, was reported to have assured Johnse that he was under the protection of the law and that no harm would come to him.[24] But as one researcher says, "Descriptions of the rescue, like other events of the feud, vary so greatly that there is no way of determining exactly what happened."[25]

Tolbert McCoy was so outraged by whatever occurred on that mountain path with the Hatfield posse that he rushed to a justice of the peace and obtained warrants for the arrest of Devil Anse Hatfield and all the others who had rescued Johnse. Three months later, reluctant feudist Good Elias Hatfield and his cousin Floyd Hatfield of Hog Trial fame were arrested and incarcerated. A Kentucky Hatfield bailed them out, and some McCoys testified in their defense. The charges were dropped, further humiliating the enraged Tolbert.[26]

Meanwhile, Roseanna McCoy's warning to Devil Anse Hatfield about Johnse's arrest—which could easily have resulted in the deaths of whichever male relatives were Johnse's captors—estranged her even more from her family and neighbors. Especially cold and unforgiving, her father was disgusted by her liaison with Johnse Hatfield, her efforts to save him at the expense of her own brothers, and her pregnancy.[27]

In the spring of 1881, aided by her aunt Betty, Roseanna McCoy gave birth to a daughter, Sarah Elizabeth.[28] Johnse Hatfield was nowhere to be seen. It was said that Roseanna's father and brothers had threatened him with death if he came sniffing around again—but he was also otherwise engaged: drinking too much moonshine and courting Roseanna's cousin Nancy McCoy, who was sixteen.[29]

"Tall and lithe with a strange dark beauty all her own," Nancy McCoy had black hair so long that she could reportedly sit on it.[30] Many young women in the mountains married by age sixteen, and some as young as fourteen. But Nancy was still a schoolgirl, and Johnse Hatfield was courting her by giving her rides to the schoolhouse on the back of his horse.[31] It was Nancy with whom Patty Cline McCoy had been pregnant when she discovered Harmon's bullet-riddled body in the forest and dragged him home through the snow. Bad Jim Vance, Harmon's purported murderer, was Johnse Hatfield's great-uncle. Patty opposed her daughter's romance with Johnse for this reason.[32] Johnse's father, Devil Anse, had also recently taken five thousand acres of Patty's father's land from her brother Perry Cline.

But the horseback courtship succeeded, and the couple married on May 14, 1881, despite the objections of Nancy's mother.

The winter after Johnse Hatfield's marriage to Nancy McCoy, his woods-colt daughter with Roseanna McCoy, Sarah Elizabeth, died of measles and pneumonia. Roseanna mourned for hours every day beside the child's grave on a pine-treed hillside behind Aunt Betty's house. When Roseanna's sister Alifair contracted typhoid, Sarah McCoy finally persuaded Roseanna to come home and nurse her ailing sibling. After Alifair's recovery, Roseanna moved to Pikeville to nurse another child with typhoid, this one belonging to Perry Cline, whose niece Nancy McCoy had just married Johnse Hatfield. Roseanna remained with the Clines to help them care for their six children.[33] It must have been difficult for her to accept the role of spinster aunt after the passion she had so recently experienced with Johnse.

Truda McCoy reports a dramatic, perhaps dramatized, episode recorded by no one else in which Johnse Hatfield comes to the Cline house in Pikeville and begs Roseanna McCoy to marry him, which she refuses to do.[34] This scenario seems unlikely since Johnse was presumably married to Roseanna's cousin Nancy by this time, but who knows? A well-known womanizer, Johnse may have continued to pursue Roseanna while he was married to Nancy, just as he had pursued Nancy when Roseanna was living with him and his family. He could never get enough, of alcohol or of women. Truda McCoy calls him a "chronic lover."[35]

Truda McCoy also reports that, before his marriage to Nancy McCoy, Johnse Hatfield had assuaged his grief over the loss of Roseanna in the arms of Belle Beaver of Happy Hollow, West Virginia. Belle had previously been tarred and feathered and ridden out of a North Carolina town on a rail by obedient husbands of jealous wives. The upright wives of the Tug Fork Valley also insisted that their menfolk get rid of her. So some men bound her hands, tied the skirt of her dress over her head in a knot, and suspended her—naked from the chest down—from the rafters of her shack by a rope under her armpits. When someone finally freed her twenty-four hours later, she announced that she had decided to leave Happy Hollow.[36]

Some researchers downplay the significance of the romance between Roseanna McCoy and Johnse Hatfield as a cause for the brutal, bloody feud violence that followed.[37] Coleman C. Hatfield maintains that their blighted romance played little part in the course of the feud—until the tabloids got hold of it at the end and turned it into a hillbilly *Romeo and Juliet* to titillate their prim Victorian readers in Northern cities.

Roseanna may have behaved like Juliet, but Johnse was no Romeo, with or without his yellow boots and celluloid collar.

6

Pawpaw Murders

The tragedy that ensnared Roseanna McCoy when she met Johnse Hatfield at the 1880 Election Day didn't teach the McCoys to avoid the polls. On Monday, August 7, 1882,[1] they traveled across their ridge and down to the polling grounds under the beech trees for an Election Day even more lethal than the last.[2]

Meanwhile, Good Elias and Ellison Hatfield rode their horses across the Tug Fork to join the festivities and to support a kinsman running for office.[3] By afternoon most of the men in attendance were drunk and napping in the shade of the beech trees when the handsome war hero Ellison Hatfield got into a scuffle with three of Ranel's more obstreperous sons, Tolbert, Pharmer, and Bud.

Tolbert McCoy was twenty-eight years old and, like his brothers, owned no land. He and his new wife lived with another family, for whom Tolbert worked as a farm laborer. One writer describes him as "a handsome man with a beard like General Winfield Scott Hancock of Civil War fame."[4] Another researcher observes that "Tolbert would fight at the slightest provocation, especially after downing a few drinks."[5]

Tolbert McCoy must still have felt chagrined by the Hatfields' rescue of Johnse Hatfield following Roseanna's bareback ride across the river to warn Devil Anse. If Devil Anse really had ordered Tolbert to kneel, and he had done so while his older brother Jim then refused and remained standing, Tolbert's sense of humiliation would have doubled. When his own McCoy relatives testified in defense of Good Elias and Floyd Hatfield after Tolbert had arranged to have those two arrested for their role in freeing Johnse, his humiliation would have been complete.[6]

Ranel McCoy was said to be gunning for Ellison Hatfield that day because of Ellison's testimony against Paris and Squirrel Hunting Sam McCoy, nephews of Ranel, in their trials for the murder of Bill Staton two years earlier.[7] Perhaps Ranel was also still angry about Devil Anse's appropriation of Perry Cline's land; about the loss of what Ranel claimed were his hogs to Floyd Hatfield; about Devil Anse's supposed refusal to let his son Johnse marry Roseanna; and about Johnse's subsequent marriage to his niece Nancy McCoy, the daughter of his murdered brother, Harmon. It was a significant collection of aggrievements, and he had no doubt been filling his sons' ears with recitatives concerning all these Hatfield transgressions and more.

The three McCoy sons, Tolbert, Pharmer, and Bud, already liquored up, came racing up on their horses, shouting. Ellison Hatfield was wearing a large straw hat, which he jokingly offered as feed for their horses. Tolbert, sporting his luxuriant beard, leapt off his horse.

"I'm hell on earth!" he announced.

"You're a damned shithog," replied Ellison—shithogs being those that fed on undigested grain from manure in the roads, as opposed to the more noble hogs that fed on chestnuts high up the mountainsides.[8]

Enraged, Tolbert McCoy slashed Ellison Hatfield with his knife. Bud McCoy joined in with his pocketknife, and then Pharmer McCoy shot Ellison in the back.[9] Some claim that Ranel McCoy was holding a piece of fence post with which he intended to wallop Ellison once he was down, but that the crowd restrained him.[10] But this is an account of Ellison's murder, as told by his great-nephew, Coleman A. Hatfield.[11] Truda McCoy insists that Ranel wasn't even present at this fight.[12]

Truda McCoy's version has Tolbert buck dancing to a banjo on a platform for a long time. He was evidently widely admired for his clogging, if for nothing else. Black Elias Hatfield, Preacher Anse Hatfield's brother, an ornery fellow with a drinking problem,[13] joined Tolbert. Black Elias, said to have a swarthy complexion, outweighed Tolbert by twenty pounds.[14] Tolbert was a head taller, with a fair complexion and light brown hair. Tolbert repeatedly accused Black Elias of owing him money for a fiddle.[15] Black Elias repeatedly insisted that he had already paid this debt. Eventually Black Elias slugged Tolbert in the chin to shut him up. They began to fight, and Tolbert knocked Black Elias out.

Annoyed to see his cousin defeated (or possibly trying to break up the fight),[16] Ellison Hatfield took to the dance floor. One researcher speculates what might have been going through Tolbert McCoy's liquor-benumbed brain at this point: "Ellison was everything Tolbert was not: a large, physically strong man; a war hero; a respected officer of the law in Logan County; a landholder; and, most important, Devil Anse Hatfield's brother. All the stories drummed into Tolbert by Ole Ranel must, at that moment, have congealed into an irrational fury. The Hatfields cheated and lied but they were successful, feared, respected and admired. Tolbert was going to give them what they deserved."[17]

So Tolbert McCoy taunted Ellison Hatfield by calling him "a cross between a gorilla and a polecat."[18] Tolbert and Ellison started fighting as though their lives depended on the outcome—which, as it turned out, they did. Tolbert was exhausted from buck dancing and his struggle with Black Elias, and Ellison, carrying two hundred pounds of well-positioned muscle, was taller and larger than Tolbert. Tolbert and his brothers, however, were carrying knives.

Ellison Hatfield began to force Tolbert McCoy's head backward, trying to break his neck, in a ploy not uncommon in frontier fighting, during which noses and ears were sometimes bitten off and eyes gouged out. Tolbert reached for the knife in his belt and stabbed Ellison in the stomach several times. Tolbert's brother Bill also started slashing at Ellison with his pocketknife.[19]

Ellison Hatfield, his shirt soaked in blood, threw Tolbert McCoy to the ground and reached for a rock with which to bash his head. Someone in the crowd tossed a pistol to Pharmer McCoy, who shot Ellison, saving Tolbert's life—for the time being.

Reluctant feudist Good Elias Hatfield (not to be confused with his cousin Black Elias Hatfield, the fiddle debtor presumably still lying unconscious on the dance floor), who had tried to stay home when Devil Anse organized the posse to rescue Johnse from his McCoy captors, forced the pistol from Pharmer McCoy's hand. Then he tried to shoot Pharmer with it but missed, making him an incompetent feudist as well as a reluctant one. The McCoy sons raced for the woods but soon returned to face their fate.[20]

Good Elias Hatfield had his severely wounded brother Ellison placed on a stretcher fashioned from two saplings and a blanket and carried to a friend's house near the river. He also sent messengers to his brothers Devil Anse and Wall in West Virginia to inform them of the situation.

Preacher Anse Hatfield, a justice of the peace for Blackberry District, ordered local constables Tolbert Hatfield and Joseph Hatfield to escort the three McCoy brothers to the Pikeville jail some twenty-five miles distant.[21] Although the constables were themselves Hatfields, they were Kentucky Hatfields, normally sympathetic to the McCoys, several later testifying on their behalf in the trials that ended the feud. Some were also related to the McCoys through their mothers.

Preacher Anse Hatfield warned the McCoys that they needed to get to the Pikeville jail quickly, lest the West Virginia Hatfields cross the river and take vigilante revenge on them. Ranel McCoy and his son Bill replied that the McCoys were fighters, too, and had "plenty old axes 'n' things to fight with."[22] Ranel mounted his horse and rode ahead to Pikeville to hire a lawyer for his sons' defense.[23]

Apparently not feeling Preacher Anse Hatfield's urgency, the Hatfield constables and their prisoners stopped en route to the jail to eat supper and spend the night. In any case, it would have been dangerous to travel the twisting mountain paths in the dark. Sarah McCoy arrived to comfort her captive sons, but they shrugged off her concerns.[24] She and Tolbert's wife stayed overnight with the insouciant young prisoners.[25]

The next morning, Devil Anse Hatfield arrived at the house where his mortally wounded younger brother Ellison was being cared for and arranged to have him taken across the river to the house of another friend in West Virginia. Meanwhile, Good Elias and Wall Hatfield went in pursuit of the McCoy sons and their guards on the trail to Pikeville. They soon caught up with them, as the constables and their prisoners had traveled only about a mile from the house in which they had stayed overnight. Sarah McCoy and Tolbert's wife had returned home, but Jim, Sam, and Floyd McCoy had arrived to accompany their brothers to Pikeville.[26]

Wall Hatfield was Devil Anse's older brother and a justice of the peace in the Magnolia District of West Virginia. Called "The Old Man" by his relatives, he was known as "the most dependable and conservative member of the clan,"[27] this despite rumors that he had more than one wife.[28] He was "tall, powerful, well proportioned, with iron-gray hair, a full mustache, and rough, shaggy eyebrows, the last a screen from behind which eyes peeped rebelliously and made it difficult for him to maintain the proper degree of decorum as a justice of the peace."[29]

Wall Hatfield persuaded his Kentucky Hatfield constable cousins that the three McCoys needed to be tried in the Tug Fork Valley, where the fight had occurred and where some elderly witnesses to it resided.[30] He also expressed the wish of the Hatfield brothers to be near Ellison as he struggled for his life.[31] In light of the tragedy to come, preventing the McCoy sons from reaching the safety of the Pikeville jail seems a somewhat sinister move on Wall's part, but his overall behavior during the feud suggests idealism and naïveté more than cunning.

So the three McCoy prisoners were taken back toward the Tug Fork in a horse-drawn wooden box on runners that was used to haul harvested corn.[32] When they reached Preacher Anse Hatfield's house, Devil Anse and two dozen supporters were milling around the yard. Preacher Anse invited the constables, the Hatfield brothers, and several others to dinner and a discussion of what should happen next. The conversation no doubt involved a debate between Preacher Anse Hatfield, who felt the McCoy sons should be taken to Pikeville for trial, and Wall Hatfield, who wanted them tried in the Tug Fork Valley.

Fed up with the fine points of this legal debate, Devil Anse Hatfield abruptly ordered all the Hatfields to "fall into line."[33] The talking was over, and Devil Anse Hatfield, former leader of the Logan Wildcats, was taking charge. The McCoy sons were loaded back into the corn sled, tied into place, and dragged down the path toward the river.[34] Devil Anse then dismissed Jim McCoy, who had remained with his brothers up to this point.

Ellison Hatfield, still alive after twenty-six knife wounds to his bowels and a gunshot wound in his back, was being tended by his mother and his pregnant wife at a friend's house near the river in West Virginia. Toward dusk, under amassing storm clouds, Devil Anse's band ferried the three McCoy sons across the river in an old skiff and marched them to an abandoned schoolhouse, forcing them to lie on the floor, their hands bound.[35] What happened to them next would depend upon whether Ellison lived or died.

It was raining heavily by now, and the only light came from a flickering lantern at the door. Armed Hatfields guarded the schoolhouse and patrolled the yard, on the lookout for an assault by the McCoys to rescue the three prisoners.[36] Twelve years earlier Good Elias Hatfield, aided by Devil Anse and a community leader named Dr. Elliot Rutherford, had arranged to have this schoolhouse, now deserted, built on land Elias had donated. The teacher had been a man named Charlie Carpenter, soon to play a crucial role in the unfolding feud drama.

Sarah McCoy, the boys' mother, again accompanied by Tolbert's young wife, rode through the rain to the schoolhouse and pleaded with Devil Anse for her sons' lives. He assured the sodden women that he would return the young men to Kentucky alive, regardless of whether his brother Ellison lived or died. But he warned them that the prisoners would die if any McCoys tried to rescue them.

Devil Anse allowed the two women to talk with the McCoy sons. Ending up in tears, Sarah McCoy and her daughter-in-law spent the night at a nearby house and returned in the morning. Jim McCoy also arrived at the schoolhouse, standing silently, watching and waiting to see if he could help his captive siblings.[37]

Ellison "Cottontop" Mounts, illegitimate son of Ellison Hatfield and his first cousin Harriet Hatfield Mounts, was tall and muscular, with pale blond hair and light gray eyes. Said to be albino, he had the intelligence of an eight-year-old and a strident laugh that irritated the other Hatfields, who manipulated him into taking the fall for a murder probably committed by Devil Anse Hatfield's son Cap. COURTESY OF PAUL C. MAYS, PIKEVILLE, KENTUCKY

Ellison "Cottontop" Mounts, a woods-colt son of Ellison Hatfield,[38] entered the schoolhouse and made threats against the McCoy brothers for stabbing and shooting his father. Tall and muscular, with pale blond hair and light gray eyes, Cottontop was said to be albino, with the intelligence of an eight-year-old and a strident laugh that irritated the other Hatfields.[39] A photo of him from the end of the feud shows a nice-looking young man with close-cropped hair and a surly curl to his full upper lip. He was later manipulated into taking the rap for a murder thought to have been committed by Devil Anse Hatfield's son Cap—and he hanged for it—but for now Wall Hatfield intervened and sent Cottontop away.

Preacher Anse Hatfield crossed the Tug Fork from Kentucky to plead with his cousin Devil Anse to take the McCoy sons to Pikeville for trial. Devil Anse replied that if Ellison recovered, he would do that. Tellingly, he didn't indicate what he would do if Ellison died.[40] Dyke Garrett, an itinerant preacher who had perhaps served in the war as a chaplain with Devil Anse, also visited him and urged him to release the McCoy brothers into the custody of the law.[41] (It's possible that these two visits from preachers were actually one and the same, Preacher Anse being the more likely of the two to have visited since he had been involved in adjudicating the murder right from the start.)

Rumors swirled that Ranel McCoy was approaching the schoolhouse with a posse. But Ranel instead was in Pikeville, unable to persuade authorities to assist him against the Hatfields on his sons' behalf.

Unfortunately for all concerned, Ellison died two days after his stabbing.

Coleman A. Hatfield curiously left no account whatsoever of the tragedy that ensued.[42] Perhaps he was too horrified by the roles played in it by his father and grandfather, Cap and Devil Anse Hatfield. Instead, he turned his attention to a mysterious character named Charlie Carpenter, a red-haired former schoolteacher with hyperthyroid eyes, which stayed so busy scanning the surroundings for possible danger that they never alighted on the person with whom Carpenter was talking. He carried a pistol under his coat and could shoot a walnut from the highest branches of a tree with his rifle. He claimed he had been shot at once a year for seventeen years, though he didn't say why.

After Ellison Hatfield's death, Carpenter composed a document to legitimize vigilante justice against the McCoy sons. Among other things, it said, "Now, therefore, be it resolved that . . . the guilty be punished according to their deeds, an eye for an eye and a tooth for a tooth, and that all other things which be just and proper be done for the good of our community."[43] A few men reportedly walked away from this meeting, including, perhaps, Devil Anse's older brother, Wall. Those remaining signed it with their X's.

Devil Anse Hatfield fulfilled his promise to Sarah McCoy to bring her sons back to Kentucky alive. He and some twenty of his henchmen took them across the Tug Fork—possibly because he believed that if they killed the three in Kentucky and returned to their West Virginia homes, geography would protect them from arrest by Kentucky authorities.

Once they reached the Kentucky shore, using Carpenter's document as authorization, Devil Anse ordered the three young men bound to pawpaw trees in a sinkhole where the carcasses of some sheep-killing dogs had recently been tossed. The stench of the rotting dogs was said to be suffocating.[44] The McCoys were blindfolded and told to make their peace with God. Cottontop Mounts, in the trials that later ended the feud, testified that the sinister Charlie Carpenter tied the young men to the pawpaw trees and hung a lantern on a branch above their heads so that the firing squad could see their targets. He further stated that Carpenter; Devil Anse, Johnse, Cap, and Bill Tom Hatfield; Alex Messer; and Tom Chambers fired the fifty shots that killed the three McCoy brothers.

One researcher claims that Bud McCoy, only eighteen—and innocent of Ellison's murder, at least according to Truda McCoy, because he had been mistaken for his brother Bill—begged for his life. Devil Anse Hatfield wanted to spare him. But Jim Vance walked over to Bud, put a gun to his head, and pulled the trigger, saying, "A dead man tells no tales."[45] But Devil Anse's grandson Coleman A. Hatfield insists that Jim Vance had had a falling out with Good Elias Hatfield over some timberland and wasn't even present that night when the McCoy brothers were executed.[46] Cottontop Mounts later testified that Alex Messer shot Bud McCoy in the head.

Jim McCoy heard the deadly fusillade while sitting on a friend's porch on the West Virginia side of the river. He had already learned of Ellison Hatfield's death, so he had a pretty good idea of what the shots meant. He organized a search party to cross the river in the direction of the rifle fire.

Jim McCoy found his brothers that same night[47]—Tolbert with a hand against his head, as though to fend off the bullets that had passed through his palm and entered his skull; Pharmer pitched forward from a pawpaw trunk, swaying from the ropes that bound him; and Bud kneeling, with part of his head blown off.

It was a soft summer evening, fireflies flaring lazily, mirroring the shimmering stars in the blue-black sky overhead. On a night like this, these damaged young men, murderers and the murdered alike, should have been lying in the arms of willing young lovers instead of killing one another with knives and guns. What had gone wrong with them? No one could say, and the river just kept on flowing.

Ellison Hatfield was buried in West Virginia the day after his death. On an ox-drawn sled, the bodies of the McCoy sons were hauled the six miles to their parents' home above Blackberry Fork. They were buried that day in separate coffins in a single grave on a shelf of land next to the cabin.[48]

Soon after, Charlie Carpenter, the evil schoolmaster, was spotted heading south through the West Virginia hills toward Tennessee. Half a century later one of his former students had a friendly encounter with him in Washington State, but nothing more was ever heard from or about him.[49] A friend of the Hatfields later blamed the entire feud that ensued on "that bull-eyed Charlie Carpenter" and his vigilante resolution.[50]

Devil Anse's great-grandson Coleman C. Hatfield relates the story of the Pawpaw Murders in one succinct sentence: "Someone took the McCoy brothers across the Tug where they bound them to pawpaw bushes and shot them dead."[51]

Someone, indeed.

As though attempting to explain why Ranel McCoy didn't organize a posse to rescue his sons, Truda McCoy repeatedly stresses that Ranel raced to Pikeville to arrange bail and to hire a lawyer to represent them. He appears to have believed that he was still dealing with the modern justice system—which had served the valley well with regard to stolen livestock—rather than with a reversion to blood feud vengeance. Truda also emphasizes that Sarah McCoy didn't summon Ranel home from Pikeville when Devil Anse Hatfield seized their sons because Devil Anse had assured her of their sons' safe return to Kentucky but also of their immediate death if armed McCoys tried to rescue them.[52]

After his unsuccessful visit to Pikeville, Ranel McCoy returned to his cabin on Blackberry Fork, accompanied by Roseanna, who was still working for the Clines. The morning after the execution, Ranel and Sarah learned of their sons' murders in the pawpaw patch.[53]

Beside himself, Ranel started assembling a posse of relatives and neighbors, but Sarah begged him not to participate in any more killing, to let the courts mete out justice to the Hatfields. She had heart problems and punctuated her plea by passing out. Ranel obliged his wife, canceled his posse, and stayed home to grieve, which many of his kinsmen felt was a mistake, believing the Hatfields could be stopped only by an equivalent show of force. One neighbor was quoted as saying, "If they think they've got ye on the run, they'll keep after ye."[54]

And they did.

7

Devil Anse and the Hellhounds

Once again, the Tug Fork Valley froze with horror. Three sons of Ranel McCoy had killed Devil Anse Hatfield's younger brother Ellison, and a group of twenty-three Hatfield supporters had executed the McCoy boys in return. Good Elias Hatfield, the reluctant feudist, called these Hatfield supporters who always did his older brother's bidding "Anse's Hellhounds."[1] The pack was poised for further pursuits.

But for the moment the only man in motion was Ranel McCoy, who made several trips to Pikeville to initiate legal proceedings against Devil Anse and the Hellhounds.[2] In September 1882, a grand jury finally issued indictments against Devil Anse and twenty Hatfield supporters. Four days later bench warrants were issued for some seventeen witnesses for the state.[3]

At the next session of the court several months later, however, the Pike County sheriff reported himself unable to arrest any of the indicted. He wrote "not found in this county February 19, 1883" beside each name in the records.[4] Perhaps the sheriff felt that justice had already been served by the murders of Ellison Hatfield's killers and that it was best to let sleeping hellhounds lie. Or perhaps he and his deputies feared confronting the armed bands of Hatfields who continued to visit Kentucky whenever they pleased. One reporter wrote that "there are none of the local authorities brave enough to try" to capture the Hatfields.[5] Whatever the case, every last indicted Hatfield or Hatfield supporter evaded arrest for the next five years.

"It was known throughout Kentucky and West Virginia," one researcher explained, "that any judge who lifted his gavel in the mountain regions did so at the risk of his life, that civil authorities were not powerful enough to combat family or clan rule, that the instructions of the court could be carried out only if people to whom they applied were in a mood to comply." Because the Tug Fork split the valley in which both the Hatfields and the McCoys lived, geography introduced thorny issues about jurisdictions and—the reunited nation still mired in Reconstruction—states' rights.[6] Law officers from one state weren't supposed to apprehend suspects in the other state, so those who committed crimes had only to cross the river in order to avoid arrest, as Devil Anse Hatfield's crew had done after murdering the McCoy sons in the pawpaw patch.

Ranel McCoy didn't agree with the sheriff's assessment of the situation and kept agitating for the Pike County court to require West Virginia to deliver the indicted murderers to Kentucky. He also worked to assemble a posse to enter West Virginia and hunt them down. But his wife, Sarah, kept urging him to turn the other cheek, as advised in the New Testament, in stark contrast to the Old Testament eye-for-an-eye resolution adopted by the Hatfields that fatal night in the pawpaw patch.

†

A Hatfield historian maintains that "nearly everyone who has written about the Hatfield and McCoy feud has had to deal with the fact that very little happened between February 1883 and January 1887."[7] Such a statement would surely have come as news to several who were terrorized, beaten, shot, and killed during this period, as well as to those who fled the strife-torn area. An editorial in the Louisville *Courier-Journal* on June 30, 1885, stated, concerning the feud regions of Kentucky, "A reign of terror prevails. The quieter citizens are cowed, and those peaceably disposed are leaving that section and coming down within the confines of civilization."[8]

Truda McCoy notes that it was almost impossible to figure out what actually did happen during the years immediately following the Pawpaw Murders because no one kept track of the events at the time. She reports, without details, that a young son of Larkin "Lark" McCoy, Harmon's second son, was ambushed and murdered by someone associated with the West Virginia Hatfields. She describes his funeral, with armed Hatfields watching from the far bank of the Tug Fork and armed McCoys expecting them to attack at any moment.[9]

Another episode during this supposedly quiescent period was the ambush of John and Hense Scott, two cousins of Ranel McCoy, whose family was trying to remain neutral. While riding their horses along a road, Hense was shot in the shoulder and John in the knee, such that he limped for the rest of his life. Both their horses were killed.[10]

Some Hatfields later explained to the Scott brothers that they had mistaken them for Ranel McCoy and Ranel's older brother Big Jim[11] (or for Ranel's son Calvin[12]). Learning that Ranel was planning to travel to Pikeville to consult with Perry Cline about the stalled indictments against the Hatfields for the Pawpaw Murders, the Hatfields had intended to kill Ranel to avoid the resuscitation of the warrants. Apparently they didn't consider the possibility that new indictments for the murders of Ranel and his companion might take their place.

Following the Pawpaw Murders, Devil Anse Hatfield seemed to stay out of the spotlight, behaving like a mountain padrone, sending forth his Hellhounds to execute his instructions. His primary deputy was his second son, Cap, a grim-faced, heavyset young man who had received his first serious wound at age fifteen at a drunken Christmas Eve dance when he was mistaken for his brawling brother Johnse and shot in the abdomen. A portion of his colon was destroyed, and for a long time anything he ate would spill out of his wound rather than continuing to pass through his intestines.[13] Such an injury would make anyone grim. It would certainly have made it hard for him to get dinner dates.

In photos of him as a young man, Cap Hatfield wears a trimmed beard and mustache, and bangs slicked down across his forehead, in addition to a pistol in a shoulder holster. He looks a bit like Hitler, only gloomier.[14] Cap was blind in one eye from an accident with a percussion cap in his youth; his good eye was blue. The feud reporter who described Devil Anse Hatfield as resembling Stonewall Jackson disliked Cap immensely, for reasons unknown, saying, "I do not think that I ever saw a more hideously repulsive face in all my life." He also labeled Cap "quarrelsome and vindictive," claiming that he was "simply a bad young man, without a single redeeming point."[15]

Though some of the worst excesses of the feud have been laid at Cap Hatfield's feet, he appears uneasy and unhappy in his role as his father's deputy. The same reporter who despised Cap also observed that Devil Anse seemed to regard him as "a very useful tool for carrying out his purposes."[16] Like all narcissists, Devil Anse had the time of day only for those who advanced his own agenda, incapable of caring that Cap might have had goals of his own that service to his father was preventing him from pursuing. Cap Hatfield's grandson Coleman C. claimed that Devil Anse "sent Cap out to raid the McCoys and commit other frighteningly violent acts while remaining in the background. Such decisions embittered Cap, who carried the bitterness to his grave."[17] Cap's son Coleman A. concurred that his father "seemed haunted by the experiences of his youth."[18]

†

One night while the McCoy men were busy plotting elsewhere, Martha Jackson McCoy, the wife of Ranel's fourth son, Sam, and the eventual source for much of Truda McCoy's feud information, came to stay with Ranel's wife, Sarah, and daughter Roseanna, who was visiting, at the McCoys' cabin on Blackberry Fork. In the middle of the night, they heard noises. Roseanna and Martha climbed into the loft to look down through some loopholes into the yard, where they counted fifteen armed men on horseback in the moonlight. One dismounted and stepped onto the porch. Terrified, the two young women fell over a pile of new lumber and sent it crashing to the floor. Then Martha tripped over a water bucket that also clattered across the floor. Convinced the house was full of armed McCoys, the men raced off into the darkness.[19]

✝

Meanwhile, Johnse Hatfield's marriage to Nancy McCoy was not faring well, even though they had produced two children, naming their firstborn son William Anderson after Devil Anse. A schoolgirl no longer, Nancy "wore her raven black hair parted in the middle, drawn tightly back and twisted into a knot at the nape of her neck. Her luminous black eyes were shadowed by long black lashes and arched brows, but she possessed the fair complexion that rarely ever combines with this color of hair and eyes."[20]

Johnse, ever the Hatfield family Lothario, had, however, grown impervious to Nancy's beauty and was continually being summoned to feud-related shenanigans. Like his younger brother Cap, he seemed unable to say no to his father, just as he had proved himself unable to defy his father in order to marry Roseanna McCoy—if marriage was, in fact, what both Johnse and Roseanna had wanted, which is impossible to say. Johnse was also drunk much of the time, which of course didn't help matters. Belle Beaver may have fled Happy Hollow, but he had found other women to take her place. Nancy, for her part, didn't hesitate to lash him with her sharp tongue. For all his womanizing, Johnse had a reputation for being henpecked. As one researcher put it, Nancy McCoy "had taken the powder out of his gun."[21]

Twice when drunk, Johnse Hatfield tried to kill Nancy, first by sneaking into her bedroom with a rifle in the middle of the night.[22] The second time, he led her into a field where his brother Cap was hiding behind a stump with a gun, poised to pick her off. Once she spotted him, Nancy informed Cap that if she ever saw him on her property again, she would kill him.[23] No one who knew her doubted that she would. Cap did his best to avoid her after that. Truda McCoy refers to her as a "Hellcat," a worthy match indeed for any Hellhound.[24]

Nor were Nancy McCoy's other in-laws happy with her. In the autumn of 1886, Devil Anse Hatfield became convinced that a spy was betraying the Hatfield camp. Someone was supplying the McCoys with information about Hatfield activities, thereby making them more vulnerable to arrest under the outstanding indictments for the Pawpaw Murders. The McCoys had discovered a Hatfield hideout, and they had also burned down a remote cabin that the Hatfields used as a refuge.[25] The Hatfields concluded that Nancy was the source, conveying information acquired from her drunken husband, Johnse, to her sister, Mary McCoy Daniels (like Nancy, a daughter of the murdered Harmon McCoy), who lived across the river in Kentucky. Mary, in turn, was conveying it to their uncle Ranel. As one writer later put it, in the hills the best ways to spread news are to "telegraph, telephone, or tell-a-woman."[26]

One night when Mary's husband, Bill Daniels, was gone, twelve masked men broke into their house and kicked and beat Mary unconscious.[27] Then they whipped Daniels's elderly mother with the tail of a recently butchered cow. The old woman fell over a chair, broke her hip, and passed out.

The next morning Bill Daniels returned home to find his wife and mother, both still unconscious, covered with contusions and clotted wounds. When they came to, they could positively identify only Tom Wallace, who had a white streak through his hair that his mask hadn't concealed. They assumed that the cowardly Cap Hatfield was with him since Wallace worked for Cap. Besides, who else could have dreamed up the idea of donning masks to beat women unconscious with a cow tail? Old Mrs. Daniels was crippled for the rest of her life.[28]

Cap Hatfield's son admits that Cap conducted this raid and agrees that the men used a cow's tail whip, but he maintains that Bill Daniels, a mild and peaceable man, was present and had to be restrained by the raiders—understandably—while both his wife, Mary, and her sister, Nancy McCoy Hatfield, were beaten. In this version, old Mrs. Daniels wasn't present and wasn't crippled for life.[29]

Then again, this attack may not have been related to the feud at all. Tom Wallace had been living with the daughter of Bill and Mary Daniels, who had recently rejected him because he had faked a marriage ceremony in which he had pretended to marry her.[30] What is clear, though, is that the Hatfields had shown a willingness to harm women as well as men, setting an unfortunate precedent.

Soon after, Nancy Hatfield's and Mary Daniels's brother Jeff McCoy, third son of Harmon, killed a postman for calling him a liar at a Kentucky dance.[31] To escape arrest, Jeff crossed the river to West Virginia, where he first heard about the beatings of his sisters (or of Mary and her mother-in-law, depending upon which version he heard) by Tom Wallace and Cap Hatfield.

Jeff McCoy and an accomplice went to Cap Hatfield's house, seized Tom Wallace, put him on a horse, and were leading him to the Pikeville jail when Tom jumped off the horse and escaped into the woods. Jeff shot him as he fled, grazing his hip. Jeff trailed Tom back to Cap's house, where he fired many bullets into the logs of the cabin in an attempt to retrieve his escaped prisoner.[32]

Furious that his ill wife had been exposed to gunfire and his house had been shot up, Cap Hatfield had his uncle Wall Hatfield, justice of the peace for that district of West Virginia, appoint him constable. Cap issued a warrant for Jeff McCoy's arrest for shooting Tom Wallace and then apprehended Jeff.

This time, as Cap Hatfield and Tom Wallace escorted Jeff McCoy to the Logan, West Virginia, jail, Jeff escaped. He raced to the Tug Fork and plunged into it—even though it was winter and the water was freezing. He swam across, mostly underwater, while bullets from Cap's and Tom's guns pocked the water all around him. As he rose from the river on the Kentucky side to grab a sapling and haul himself up the bank, one of the men shot him dead.

As Truda McCoy tells it, with her flair for vivid detail, a gang of the Hatfield Hellhounds first captured Jeff McCoy and tied him to a tree.[33] While they were playing cards to determine who would shoot him, his sister Nancy McCoy Hatfield heard from a neighbor that the Hatfields had seized Jeff. Nancy tied her toddler to a bedpost at home and raced to her brother's rescue, creeping up and untying him from the tree. Jeff made a dash for her house while she climbed a tree to rest and to enjoy the consternation of the Hatfields down below as they discovered that their prisoner had escaped.

Jeff McCoy then stalked Cap Hatfield and Tom Wallace through the winter woods, and they him. They won, creeping up on him by his campfire one night. They dragged him to the West Virginia bank of the river and told him that if he could swim across they would let him go. After he had successfully reached the Kentucky shore, they shot him in the back as he scaled the bank.

Lark and Jake McCoy, Jeff's brothers and Harmon McCoy's first and second sons, vowed to avenge Jeff's death. They rode to West Virginia, tracked down Tom Wallace, arrested him, and escorted him to the Pikeville jail. Tom escaped.[34] Some say he hit the peg-legged jailer over the head with a coffeepot and swam the river to West Virginia.[35] Others say that the jailer, a friend or the recipient of a bribe, released him.*[36]

The day after Christmas in 1886, perhaps feeling the spirit of the season, a chagrined Devil Anse Hatfield asked his son Cap's wife, Nancy, to write a letter to Perry Cline in which Devil Anse apologized for the death of Jeff McCoy. He insisted that it was Tom Wallace and not Cap who had shot Jeff. He also placed blame at the feet of Nancy McCoy Hatfield and Mary McCoy Daniels for being such busybodies. Forswearing any animosity toward the McCoys, Devil Anse signed his letter to the man from whom he had wrung five thousand acres, "Your friend." He expressed hope that the hostilities were at an end.[37]

They weren't.

In the spring of 1887, the skunk-haired Tom Wallace was found shot through the heart in West Virginia.[38] By Jake and Lark, some said.[39] By Bud McCoy, their dangerous younger brother, others said. By two bounty hunters who brought Wallace's scalp with its distinctive white streak to Jake and Lark for a reward, say others.[40] But Coleman C. Hatfield claims that Tom Wallace fathered a child in West Virginia in 1921.[41] So who

....

* All these endless comings and goings to and from jails, arrests, incarcerations, and escapes make me wonder if the feudists might have provided the inspiration for the Keystone Kops of silent film fame early in the twentieth century.

Simon Bolivar Buckner, governor of Kentucky, promised to bring the West Virginian Hatfields to justice if McCoy supporter Perry Cline delivered the Kentucky McCoy vote to him. Trying to rule a state overrun with feuds, Buckner liked the idea of being able to blame West Virginians for some of the mayhem. COURTESY OF LIBRARY OF CONGRESS

knows who this unfortunate Tom Wallace look-alike with the skunk-pelt hair, shot through the heart by assassins unknown, really was?

But more was afoot than just the murder of a nonrelated Hatfield supporter.

Perry Cline had recently become a lawyer, one unmoved by the apologies of his new pen pal concerning the murder of his nephew Jeff McCoy by his old nemesis's son and his son's skunk-haired sidekick. Around this time, Cline was described by a Louisville newspaper as "a tall, rather stoop-shouldered man, with a pale face and full, long, black beard,"[42] one with an "intelligent, gentlemanly bearing."[43] Cap Hatfield's son Coleman A. Hatfield says rather uncharitably that Cline's "ill-fitting clothes made him appear more ancient than his years." He also ridicules his legal training, claiming that he read law in a chimney corner at night, rather than at a certified law school.[44]

During the run-up to Kentucky's 1887 gubernatorial race, Cline had promised to deliver the McCoy vote to Simon Bolivar Buckner in return for Buckner's assurance that, if elected, he would bring the Hatfields to justice.[45] Buckner won the race, so Perry Cline, the Pike County prosecuting attorney, and Frank Phillips (on whom, more later) traveled to Frankfort, Kentucky, to meet with him. They described how the Hatfields were endangering citizens in their area and discouraging outside investment.[46] Rather than pursuing indictments of Cap Hatfield and Tom Wallace for the recent murder of his nephew Jeff McCoy, Cline sought the reactivation of the five-year-old indictments of Devil Anse Hatfield and his followers for the Pawpaw Murders.

Governor Buckner, trying to rule a state overrun with feuds (see chapter 12), took a shine to the notion of being able to blame West Virginians for some of the mayhem. There had been talk of railroad lines in southeastern Kentucky, which would facilitate the extraction of timber and coal, but no industrialist wanted to invest in a region so rife with violence.[47]

One Pikeville businessman working to bring mining and timber interests to the area was Col. John Dils. He had survived the Civil War, despite being dragged down a hill by his horse during a battle and left for dead by Confederate soldiers. Having supported his Union regiment with his own money, he sold some supplies confiscated during raids and kept the proceeds. Charged with fraud as a result, he received a dishonorable discharge from the Union army.

Colonel Dils joined a partisan band run by the notorious and aptly named Union guerrillas Alf Killen and Joel Long (ancestors-in-law of the author), who were loosely affiliated with Dils's 39th Kentucky Mounted Infantry. It's believed that Dils was captured by the equally notorious Confederate guerrillas Rebel Bill Smith and Vincent Witcher.[48] Devil Anse Hatfield's Logan Wildcats were allied with Rebel Bill, as noted earlier, and Bad Jim Vance had served under Vincent Witcher prior to joining the Logan Wildcats. No one knows how Dils managed to avoid execution by Rebel Bill and regain his freedom.[49]

Now that the war was over, Colonel Dils was partially deaf from being dragged down the hill by his horse, and some of his ribs were damaged. But he had managed to become the second richest man in Pikeville, buying 15,000 acres of land for 2.5 cents an acre. By the time of Jeff McCoy's murder, he was worth some $40,000 (almost $1 million today).[50]

Col. John Dils, a businessman, led Union forces in southeastern Kentucky and southwestern Virginia during the Civil War. Although he didn't participate directly in feud events, he pulled strings behind the scenes to dismount his old Civil War rival, Devil Anse Hatfield. FROM ELY, *BIG SANDY VALLEY*

In a drawing of Colonel Dils done about this time, he sports a glossy, shapely mustache and beard that make him resemble a Shih Tzu—this in contrast to the messy, scraggly bird's nests on the feudists' faces. A sketch of his Pikeville house shows an elegant Victorian mansion with a widow's walk, front porticos upstairs and down, and a wrought-iron fence[51]—this in contrast to the dogtrot log cabins in the Tug Fork Valley.

Although Colonel Dils didn't participate directly in feud events, there is little question that he was pulling strings behind the scenes in an effort to dismount his old Civil War rival Devil Anse Hatfield.[52] Former guardian of both Perry Cline and Frank Phillips, two emerging young leaders of the McCoy cause, Colonel Dils no doubt applauded and encouraged, perhaps even actively engineered, their decision to revive the Hatfield indictments for the Pawpaw Murders.

Alarmed by Perry Cline's visit to Governor Buckner and by the former's apparent determination to reactivate the indictments, Devil Anse Hatfield regressed to his Wildcats days. You might say that he lapsed into paranoia—except that his fears and suspicions were justified. He wrote a threatening letter to Perry Cline, again via his daughter-in-law, signing himself fictitiously as the "President and Secretary of the Logan County Regulators." The letter said, among other things, "We have plenty of good strong rope left, and our hangman tied a knot for you and laid it quietly away until we see what you do. We have no particular pleasure in hanging dogs, but we know you and have counted the miles and marked the tree."[53] Feeling the need for a show of force in the face of disapproval from the entire state of Kentucky, Devil Anse claimed to have forty-nine supporters, even though most put the number at about a dozen fewer than that.[54]

Around this same time, Ranel McCoy was standing in the doorway of his cabin on a ridge above Blackberry Fork, looking out to the graves of his sons who had been executed in the pawpaw patch. A bullet fired from the woods sank into the molding right beside him.[55]

In consequence, Perry Cline surrounded himself with armed bodyguards.[56] On September 10, 1887, Governor Buckner fulfilled his campaign promise to Cline by posting rewards for the indicted Hatfields, ensuring that bounty hunters from all over the country would arrive to

Frank Phillips, the second husband of Nancy McCoy, daughter of Harmon. Perceived as a roughneck, Frank was a grandson of one of the wealthiest men in Pike County, Kentucky. He led the Kentucky posses that invaded West Virginia to arrest the indicted Hatfields, killing Jim Vance and Bill Dempsey.

participate in their pursuit. He also sent an extradition demand for the indicted Hatfields to the governor of West Virginia, E. Willis Wilson, and authorized Pikeville to appoint a special deputy to receive them.[57]

The man selected as special deputy, Bad Frank Phillips, a rowdy twenty-five-year-old, already had two ex-wives and four children. His father, Billy Phillips, had been killed while serving heroically—some might say suicidally—as a sentinel for Colonel Dils's 39th Kentucky Mounted Infantry. During a battle, the elder Phillips received an order to retreat because area Confederates were advancing. But brave Billy refused to abandon his post or to run from rebels. So a bunch of them swarmed him, and he was never seen or heard from again.[58] Billy Phillips had been a friend of Harmon McCoy, and Billy's son Frank was friendly with some of the younger McCoys, who lived across a ridge from his home on Johns Creek.[59]

Colonel Dils was, for a time, the guardian of Frank Phillips, who was born in 1862, not long after his father left Johns Creek to fight in the war.[60] Frank appears to have inherited the courage and foolhardiness of his father, whom he never met. A representative sent by Governor Buckner to assess the feud described him as "a handsome little fellow, with piercing black eyes, ruddy cheeks, and a pleasant expression, but a mighty unpleasant man to project with."[61] Said to enjoy shooting at innocent strangers' feet to make them dance,[62] he had a drinking problem and a way with women that rivaled Johnse Hatfield, who was the same age.[63]

A strange undated photo of Frank Phillips that looks like a publicity still for a Western movie features a drooping coal-black mustache, a cowboy hat, a bone- or ivory-handled pistol hanging across his abdomen, and a rifle in one hand.[64] Although perceived as a roughneck, Frank was a grandson of one of the wealthiest men in Pike County.[65] This leaves us with the rather touching impression that he was constantly trying to live up to his unknown father's reputation for fearlessness.

Perry Cline, Frank Phillips, and Ranel McCoy settled down to wait for the indicted Hatfields to arrive for trial from West Virginia. But Governor Wilson found various reasons for delay in sending them, largely because an old friend of Devil Anse, John Floyd, assistant secretary of state to Governor Wilson, was championing the Hatfield cause.[66] John Floyd's father and uncle had been among Devil Anse's Confederate commanders during the Civil War.[67]

Floyd instructed the Hatfields to assemble character references, petitions, and affidavits from their friends and neighbors proclaiming their good character and their innocence of the charges of which they had been accused, for delivery to Governor Wilson. He also informed the governor of the McCoys' culpability for the murders of Bill Staton and Ellison Hatfield, and he emphasized the miscarriage of justice that would result if Hatfields were tried in the Pikeville court with Kentucky jurors. He further explained to the governor the origin of Perry Cline's animosity toward Devil Anse in the settlement that had forced Cline off his inherited land.[68]

Overcome by impatience at West Virginia's failure to hand over the Hatfields, Perry Cline wrote Governor Wilson a letter itemizing their depredations, including the one against himself in taking his land, in language often misspelled and ungrammatical. Cline maintained that the Hatfields were "the worst band of meroders [marauders] ever existed in the mountains," asserting that they had no doubt forced their neighbors to sign petitions and affidavits on their behalf. He explained that the Hatfields were constantly crossing into Kentucky to interfere in local elections and to buy votes with their moonshine. But Cline promised that his only goal was to subject them to impartial, official justice.[69]

When Governor Wilson failed to reply, Perry Cline and Frank Phillips secured warrants for the arrest of twenty Hatfields involved in the Pawpaw Murders and headed to West Virginia with a posse on December 12, 1887. They returned with Selkirk McCoy, the turncoat who had voted against Ranel at the Hog Trial almost a decade earlier.[70]

Phillips planned more raids, but the sheriff of Pike County, Basil Hatfield, requested Phillips's removal as special deputy because the raids were widely regarded as illegal, involving citizens from one state shanghaiing those from another—despite the fact that Devil Anse Hatfield had done the exact same thing to the McCoy brothers after they killed his brother Ellison. A distant cousin of Devil Anse, Basil Hatfield was said not to be a supporter of his,[71] even while seeking the ouster of

Frank Phillips. Phillips was relieved of his position, but he and Cline resumed their raids anyway.[72]

In response, Devil Anse Hatfield sent a relative and an attorney to Perry Cline in Pikeville, offering him $225 to cancel these raids. Cline accepted the money, supposedly earmarked to reimburse Cline for the expenses he had incurred in securing the extradition documents.[73] But Kentucky posses continued to prowl the West Virginia side of the Tug Fork. Cline no doubt felt that $225 was small change compared to what the five thousand acres that Devil Anse had wrested from him were worth, especially now that politicians and businessmen were considering a rail line up the Tug Fork through that same property.

Thwarted in his peaceful attempts to avert the seizure of himself and his henchmen under the Pawpaw Murders indictments, Devil Anse Hatfield or one of his supporters came up with another plan worthy of the Keystone Kops.

The results proved anything but amusing.

New Year's Night Massacre

On the sun-dappled Christmas afternoon of 1887, anxious that Frank Phillips's posse would abduct all the indicted Hatfields to Kentucky for trial, the Hatfield feudists gathered at Bad Jim Vance's house on Thacker Creek in West Virginia. Devil Anse, obsessed with the memory of the hanging of his great-grandfather Abner Vance, "thought that he and his loved ones would not receive justice, but would be met with mere vengeance."[1] Sitting in the yard with their feet propped up on logs, the Hatfields devised a plan taken from the playbook of the Logan Wildcats.[2]

Their harebrained scheme would eliminate the threat posed by the raiders from Kentucky by eliminating sixty-two-year-old Ranel McCoy. In their eyes, he had started the trouble, had kept the cauldron of bile bubbling, and would testify for the prosecution if the Hatfields ever came to trial. They didn't appear to realize that Sarah McCoy and Tolbert's wife posed more of a threat to them than Ranel, since those two women had witnessed the McCoy boys trussed like roasting hens on the schoolhouse floor just before the Pawpaw Murders. But the Hatfields longed to find a way to come in from the cold. They were sick of sleeping in the woods and in caves, always alert for sounds of pursuit, always poised for flight, not unlike the wild animals that they themselves loved to stalk.[3]

Truda McCoy insists that the Christmas Day plan was Devil Anse's and that he told his Hellhounds, "Ranel has got to die."[4] Devil Anse's grandson Coleman A. Hatfield, however, states that "Anse Hatfield did not think it was a good idea to attack the McCoys and felt that they should forget the whole matter."[5] But Coleman's son maintains that "Anse turned to his well-remembered Civil War tactic of a preemptive strike at the heart of his perceived enemy and sent a small band of raiders to attack Randal McCoy's home."[6] Devil Anse's own descendants can't seem to agree on who hatched this cowardly plot. Some researchers even lay the blame on Cap Hatfield's doorsill, like a decapitated mouse.[7]

Coleman A. Hatfield, who tends to shift any culpability away from his grandfather and father, Devil Anse and Cap, holds Good Elias Hatfield responsible for the ill-advised midnight jaunt. He claims that Good Elias was convinced that the McCoys had his farm under surveillance and planned to assassinate him. On a hill above his house, he had found a sapling with a branch trimmed down to a fork, on which were marks indicating that a rifle had rested there, trained at his yard. Brush had been mounded up around the tree trunk to conceal the shooter. Good Elias insisted that an attack on Ranel McCoy's cabin "would have to be did." Still the reluctant feudist, he deeply regretted that his poor health would prevent him from accompanying the Hellhounds, but he told them that they would have to carry out this attack in order to protect their "old uncle," who was just forty at the time. Jim Vance, over two decades older than his elderly nephew, rose to the occasion and assumed leadership of the mission. But Cap's son considered Good Elias "the main agitator who rekindled the smoldering feud fires."[8]

Whoever proposed this idiotic plan, feud legend maintains that Devil Anse didn't participate in it because he was, once again, sick in bed.[9] But one researcher, showing more confidence in Devil Anse's character than some possess, disputes this notion, insisting that "such behavior would have been out of character. If Anse had instigated the raid, he would have led it. . . . Anse's brothers Valentine ['Wall'] and [Good] Elias declined involvement. . . . One must suspect that Devil Anse and most of his group were not willing to take such drastic action or even to sanction it—possibly they didn't even know when or where it was to occur."[10] But the rumor around Pikeville after the midnight attack held that Devil Anse was angry that his brother Wall had refused to participate.[11]

It's true that only nine Hatfield goons out of thirty-seven took part in the upcoming outing.[12] Many of the missing were hiding in the West Virginia hills, perhaps hoping to avoid conscription into this squadron of assassins.[13] But Cap Hatfield's son states that Devil Anse believed a preemptive strike—meaning murder, of course, such as he had conducted against Gen. Bill France during the Civil War—was necessary to deal with Ranel McCoy, which required secrecy and a limited number of men.[14]

Cap's son relates that the Hatfield patrol first sneaked up on the McCoy house on New Year's Eve of 1887. But someone leaned against a split rail fence and sent it crashing down the hill, alerting the McCoys to their presence, so the Hatfields fled.[15] God knows they wouldn't have wanted to give the McCoys fair warning of their impending deaths.

The next evening, after dinner at Cap Hatfield's house, Jim Vance raised his arms and said, somewhat histrionically, to his eight henchmen, "May hell be my heaven, I will kill the man that goes back on me tonight, if powder will burn."[16] Then he led his death squad—Devil Anse's three oldest sons, Johnse, Cap, and Robert E. Lee (Bob); Elliott Hatfield and Cottontop Mounts, sons of the murdered Ellison; French Ellis, who was Devil Anse's nephew-in-law;[17] Tom Chambers; and the teenaged Charlie Gillespie[18]—under a full moon across the Tug Fork and over the ridge to Ranel McCoy's cabin.[19] Bob Hatfield may have turned back because his mother, Levicy, begged him to,[20] suggesting on at least this one occasion that she, like Sarah McCoy, might have tried to oppose the conduct of her feudist sons and husband. Every one of these men was under thirty-five years of age except Jim Vance, who was sixty-one and should have known better.

After tying their horses up in the woods under the first full moon of 1888, Cap and Johnse Hatfield and Jim Vance donned masks.[21] One wonders who else the McCoys might imagine were attacking them in the middle of the night—although masks could, of course, allow the Hatfields later to shift blame wherever they wanted it to fall. They advanced on foot to the McCoy cabin, inside which everyone was fast asleep. The dogtrot log cabin had a story-and-a-half main structure connected to a smaller one-story kitchen by a roofed porch. Hoarfrost on the roof sparkled in the moonlight.[22]

The Hellhounds stationed themselves across from all the entrances. Jim Vance called for the McCoys to come out and surrender. He had ordered his comrades not to fire until he directed, but a nervous or perhaps drunk Johnse Hatfield fired into the house anyway. Coleman A. Hatfield, son of Cap, who was present at the cabin, insists that Calvin McCoy, Ranel's twenty-five-year-old son, who loved learning and wanted to become a politician,[23] fired first from inside the house.[24] Whichever the case, the attackers riddled the house with bullets, and Ranel and Calvin McCoy returned fire, hitting Johnse Hatfield in the shoulder.[25]

Then Bad Jim Vance set the cabin on fire—on purpose, say most;[26] by accident, says Cap's son.[27] Tom Chambers tried to stuff a flaming pine knot under a shingle. Ranel shot at him from inside and blew off three of his fingers. Ranel's daughters Alifair, Fanny, and Adelaide tried fruitlessly to quench the flames with water and buttermilk stored inside the house, and the stench of scorched milk filled the thickening air.[28]

When twenty-nine-year-old Alifair, lame from polio, limped out to draw water from the well, she was shot dead—by Cap Hatfield, said her sister Fannie and later, at trial, her mother.[29] Some researchers insist Cottontop Mounts shot her.[30] Her mother, Sarah McCoy, nearly sixty and ill with influenza, rushed out to Alifair's fallen body. Jim Vance clubbed her to the ground with his rifle butt, breaking her arm and hip.[31] Then, with his pistol butt, someone—either Jim Vance, Johnse Hatfield, or Cottontop Mounts[32]—bashed in the skull of Sarah McCoy, the woman they had called "Aunt Sally" in happier days.

With the house burning, Calvin McCoy raced out, trying to distract the attackers' attention so that his father, Ranel, could escape from another door with a young grandson named Melvin, son of the Tolbert murdered in the pawpaw patch. Forgetting that a corncrib where he meant to seek shelter had recently been moved,[33] Calvin was trapped in the open and shot in the head.[34] Ranel and Melvin fled the conflagration and hid either in a haystack[35] or in the pigpen.[36]

Upon their departure, the Hatfields also set fire to Ranel McCoy's smokehouse, full of food stored for winter.[37] They ran back to their horses, one of which bolted,[38] no doubt appalled by the behavior of its owner. As the raiders rode over the ridge toward the Tug Fork, the McCoy house and smokehouse at their backs were engulfed in flames. They could hear the McCoy daughters calling for help. The odor of burnt meat floated on the smoke that wafted from the smokehouse.

Cottontop Mounts, though he may have been mentally challenged, recognized the horror of what had just happened. He had been shot in the arm, and the bone had been broken.[39] But before passing out from the pain, he said to the young man who rode double with him on his horse, "Well, we killed the boy and the girl, and I am sorry of it. We have made a bad job of it. . . . There will be trouble over this."[40]

He was right.

A neighbor of the McCoys later claimed to have watched the Hatfields retreat toward the Tug Fork on their horses, "their guns glistening in the moonlight," and to have wondered what they were up to.[41]

Her house destroyed, Sarah McCoy lay unconscious in the yard until dawn, alongside the body of her dead daughter. Alifair's hair froze to the ground in her own blood.[42] Ranel's and Sarah's seventeen-year-old daughter, Adelaide—said, in a probably inaccurate (though certainly understandable, if true) newspaper report, to have gone insane shortly after this attack[43]—built a fire nearby to keep her mother warm.[44] Fanny, her sister, and Cora, a young daughter of Tolbert's, who had also escaped the burning house, emerged from hiding after the Hatfields departed.[45]

Summoned by the glow from the conflagrations, the wails of the McCoy daughters, and the stench of burning meat, wary neighbors gathered. They carried Sarah on a makeshift stretcher to her son Jim McCoy's house a mile away.

A couple of days later, Calvin and Alifair McCoy were buried with their brothers who had been shot in the pawpaw patch—Tolbert, Pharmer, and

Bud—in the family plot on the shelf of land below the charred skeletons of the McCoy cabin and smokehouse.[46] Ranel McCoy loaded his severely injured wife into a cart and headed to Pikeville, placing her in the care of their daughter Roseanna at Perry Cline's house.

Ranel's sons Sam and Jim McCoy also packed up their households in the Tug Fork Valley and moved their families to Pikeville, trying to put as much distance as possible between themselves and Devil Anse's Hellhounds.[47] The governors of Kentucky and West Virginia previously had advised both the Hatfields and the McCoys to move away from the valley as a way of ending the feud.[48] It's regrettable that it took the deaths of five of their children to persuade Ranel and Sarah McCoy to do just that.

Devil Anse Hatfield was said to be alarmed when he learned that his cadre had failed in its assignment to eliminate Ranel McCoy. His great-grandson Coleman C. Hatfield says, "I do not think he knew that the retaliation would come as quick and as hard as it did."[49] Coleman C. rather coldly and callously categorizes the destruction of the McCoy home and the deaths of two of their children as "another public relations disaster"[50] for the Hatfields.

Ranel McCoy urged the Pike County sheriff to form a posse to pursue the Hatfields, regardless of whether he had warrants and extradition papers for them. The sheriff refused. Bad Frank Phillips did not.

Phillips and Perry Cline resumed their forays into West Virginia on January 8, 1888, a week after the New Year's Night Massacre, with a posse of twenty that included three sons of the murdered Harmon McCoy.[51] On a mountain path that day, they came across Cap Hatfield, Bad Jim Vance, and Jim's wife, carrying a bucket of dressed squirrels.[52] Although hiding from the posses, Vance sometimes rendezvoused with his wife for food. This particular day he was said to have been ill from eating too much raccoon meat.[53]

Bad Jim Vance and Cap Hatfield ducked behind some rocks and started shooting, while Jim's wife ran to summon Hatfield reinforcements. Jim McCoy, de facto head of the McCoy feudists while Ranel was grieving, shot Bad Jim[54] in his gun arm.[55] Bad Jim ordered Cap Hatfield to flee so he could warn the other Hatfields about the Kentucky posse.[56]

After Cap's departure, Vance lay bleeding on the ground, aiming his wavering pistol at the approaching Frank Phillips. Not taking any chances,

Phillips shot Jim Vance in the head. The man who had murdered Harmon McCoy over twenty years earlier*—who had led the New Year's Night Massacre and had beaten Sarah McCoy almost to death—finally lay dead himself, a victim of the violence he had so often perpetrated.

Cap Hatfield's son reports that Bud and Lark McCoy shook hands over the corpse of their father's murderer. Then they "waded in Jim's blood and dipped a corner of a handkerchief in blood-feud revenge."[57] Another Hatfield researcher, in an anecdote that sounds equally far-fetched, maintains that Bud McCoy dipped his finger in Jim Vance's brains, used it to polish his boots, and then licked his finger clean.[58] Yet another claims that Dave Stratton (more about him later) and Bad Frank Phillips shook hands over Vance's body.[59] Whoever rejoiced, the McCoy team clearly gloried in its vengeance.

Sam McCoy, Ranel's fourth son and Martha McCoy's husband, spotted Cap Hatfield's overcoat, which he had shed so as to run faster. Sam picked it up and took it home with him. Young women in Pikeville later asked him for buttons from it as souvenirs, until his wife, Martha, grew jealous of all the admiring young women and made him get rid of it.[60]

The coatless Cap Hatfield, meanwhile, was now also barefoot, having removed his boots so that the McCoys couldn't track him. Had he continued his search for Hatfields to come rescue the already-dead Jim Vance, he might have ended up stark naked. Instead, he shot a neighbor's steer, mistaking its white face for the shirt of a McCoy and its long horns for a rifle.[61]

Half a dozen raids during the next ten days netted seven more Hatfield feudists—but not Devil Anse.[62] All of Pikeville panicked, convinced that the Hatfields would rescue their confederates from jail, burning the town and murdering innocent civilians in the process.[63] But they overestimated the Hatfields' courage and concern for their captured comrades.

Wall Hatfield, Devil Anse's older brother, wrote to Frank Phillips, offering to surrender. Not one to wait for what he wanted, Phillips arrested Wall at his home.[64] As a justice of the peace in his district, Wall apparently had faith in the legal system—unwarranted, it turned out—and expected to be exonerated since he claimed not to have participated in either the New Year's Night Massacre or the Pawpaw Murders.

* And my own ancestor Harmon Artrip after that.

Rather than riding to Pikeville and freeing his incarcerated followers, Devil Anse rode to Logan, West Virginia, and persuaded county officials there to issue indictments for the twenty men in Frank Phillips's posse who had murdered his uncle Bad Jim Vance. These same officials also organized a posse of their own to patrol the West Virginia banks of the Tug Fork and to arrest Frank Phillips's band, should it cross the river from Kentucky again.

†

On January 19, 1888, eighteen days after the murders of Alifair and Calvin McCoy outside their family cabin, and eleven days after the murder of Jim Vance on the West Virginia mountainside, Frank Phillips returned to West Virginia with eighteen men.[65] It was said the Phillips posse had dynamite in their saddlebags for blowing up any barricades the Hatfields might have erected.[66]

On the banks of Grapevine Creek, the Pike County posse met thirteen Hatfield supporters intent on arresting those responsible for the murder of Bad Jim Vance. The battleground on which they stood had once belonged to Rich Jake Cline, then for a time to his son Perry Cline. Now it belonged to Devil Anse Hatfield and fourteen others to whom he had sold parcels.[67]

Like every other episode in the feud, it's almost impossible to figure out from conflicting accounts what actually happened during the battle.* The Hatfields lined up in battle formation as the Phillips band rode from the Kentucky side of the Tug Fork, down the river toward Grapevine Creek. The Kentuckians tied their horses near the mouth of the creek to advance on foot, but rifle shots from a party of squirrel hunters stampeded their horses.[68] While part of the Kentucky group chased the panicked horses, Frank Phillips led another group up the creek toward Cap Hatfield's house.

They found a man named Bill Dempsey hiding in a fodder pen. Shot in the leg, through an artery, he begged them to spare him because he had nothing to do with the Hatfields and was only an appointed deputy. Some say Dempsey mistook the McCoy posse for friends and asked for water.

"I'll give you water," Bad Frank Phillips replied, and then he blew Dempsey's brains out.[69]

---

* But that hasn't stopped me from trying so far.

Truda McCoy says that Jim McCoy chastised Frank Phillips for the unnecessary killing and that Phillips replied contemptuously, letting Jim know who was actually in charge now of the McCoy allies.[70]

Truda McCoy's version of this battle puts the McCoys in the woods, slipping from tree to tree like natives, when they spotted half a dozen of the principal Hatfield feudists crossing a cornfield.[71] They agreed to hold their fire until the Hatfields reached the middle of the field, where they would have no shelter to which to retreat. But Harmon McCoy's son Bud (not Ranel's Bud, already killed in the pawpaw patch), widely known as one of the most dangerous men in Kentucky, couldn't restrain himself.[72] He leapt up, pointed his rifle at the Hatfields, and demanded their surrender.

Bud McCoy, fourth son of Harmon, had vowed revenge on the Hatfields for the murder of his father and his older brother Jeff. Present when Frank Phillips killed Jim Vance, he took a bullet in the shoulder during the Battle of Grapevine Creek.
COURTESY OF WEST VIRGINIA STATE ARCHIVES

Said to be "cruel, vindictive, and quarrelsome,"[73] Bud McCoy, fourth son of the murdered Harmon, had vowed revenge on the Hatfields for the death of his brother Jeff after his swim across the Tug Fork to Kentucky.[74] Having your father murdered when you are three years old, and your older brother when you are twenty-four, might put anyone in a permanently bad mood. A photo shows a young man with very dark hair and eyes, and a full mustache. He looks crazed, but possibly because his ears stick out like handles on an urn.[75]

Once Bud McCoy had ruined the trap that the McCoys had prepared for the Hatfields, he kept exposing himself unwisely during the ensuing gun battle, like a jack-in-the-box on too much caffeine. Finally, Bob Hatfield, who had purportedly avoided the New Year's Night Massacre because of his mother's pleas, obligingly shot Bud in the shoulder.[76] After the Hatfields had withdrawn into the mountains for the night, Bud expressed relief to his comrades that he had been hit in his gun shoulder and not in his dynamite pouch.[77]

Bud McCoy was clearly a fellow who knew how to see a glass as half full.

9

ALL OVER BUT THE SHOUTING

THE BATTLE OF GRAPEVINE CREEK DIDN'T ACCOMPLISH ANYTHING. Neither side killed or captured any of the indicted feudists. Bill Dempsey, a West Virginia deputy who had nothing to do with the feud, had been killed, and Bud McCoy had sustained a bullet wound in his gun shoulder.

The Hatfields did realize, though, that their muzzle-loaders and one-shot rifles from Civil War days paled in the face of the Winchester repeating rifles that the McCoys had recently bought from riverboats that came up the Levisa Fork of the Big Sandy River to Pikeville. So Devil Anse Hatfield instructed his deputy, Cap, to order twenty-five new Winchesters and ten thousand rounds of ammunition. They arrived at the nearest railway station, one week's journey by wagon from Devil Anse's house. Unfortunately, Cap's wife, Nancy, who had written the order, accidentally omitted a zero. Then again, perhaps she omitted it on purpose, doing her best to strangle her family's retribution with her pen. Either way, only one thousand cartridges arrived. But even these turned out to be superfluous, because it was all over but the shouting.[1]

Prior to the New Year's Night Massacre, newspapers from outside Kentucky and West Virginia simply reprinted material from local Kentucky newspapers, most of it hostile to the Hatfields. After the massacre, though, the feud became front-page fodder in such cities as Cincinnati, Pittsburgh, and New York. Papers there portrayed the Hatfields as ruthless desperados and the McCoys as the good guys in white hats trying to uphold the rule of the law.[2]

The *Pittsburgh Times* was the first prominent newspaper outside the region to send a reporter to feud country for a firsthand account. Charles Howell stayed in Pikeville for three days, making no effort to venture into the wilds of West Virginia. Instead, he visited Ranel and Sarah McCoy in a house devoid of furniture, since theirs had burned in the fire that had destroyed their Blackberry Fork cabin. He described Ranel as "a man who has been bent and almost broken by the weight of his afflictions and grief."[3]

Howell also visited the jail and interviewed Wall Hatfield. He described Wall's shaggy eyebrows as almost concealing "eyes of a greenish gray that are forever evading the person with whom the owner may be talking."[4]

Howell's overall assessment of the feud was that the Hatfields were destroying the smaller and weaker McCoy clan: "Given, on the one hand, a family with its contingents of the same blood, allied and cemented by a common desire to avenge an imaginary affront, and on the other another family, small in the matter of alliance and collateral sympathies, doomed to destruction by the larger one, and the case is stated."[5] Many newspapers outside the region syndicated Howell's account, further coloring public opinion against the Hatfields.[6]

†

Sensing that Devil Anse Hatfield was now vulnerable because of the successes of the Kentucky posses, the creditors from his timbering operations in West Virginia swooped down on him only days after the Battle of Grapevine Creek. They had been hounding him to settle his debts for a long time. He and his men had charged supplies at some stores, and the store owners had marked up the goods higher than Devil Anse felt he had agreed to.[7]

Devil Anse had been wanting to move to a spot more easily defensible from Kentucky raiding parties and bounty hunters, in any case,[8] so he sold for $7,000 the remaining land he had acquired from Perry Cline. The purchaser, a coal agent for a consortium of capitalists from Philadelphia, paid off Devil Anse's timbering debts, and the Norfolk and Western Railroad began surveys for railroad tracks up the Tug Fork Valley.[9]

In two years' time, Perry Cline's land on Grapevine Creek would be worth ten times the amount that Devil Anse received for it, since it turned out to be located in the heart of a rich coalfield. Soon the valley filled up with outsiders: land speculators and surveyors, engineers and construction workers for the railroad line. Their off-hours drinking and recreational gunplay introduced even more chaos to the already strife-torn region.[10] Country living isn't always the bromide for stress that many city dwellers believe it to be.

Devil Anse bought several thousand acres inland from the Tug Fork from an eccentric wanderer named Old Hawk Steele, who had flowing hair and a long beard. Steele sold his land in return for a portion of the profits Devil Anse would earn from timbering it, which turned out to be considerable.[11] Just as Ranel McCoy and his family had moved away from the Tug Fork Valley to escape the feud, so was Devil Anse moving inland and upland from the valley to distance himself from the ongoing ramifications of his prior feud activities.

Devil Anse Hatfield built his new cabin in a valley between two ridges running atop a tall mountain. Nearby he constructed a fort of logs two feet in diameter, the walls six logs high.[12] The structure featured only one entrance and portholes in all the walls. He stocked it with food, water, fuel, arms, and ammunition, rather like a Cold War bomb shelter.[13] He organized an army of supporters and a system for summoning them with a code of rifle shots, whistles, birdcalls, and animal cries.[14] He also installed a drawbridge over the creek in front of his new house.

Resuming his life of hunting, farming, moonshining, and timbering, Devil Anse hid out from pursuers when necessary, waiting to see what would happen to his comrades in the Pikeville jail, as well as to those not yet apprehended.

✝

A month after the bootless Battle of Grapevine Creek, Devil Anse Hatfield's wife, Levicy, gave birth to their twelfth child, a son. In a masterpiece of public relations, they named him E. Willis Wilson Hatfield after the governor of West Virginia, who was emerging as Devil Anse's champion in the legal battles over extradition.

Much maneuvering and posturing ensued between the governors of Kentucky and West Virginia, each naturally supporting his own citizens.[15] A populist, Governor Wilson, whom one observer described as a "fiery but humorless orator," often chewed his red mustache when agitated. A reporter described him as "a small, rather slender man who has the thin and wrinkled face of one who habitually suffers from ill health."[16] His nickname was Windy, and one can't help but wonder if it stemmed from the nature of his oratory or the operation of his bowels.[17]

Governor Wilson wrote to Governor Buckner of Kentucky, informing him of the bribe that Perry Cline had accepted (and then ignored) not to pursue the Hatfields. Wilson refused to extradite the Hatfields from West Virginia, claiming that they couldn't receive an impartial trial in Kentucky. He also protested the killing in the fodder pen of Bill Dempsey, who wasn't a feudist and had been deputized merely to arrest Bad Frank Phillips and several McCoys for the murder of Bad Jim Vance.

All the bloodshed and stray bullets panicked ordinary citizens on both sides of the Tug Fork, who petitioned their respective governors for protection. Both states ordered their militias to prepare to defend their borders, and they sent representatives to the feud areas to assess the situation.

West Virginia's representative reported that the situation had calmed down and that the Hatfields were models of probity being persecuted by Phillips and Cline. Kentucky's representative agreed that tensions had abated but insisted that the Hatfields were the aggressors, and the McCoys fine upstanding citizens. Both governors countermanded their orders for deployment of their militias.

Local newspapers, meanwhile, had jumped into the fray. The Kentucky papers portrayed the Hatfields as sadistic banditos. The West Virginia papers insisted that the Kentuckians had started the feud and that most of the outrages had occurred there, so it was the McCoys who had a problem with anger management and not the Hatfields.[18] The West Virginia papers don't seem to have put much stock in the fact that the outrages in Kentucky had mostly been perpetrated by West Virginians.

Governor Wilson sent a document to Governor Buckner requisitioning Bad Frank Phillips and twenty-seven members of his Kentucky posse for the deaths of Bad Jim Vance and Bill Dempsey. Wilson also posted rewards of $500 for Phillips and $100 each for the others, many of whom went into hiding around Peter Creek in the Tug Fork Valley, near where Harmon McCoy had been murdered so many years before.[19] The uncaptured Hatfields were also hiding out in the West Virginia mountains.[20] All these men on both sides were no doubt delighted to leave the boring chores of farm life to their long-suffering wives and children.

Governor Buckner replied to Governor Wilson, defending the Phillips raids and demanding extradition of the remaining indicted Hatfields. Governor Wilson, in turn, requested that the US district court in Louisville issue orders releasing the Hatfields held in the Pikeville jail because the Kentucky invaders had unlawfully transported them across state lines. Wilson also maintained that the Hatfield prisoners in the Pikeville jail were in danger of attack from enraged McCoys.

The district court judge ordered the nine prisoners in question brought to Louisville for a hearing regarding Governor Wilson's request that they be freed. Perry Cline, Ranel McCoy, and several others escorted them to Louisville by steamboat and then by train. They had been in the Pikeville jail for a month, but the terms of their imprisonment had been lenient. Wall had been allowed to roam Pikeville at will and to visit Perry Cline's family. He appears to have impressed Col. John Dils because Dils offered to pay his bail.[21] Colonel Dils evidently had issues with Devil Anse Hatfield, but not with his entire family.

Perry Cline had switched from representing Ranel McCoy to representing Wall Hatfield because, some say, Wall had offered him a higher fee.[22] Truda McCoy reports that Perry Cline privately assured Ranel McCoy that his working for Wall Hatfield was in Ranel's best interests, though he didn't explain what he meant by this.[23]

A large crowd greeted the Hatfield prisoners at the Louisville train station, eager to catch a glimpse of the infamous desperados. Perry Cline lined them up two by two, each flanked by a guard, and marched them to the jail. Half wore white shirts, a few wore collars, and all wore soft felt hats and trimmed mustaches. They were quiet and polite, and many in the crowd were disappointed to realize that these were the gun thugs supposedly responsible for so much havoc. The *New York Times*, preferring stereotypes to this less dramatic reality, said on its editorial page, "The latest vendetta in the backwoods of Kentucky shows the purely savage character of the population more strongly than almost any previous instance."[24]

At the same time, the Louisville *Courier-Journal* helpfully suggested that the Hatfields move to Dakota Territory and the McCoys to Venezuela as a way to end the feud.[25]

In the district court the West Virginia lawyers argued that a citizen of one state couldn't enter another state to extract suspects in crimes committed in that citizen's home state. The Kentucky side replied that once a suspect was in another state, however he had gotten there, that state had a right to try him for a crime committed within its boundaries. Both sides maintained that a district court couldn't settle a dispute between two states, that only the US Supreme Court could.

The judge of the district court agreed that the case didn't lie within his jurisdiction and ordered the prisoners returned to Pikeville. West Virginia took the case to the US circuit court, which agreed with the findings of the lower court. Then the case was referred to the US Supreme Court.

The prisoners returned to the Pikeville jail, bored from a month of sitting quietly listening to a lot of legal wrangling that they didn't understand. They had enjoyed their time in the Louisville jail, though, listening intently as other prisoners read to them from books and lustily singing hymns in perfect pitch during religious services. Keeping to their mountain schedules, they had gone to sleep at dusk and arisen noisily at dawn—much to the annoyance of more urban prisoners who wanted to sleep in.[26]

Shifty-eyed Wall Hatfield had impressed the reporters with his quiet intelligence, despite the fact that one of his Pikeville guards had outed him to reporters as having five wives.[27] He steadfastly maintained the innocence of himself and of his fellow West Virginian prisoners, pinning blame for the McCoy murders on his brother Devil Anse; his nephews Cap, Johnse, and Bob; and several others, none of whom had yet been apprehended. "They are all bad men," he said. He also denied the rumor that he had multiple wives.[28]

Valentine "Wall" Hatfield, elder brother of Devil Anse, during the feud trials. *Pittsburgh Times* reporter Charles Howell described Wall's shaggy eyebrows as almost concealing "eyes of a greenish gray that are forever evading the person with whom the owner may be talking." Although he had pleaded not guilty, Wall was found guilty of the deaths of three McCoy brothers and sentenced to life in prison, where he soon died. COURTESY OF THE LOUISVILLE *COURIER JOURNAL*

A newspaper sketch of Wall Hatfield at this time shows an older man, partially bald, with a walrus mustache, the prominent Hatfield nose, and heavily lidded eyes. He looks almost as though he is wearing an ascot with his suit jacket. He gives the impression of being a thoughtful, distinguished country squire, rather than a hardened killer, which he probably wasn't.

†

As the Hatfield prisoners languished in the Pikeville jail, waiting to hear whether the Supreme Court would order their release, Nancy McCoy Hatfield decided to leave Johnse Hatfield. At the time, he was hiding out from the McCoy posses in a secret location. Fed up with his drinking and womanizing, she was also, no doubt, appalled by his role two months earlier in the murders of her cousins Calvin and Alifair McCoy, the beating of her aunt Sarah, and the burning of her aunt and uncle's cabin and smokehouse. She packed her belongings and crossed the Tug Fork with Johnse's and her two children, returning to her mother's house on Peter Creek in Kentucky.

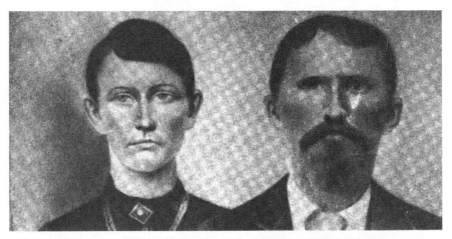

A twenty-four year-old woman with a twenty-three-inch waist, Nancy McCoy, after leaving Johnse Hatfield, caught the eye of Bad Frank Phillips, the McCoy family champion. They moved in together and had a child, even though Johnse Hatfield didn't divorce her until several months later. Her family knew that Phillips would protect her and her children from any revenge that Johnse Hatfield might take. COURTESY OF JESSE PHILLIPS

An attractive twenty-four-year-old woman with a twenty-three-inch waist, unlaced,[29] she soon caught the eye of Bad Frank Phillips, the McCoy champion who had organized the Kentucky posses that had captured the Hatfield prisoners. They moved in together that year and had a child the following year, even though Johnse Hatfield didn't divorce her until several months after that.[30] Her family rejoiced in the knowledge that Frank Phillips would protect her and her children from any revenge that Johnse Hatfield might decide to take.[31]

✝

The lawyers for Kentucky and West Virginia went to Washington for the Supreme Court hearing on April 23, 1888. The decision handed down by the justices, with two dissenters, was that prisoners, even if seized illegally, could be tried once they were detained in the state in which their crimes had been committed.

Given official permission by the US Supreme Court to kidnap people and hijack them across state lines, private detectives and bounty hunters arrived in the Tug Fork Valley in droves, hoping to claim the rewards offered by Kentucky for the Hatfields, and by West Virginia for Bad Frank Phillips's posses. By now, those rewards totaled some $8,000 (close to $200,000 today).[32]

In June two detectives from Charleston, West Virginia, set out in search of Dave Stratton, a West Virginian who had joined Bad Frank Phillips's posse because of a political grudge against Devil Anse Hatfield. Stratton had been with Bad Frank when Phillips shot both Jim Vance on the mountainside and also Bill Dempsey in the fodder crib. The detectives found Stratton, now living in Kentucky, asleep on a sandbar just inside the West Virginia state line, his flatboat beached beside him. One pounced on him and put a gun to his temple. Stratton surrendered, and the detectives delivered him to the Logan County jail and collected the reward.[33]

A detective who wore fringed buckskins and asked to be called Wild Bill—claimed by one researcher to be the notorious Confederate guerrilla leader Rebel Bill Smith himself[34]—reported hunting near Peter Creek for some McCoys, who turned the tables and started stalking him instead. To escape, Wild Bill placed his cap and coat in a pathway well beyond a hollow log, as though they had been shed in flight. Then he returned to the log and crawled inside it. The pursuing McCoys arrived and sat down on the log to discuss what they were going to do to him when they caught him. He hid in the log for two days.[35]

✝

During this summer of 1888, when bounty hunters were haunting the hills of the Tug Fork searching for their human prey, the *New York World* sent a reporter named T. C. Crawford to West Virginia to find and interview Devil Anse Hatfield. Crawford secured permission to visit Devil Anse with the help of John Floyd, Devil Anse's friend at the statehouse.[36] Crawford wrote a book called *An American Vendetta: A Story of Barbarism in the United States,* dictating "the first chapter and the essential parts of the story" in three hours upon his return to New York, after ten days of misery in West Virginia.[37] This book, and the pen and ink sketches of mountaineers by a Mr. Graves that it included, established and circulated, more than anything else, the emerging stereotype of the venal hillbilly.[38] The primary value of the book to researchers is the descriptions it gives of some of the major feudists by someone who met them in person, unlike most other feud reporters. It also includes statements from the mouths of some of the feudists themselves about their actions and motives, however self-serving these may have been.

Devil Anse Hatfield told Crawford that he had a bodyguard of nine men and explained, "I simply will not be taken."[39] He described the hardships involved in being pursued by posses and detectives: "I have been out hiding in the brush. I have been kept away from my wife and babies many and many a time. I do not like to be kept away from my babies."[40] Temper any sympathy arising from that statement with thoughts of Harmon, Tolbert, and Jeff McCoy, who never saw their own babies ever again, and of Pharmer, Bud, Calvin, and Alifair McCoy, who never even had the chance to conceive any.

Claiming that Devil Anse Hatfield resembled Stonewall Jackson, Crawford portrayed him as a "jovial old pirate,"[41] rather like an early Keith Richards. But he described West Virginia itself as a "barbarous, uncivilized and wholly savage region."[42] Previously the *New York Times* had labeled Kentucky "Corsica of America."[43] The mythmakers of America were off and running, using mountain life as grist for their media mills.

⸸

By fall, three more Hatfields—Charlie Gillespie, Cottontop Mounts, and Alex Messer—had been caught and delivered to the Pikeville jail. Gillespie, tracked for months, was finally captured by a detective and put in jail in Ohio, until officials arrived from Pikeville with requisition papers from the governor of Kentucky. A handsome, polite teenager with dark hair and eyes, he told his story to Charles Howell from the *Pittsburgh Times,* insisting that he went along on the New Year's Night Massacre because Cap Hatfield had promised him "some fun." He quoted Jim Vance as saying that the goal was to kill Ranel and Calvin McCoy in order to eliminate all possible witnesses for the prosecution of those indicted for the Pawpaw Murders. Gillespie maintained that the plan was to lure the McCoys out of their house, but if they wouldn't come out, to shoot through the doors and windows until everyone inside was dead. He claimed that he had only stood guard and had had no part in the killings.[44]

Two detectives tracked Cottontop Mounts for days, until they ambushed him on a road near Mate Creek in West Virginia. A tall, muscular young man, Cottontop fought back, shooting one detective through the leg, but he was eventually subdued and escorted to the Pikeville jail.[45]

Widely regarded as one of the most dangerous men in the Tug Fork Valley, Alex Messer had served as sheriff of a nearby county and reputedly had twenty-seven notches on his gun. Cottontop Mounts later claimed it was Messer who had shot Bud McCoy in the head in the pawpaw patch. Two detectives traced him to a country store. Posing as friendly strangers, they got themselves invited back to Messer's lodgings, where they revealed their true identities and accepted his rueful surrender.[46]

An enterprising detective disguised himself as a tramp and went in pursuit of Devil Anse Hatfield. Warned by a neighbor, Devil Anse's henchmen apprehended the fake hobo at a corn shucking. They forcibly removed his rags to discover underneath a new suit that smelled of mothballs as well as a pistol and cartridges. They escorted him out of the mountains and put him on the road back home to Ohio.[47]

Some newspapers reported that besieged Hatfields had been spotted trekking north along the railroad tracks, fleeing West Virginia to escape the bounty hunters.[48] Other reporters stirred up more hysteria by claiming that West Virginian mountaineers would shoot on sight any Northern sportsman, from a suspicion of strangers due to the presence of so many detectives, and also from a wish to steal his superior firearms.[49]

In January 1889 two detectives announced their intention to shoot Devil Anse, Cap Hatfield, and French Ellis, and to accost the other indicted Hatfields. The Hatfields took out warrants against the detectives for these threats and managed to capture them in the woods. Then Devil Anse and his followers marched their prisoners to Logan, West Virginia. The Hatfields made the detectives carry them on their backs across streams so that they wouldn't get their boots wet. In Logan, the Hatfields had the detectives locked up in jail so they could see how much they liked it.[50]

After this prank, the "jovial old pirate" went back up to his fort in the sky and concentrated on making sure that he and his family weren't caught. Later, an arsonist believed to be one of the jailed detectives set fire to Devil Anse's barn, destroying a valuable horse and 150 bushels of corn.[51]

†

Sometime in the spring of 1889, Roseanna McCoy, who had been wasting away for a long time, took to her bed and never got up again. Her young life had been one of loss—of her uncle Harmon; Johnse Hatfield; her woods-colt baby, Sarah Elizabeth; her cousin Jeff McCoy; and five of her siblings. She felt partially responsible for some of the disaster that had befallen her family because of the role her romance with Johnse had played in inflaming the feud. Her mother had been permanently disabled and their cabin and smokehouse incinerated. Her father remained remote and unforgiving. She had many regrets about her past and could see nothing to look forward to in the future.

Some in the feud had already died of broken bodies, but Roseanna died of a broken heart, "jilted to death by Johnse,"[52] collateral damage in a war in which she had made the mistake of loving one of her family's enemies.

10

"The Hatfields Made Me Do It!"

In April 1889, the incarcerated Cottontop Mounts confessed.

He stated that Charlie Carpenter, the former schoolteacher who had composed the document authorizing vigilante justice against the three McCoy sons, had tied them to the pawpaw bushes and hung a lantern over their heads so that their executioners could see their targets. Mounts said that before Tolbert and Bud had finished praying, Johnse Hatfield shot Pharmer, Devil Anse shot Tolbert repeatedly, and Alex Messer shot Bud, adding a twenty-eighth notch to his gruesomely overwrought gun. Several others then riddled the bodies with bullets.

Cottontop also claimed that Wall Hatfield swore the participants to secrecy afterward. Then he gave equally detailed accounts of Jeff McCoy's murder, as told to him by Cap Hatfield, and of the New Year's Night Massacre.[1]

The trials of the Hatfield prisoners for the Pawpaw Murders began in late August 1889.[2] Spectators from all over the area packed the courtroom. The mules and horses that had brought them to town filled the livery stable and lined the banks of the river.[3] As when Joseph and Mary arrived in Bethlehem to be counted in the Augustan census, all the inns were full.

Perry Cline was representing Wall Hatfield and his three sons-in-law now. In a truly ironic twist, Wall was paying for Cline's services with the promise, in the event that he couldn't raise the necessary cash for the legal fees, of some of the land on Grapevine Creek that Devil Anse had won from Cline in the settlement eleven years earlier and had then sold to Wall.[4] No one has ever been able to say whose side Perry Cline was actually on, but he lost the case, so perhaps he really was working in secret for the McCoys.[5]

The prosecution produced nineteen witnesses, eight of them named Hatfield, including Preacher Anse, further proof that not all Hatfields sided with Devil Anse.[6] Ranel McCoy told of accompanying his sons as the Kentucky Hatfield constables escorted them to Pikeville after they killed Ellison Hatfield during the Election Day Brawl, and of their counterseizure by Wall Hatfield and others. His memory of the events was vague and contradictory,[7] perhaps a symptom of what today we would call post-traumatic stress disorder.

The only known likeness of Sarah McCoy comes from a newspaper sketch at the time of the trials that ended the feud in 1890. By this time, she had lost six children to the feud, had been beaten senseless and burned out of her home, and was handicapped for life, needing a cane to walk. She died a few years later. COURTESY OF THE LOUISVILLE *COURIER JOURNAL*

Sarah McCoy spoke of her visit to the schoolhouse in which her sons were held captive and quoted Wall Hatfield as saying that if his brother Ellison died, her sons would be shot as full of holes "as a sifter bottom."[8]

The stalwart Jim McCoy, now forty years old, recounted sitting on the porch of a house in West Virginia near the Tug Fork and hearing a volley of rifle shots from across the river in Kentucky. He and several others crossed over to the pawpaw patch and found the bullet-riddled bodies of his three brothers.

Wall Hatfield explained that he took the McCoy brothers from the constables escorting them to the Pikeville jail because he wanted them tried in the Tug Fork Valley so as to obtain testimonies from several older witnesses of the Election Day Brawl who lived there and would have had difficulty making the trip to the county seat. He acknowledged attending a meeting after Ellison's murder at which Devil Anse ordered all the Hatfields and their supporters to fall in line. But Wall denied telling anyone that the McCoy sons would be killed if Ellison died. He further denied crossing the Tug Fork to the pawpaw patch or administering an oath of secrecy to the execution party afterward. He insisted that he had wanted the McCoy brothers tried in a court of law and had done everything in his power to protect them while they were being held captive in the schoolhouse. He also pointed out that he had surrendered voluntarily to the Kentucky authorities in response to the indictment against him.[9]

Various witnesses confirmed the testimonies of Ranel, Sarah, and Jim McCoy. Two of the indicted turned state's evidence in return for having their charges dismissed. They had been among four who had refused to participate in the shooting of the McCoy brothers and had turned to leave as the others opened fire.

Several spoke in Wall Hatfield's defense. But in the end, the jury found him guilty, and the judge sentenced him to life in prison, the same verdict and sentence as those handed down to Alex Messer, two of Wall's sons-in-law, and five others. Wall's third son-in-law had fallen ill while in jail, and his trial had been postponed. When Messer heard the judge say that he was "confined to hard labor for the period of your natural life," he rose and explained that he hadn't been able to work worth anything for several years now. It provided a moment of comic relief in the grim proceedings.

The courtroom audience reeled, though, upon realizing that the defendants hadn't received death sentences. Ranel McCoy set about trying to organize a lynch mob, but people mostly ignored him.[10]

Eight Hatfield followers had also been indicted for the murder of Alifair McCoy during the New Year's Night Massacre, when she ran from the cabin to draw water from the well to douse the fire set by Bad Jim Vance. The Hatfields under indictment were: Johnse, Cap, Bob, and Elliott Hatfield; Cottontop Mounts; French Ellis; Charles Gillespie; and Tom Chambers.

The ringleader, Jim Vance, was already dead. The reputed mastermind, Devil Anse Hatfield, had covered his tracks that night by staying home in bed. Charlie Gillespie requested and was granted a separate trial, but he escaped from the Pikeville jail and was never found again.[11] None of the other indicted West Virginians had been apprehended, except for Cottontop Mounts.

Cottontop, though twenty-five years old, was said to have had the comprehension of an eight-year-old. He had already pled guilty to the murder of Alifair McCoy. His family was poor. His mother, Harriet Hatfield Mounts, had borne him out of wedlock. His biological father was her first cousin, the murdered war hero Ellison Hatfield, for whom Cottontop had been named. Since Wall Hatfield hadn't included Cottontop with his sons-in-law for defense by Perry Cline, and since no other Hatfields had come forward to hire him another attorney, he had a court-appointed one.[12]

The only witness called was Sarah McCoy, who hobbled to the witness stand, leaning heavily on a cane because of injuries sustained at the hands of Bad Jim Vance during the New Year's Night Massacre. She stated that Mounts hadn't killed her daughter and that Alifair had called out Cap Hatfield's name just as she was shot.

Regardless, the jury found Cottontop Mounts guilty and sentenced him to be hanged. He tried to change his plea to not guilty, explaining that he had confessed expecting mercy. But he wasn't allowed to retract his confession. He had become the designated Hatfield scapegoat. As Perry Cline told Ranel McCoy, "We've got to hang someone."[13]

Truda McCoy claims that Cap Hatfield had given Cottontop Mounts $500, a rifle, a saddle, and a promise of rescue from jail if he admitted to the crime.[14] As Cottontop waited in his Pikeville cell for the day of his hanging, he expected the Hatfields to arrive and fulfill this promise. They never did.

A newspaper article spoke of his "dull gray eyes that alternately stared and blinked at vacancy . . . his skin of ashen hue, and his countenance marked by the mental agony of one doomed to die, although madly desirous of living." He was quoted as saying that the Hatfields came after him with guns and insisted he join them in killing the McCoy brothers who had murdered his father. He claimed his guilt was not so great as those who had received only life imprisonment. "Nobody seems to be doing anything for me," he told the reporter. "My lawyers come here and talk to me; then go away and forget that I am alive."[15] They wouldn't have to forget for long.

Wall Hatfield and two of his sons-in-law were conveyed to the Lexington jail to await the results of their appeals, which were eventually denied. Alex Messer—said by Cottontop Mounts to have executed young Bud McCoy in the pawpaw patch—went straight to the penitentiary in Frankfort.

The Pikeville sheriff who delivered these prisoners to their respective jails, accompanied by twenty-five guards, admitted his fear of Hatfield reprisals to reporters: "Every man, officers as well as witnesses, in these late convictions, has taken his life in his hands and may expect to be called on at any moment to pay the forfeit. . . . To do it [maintain the peace] requires unflinching nerve and backbone to stand the fire of midnight assassins."[16] Everyone had seen what the Hatfields could do to those who stood in their way, and no one had reason to doubt that they would do it again.

In October of 1889 Ranel and Sarah McCoy's youngest son, Bill, followed Roseanna's example and died of guilt and despair. Mistaking his brother Bud for himself, the Hatfield mob had killed Bud in his place. Bill was actually the one who had helped Tolbert McCoy stab Ellison Hatfield during the Election Day Brawl, at least according to Truda McCoy.[17] Despite Bill's attempts to lead an ordinary life, he still vanished for days at a time and was sometimes found sitting by Bud's grave. Finally, he, too, went to bed and stayed there.[18] He became Ranel and Sarah McCoy's fifth son and seventh child to die from feud-related causes.

†

Devil Anse Hatfield came down from his mountain fastness in November 1889, ten days after his convicted cohorts learned of the failure of their appeals, to face federal charges in Charleston, West Virginia, of selling whiskey without paying the federal tax on it.[19]

The previous spring, Dave Stratton—evidently not jailed, or subsequently freed, following his apprehension by detectives for participating in Bad Frank Phillips's posse—had traded Devil Anse some bridles and saddles in return for calves and cowhide. After the transaction, Devil Anse generously offered him as much as he cared to drink from a barrel of whiskey.[20]

Stratton presented this story to a grand jury in Charleston and parlayed it into an indictment of Devil Anse for selling liquor without a license. Stratton and some detectives hoped to lure Devil Anse down from the mountains so they could whisk him off to Kentucky for trial, thereby claiming the reward for his arrest.[21]

Greeted at Devil Anse's mountain fortress by a pack of growling bear dogs, the marshal who delivered the warrant to Devil Anse Hatfield promised him that if he came to court voluntarily, he would be shielded from all outstanding indictments against him. The seventeen supporters[22] who accompanied him to Charleston were allowed to carry their guns—a motley collection of squirrel rifles, muzzle-loader shotguns, and new Winchesters—and to keep the firearms with them in the courtroom.

Spectators in Charleston observed an affable old man in a navy blue suit with an open-necked shirt, and trousers stuffed into the tops of high boots, instead of the cloven-hoofed Lucifer they had been expecting.[23] The judge treated Devil Anse with respect and bonhomie, and dismissed the charges against him, believing them to be, as they in fact were, a trumped-up excuse to lure Devil Anse to Charleston so that Dave Stratton and the detectives could capture him and deliver him to Kentucky for the reward.

After a chat in his chambers and an invitation from Devil Anse to come bear hunting in the hills, the judge ordered that Devil Anse be given safe conduct for the hundred miles back to his home. Devil Anse replied that he didn't need any help, that all he wanted was to "get across the river and back to the timber."[24]

Charleston treated Devil Anse like a celebrity. He gave an interview to the local newspaper in which he denied involvement in the shooting of the three McCoy sons and the burning of Ranel and Sarah McCoy's cabin. He maintained that the feud had begun with the Hog Trial. Paris and Squirrel Hunting Sam McCoy had killed Bill Staton for his testimony against Ranel McCoy. Then Ellison Hatfield had sworn out a warrant for the arrest of Paris and Sam, for which the three McCoy brothers had killed Ellison at the Election Day Brawl. Much of the interview concerning Johnse and Roseanna's romance and the Pawpaw Murders was inaccurate and garbled, probably by the reporter, who described the Hatfields as "hospitable, honest . . . peacefully disposed."[25]

Several of Devil Anse's comrades, including his older brother, had gone to prison for life, and one was about to be hanged. Yet the "jovial old pirate" was striding freely around the state capital, flaunting his firearms, heralded as "peacefully disposed." Devil Anse had not only survived but thrived when many of his followers and opponents had not—and the public admired him for it.

On the day of his hanging, February 18, 1890,[26] Cottontop Mounts was waiting in his cell for the arrival of his mother.[27] Harriet Hatfield Mounts never came, dying that morning of a heart attack on the path to Pikeville.[28] It was another broken heart and another case of collateral damage, the kind not tallied in statistics about the victims of violence.

Cottontop had also been waiting for the Hatfields to rescue him at last. Rumors were rife throughout the region that they would do so. Security at the jail had been increased, and pickets had been posted around town.[29]

The only person to appear at the jailhouse was a very drunk Bad Frank Phillips, shooting pistols into the air and announcing that he had dealt with the Hatfields and was now ready to run Pikeville.[30] Despite his drunken delusions, he was frantic that Cottontop was about to be executed for a crime Bad Frank was convinced that Cap Hatfield had committed.[31] Deputies overpowered him and confiscated his pistols. Then a drunken Bud McCoy, fourth son of Harmon McCoy, rushed to his rescue, knocking the sheriff to the ground. The sheriff summoned twenty-five militiamen,[32] who restored order and left Bad Frank lying in the jailhouse doorway to sleep it off.[33]

While his death warrant was read to him, Cottontop Mounts smoked a cigar and blew smoke rings. Then he rode in a wagon, seated on his own coffin, to the gallows. Both he and his guards kept glancing toward the mountains, waiting for his Hatfield rescuers to arrive.[34]

It was the first public hanging in Kentucky in forty years, and it would also be the last. Technically, public hangings had been banned, so a fence had been built around the gallows. But the gallows had been erected at the base of a hill, so that the seven thousand spectators who had flooded the town from surrounding counties could stand on the hilltop and watch the hanging from above. Just as though it were an Election Day, the women in the crowd sold their ginger cookies, and the men drank too much moonshine.[35]

The February 18, 1890, hanging of Ellison "Cottontop" Mounts was the first public hanging in Kentucky in forty years, and also the last. Some seven thousand people came from surrounding counties to watch. In this photograph, Cottontop kneels on the scaffold, his head bowed. Four other men kneel with him, while three officials stand aside, two shielding their faces from the photographer with their hats. When the black cap was pulled over his head, Mounts cried out, "The Hatfields made me do it!"
COURTESY OF PAUL B. MAYS, PIKEVILLE, KENTUCKY

The sun was shining, and an unseasonably warm breeze stirred Cottontop Mounts's pale hair as he mounted the scaffold. He was clean-shaven and wore an open-necked shirt with a line of embroidery down the front placket. A photograph taken just prior to the hanging shows Cottontop kneeling on the scaffold, his head bowed. Four other men are kneeling with him, while three officials stand aside, two shielding their faces from the photographer with their hats. Perhaps they feared reprisals from the absent West Virginian Hatfields should their identities become known.

When asked if he had any final words, Cottontop said that he was ready to die and hoped his friends would be good so that they could meet him in heaven.[36] As a black cap was pulled over his head, he cried out, "The Hatfields made me do it!"

The trap door dropped moments later. Cottontop's body dangled from the noose, "turning slowly, back and forth, around and around, like the pendulum of a giant clock running down." A young man who probably had very little understanding of what he was doing, and who had agreed to confess to crimes that most believe he didn't actually commit, had been killed.* Some in the watching crowd had the decency to faint.[37]

The Mounts family had been too poor to hire an attorney for Cottontop, and they were too poor to hire someone to bring his body back home to West Virginia. The McCoy boys had killed his biological father in the Election Day Brawl, and his mother had died of a heart attack the morning of his hanging. There was no one left to care about the disposition of his remains, and none of the more affluent Hatfields for whom he had purportedly taken the rap offered to help. His body was buried in the Pikeville graveyard in sight of the scaffold.[38]

The scaffold was left standing as a warning in the present, and in case its services might be needed in the future. It became the site of drunken card games and occasional fights among roughnecks apparently unimpressed by death's arm towering over them.[39]

Soon after Cottontop's hanging, Wall Hatfield, Devil Anse's oldest brother, died in prison, unable any longer to endure the confinement or betrayal. He had turned himself in. He maintained his innocence of the charges against him. Yet he was sentenced to prison for the rest of his life while his younger brother Devil Anse, the feud leader who had embroiled all the rest of them in his deadly plots, still roamed the hills of their childhood.

✝

In February 1890, Aretas Brooks Fleming took office as governor of West Virginia, replacing Devil Anse Hatfield's ally E. Willis Wilson. The Hatfields' protection from the statehouse came to an end. By early fall,

---

* Cottontop's final words—"The Hatfields made me do it!"—make me wonder if this is his confession to Alifair's murder, contradicting Truda McCoy's allegation that Cap Hatfield had bribed Cottontop to confess to the murder that Cap had actually committed. It all depends on what Cottontop meant by the word *it*. Does *it* refer to the murder itself or to the false confession that resulted in his hanging?

Governor Fleming had canceled Windy Wilson's rewards and extradition requests for the Bad Frank Phillips Kentucky posse, at which point those men were able to emerge from their hideouts around Peter Creek.[40]

A wealthy corporate lawyer with burgeoning ties to John D. Rockefeller's Standard Oil, Governor Fleming wanted to make conditions in his state more appealing to investors. Kentucky and West Virginia reached a tacit understanding that the indictments for the feudists in both states would hold but would remain unenforced so long as their targets kept their noses clean.[41] Some of the Hatfields and their later pursuers, however, appear not to have received this memo.

That spring, Dave Stratton, who had dogged Devil Anse Hatfield so relentlessly, hoping to take him to Kentucky for trial, was found unconscious near his own house with deep head wounds and a badly contused chest. He died soon afterward, with the Hatfields assumed to be his executioners. More warrants went out for the arrests of Devil Anse, Johnse, and Cap Hatfield, and four others, but further investigation revealed that Stratton had been run over by a train while drunk.[42]

Late in 1890, Bud McCoy, who had taken a bullet in his gun shoulder during the Battle of Grapevine Creek and who had struggled heroically the morning of Cottontop's hanging to rescue the drunken Bad Frank Phillips from the grasp of the Pikeville sheriff, was found dead near a lumber camp on Peter Creek. Like a brood of Chicken Littles, many feared that the Hatfields had returned to the warpath and were reviving the feud. But it turned out that a young Pleasant McCoy, probably the son or nephew of the older animal lover who was Sarah McCoy's nephew and Ranel's cousin, was responsible. Pleasant and a friend had shot Bud eighteen times over "a grudge."[43] Perhaps Bud had cracked a bad joke about a cow.

In September 1890, the Huntington, West Virginia, *Times* stated: "The famous Hatfield-McCoy feud is at an end. After partaking in the bloody butchery of all the men they could kill, after living as outlaws, with prices on their heads, defying arrest and courting meetings with their enemies, after seeing their young men shot down, their old ones murdered, with no good accomplished, they have at last agreed on either side to let the matter rest."[44] Early the next year Cap Hatfield sent to the local Logan newspaper a letter believed to represent Devil Anse's sentiments as well as his own. It read, "The war spirit in me has abated and I sincerely rejoice at the prospect of peace."[45]

A jaded editor at the *New York Tribune* responded: "Our private and entirely disinterested advice to the white-winged dove of peace is for it to fly high in that neighborhood for a while yet, lest it be served up as the principal dish at a game dinner."[46]

Rumors of the feud's resumption continued to surface off and on over the next several years, but thankfully they remained merely rumors. In 1894, the *Logan County Banner* cleverly reported, "The Hatfield-McCoy War has broken out fresh in the newspapers. The Hatfields and McCoys, however, know nothing about it."[47]

To all appearances, the feud had ended at last. If you include the victims of heartbreak, the final score was ten McCoys dead to seven Hatfields. But in fact the pointless violence hadn't ended yet. More collateral damage was waiting in the wings from young men who had learned a disrespect for life, or a lust for blood, or both, during the feud years.

PART 3:

AFTERMATH

11

SURVIVORS

RANEL AND SARAH MCCOY BOUGHT AN ATTRACTIVE TWO-STORY FRAME house in downtown Pikeville.* For the rest of his life, Ranel ran a ferryboat on the Levisa Fork, complaining bitterly about the Hatfields to any passengers who would listen. "So monotonous did his ravings become at times," says one researcher, "that his neighbors agreed among themselves it was a shame no bullet had taken him away that unforgettable night."[1]

Following injuries sustained in the New Year's Night Massacre, Sarah McCoy had to walk with a cane. Throughout the feud she had had a heart condition, and no doubt the loss of seven of her children and the burning of her home hadn't helped it any. Often short of breath, she experienced fainting spells. She died just a few years after the feud trials ended, around 1894, at age sixty-five, and was buried in Colonel Dils's family cemetery in Pikeville near her daughter Roseanna.[2]

....

* It still exists and has been turned into a very good Italian restaurant named Chirico's.

Ranel McCoy, about sixty
years old, during the height
of feud events that cost the
lives of seven of his children.
COURTESY OF LEONARD McCOY

In 1914, Ranel McCoy was visiting Melvin McCoy, his son Tolbert's son, with whom Ranel had fled his Blackberry Fork cabin when Jim Vance set it on fire. In a sad twist of irony, Ranel's clothes caught fire in front of Melvin's grate, and he was badly burned. He died two months later of his injuries and joined his wife and daughter in the Dils cemetery.[3]

Jim McCoy—Ranel and Sarah's second child, oldest son, and the de facto McCoy leader during the final throes of the feud—continued to live in Pikeville after bringing his wife and nine children there following the burning of his parents' cabin.[4] He refused to talk about the feud with his children.[5] His neighbors regarded him as "a hardworking, industrious man, easy to get along with and a friendly neighbor." He became sheriff of Pike County, later joining the police force.[6]

In his old age, Jim McCoy is rumored to have met Tennis Hatfield, Devil Anse and Levicy Hatfield's youngest son. They were seen strolling the streets of Pikeville together, arm in arm, chatting amiably. They reportedly had their picture taken there along with three friends.* Jim died of a lingering illness in 1929.

* I haven't been able to locate a copy of this photo.

After also seeking sanctuary in Pikeville following the New Year's Night Massacre, Sam McCoy, Ranel and Sarah's fifth child, bought a 250-acre farm outside town and died there of a heart attack in 1916. His dying words to his daughter were, "I don't hate anyone. I've forgiven all my enemies." His wife, Martha Jackson McCoy, continued to live on this farm until her own death in 1944. Interviews with her provided her daughter-in-law Truda McCoy with much of the information included in her book about the feud. Sam and Martha joined Ranel, Sarah, and Roseanna in the Dils cemetery in Pikeville.[7]

No records survive, if there ever were any, about what happened to the four surviving McCoy daughters—as is so often the way of the world.

Squirrel Hunting Sam McCoy, Ranel's and Harmon's nephew, who killed Bill Staton for his testimony against Ranel McCoy in the Hog Trial, moved out West in the 1890s, living in California, Kansas, and Missouri. He married four times. In the 1930s he wrote his memoirs, which tell of many deadly antics with knives and guns. He blamed the feud on the Hog Trial and on the McCoys' habit of talking too much and antagonizing the Hatfields.* Said to go barefoot in summer and winter, Squirrel Hunting Sam's feet eventually froze, and he had to have a leg amputated. He died from complications of the amputation.[8]

Perry Cline died in 1891, aged forty-two, having lived only long enough to see the end of the feud,[9] which he had perhaps helped to prolong by reviving the stalled indictments against the Hatfields for the Pawpaw Murders.

Frank and Nancy Phillips supported themselves and their eleven children—two of Nancy's with Johnse, five of Frank's with his second wife, and four of their own—in part by bootlegging.[10] Bad Frank Phillips continued to live up to his nickname. He quarreled with a younger friend over a woman and threatened to knife him. The friend warned him to back off, but he kept coming. His friend shot him through the hips.

Carried home, he set about putting his affairs in order. He requested that his first wife come to visit, and he asked her if their last two children

---

* It's hard for an outsider to understand how Ranel McCoy's being a yenta could have been an acceptable excuse for the death of five of his children, but perhaps other familial grudges were at work behind that opinion.

were really his. She said yes, but he must not have believed her because he left money to all his children except for those two.[11] He also left five hundred acres of land to Nancy. After lingering for a couple of weeks, he died of his wounds in 1898 at the age of thirty-six.[12]

Bad Frank's wife, the "Hellcat" Nancy McCoy Hatfield Phillips, died of tuberculosis three years later, also thirty-six years old. Devil Anse Hatfield's wife, Levicy, came to Pikeville to retrieve the two children Nancy had had with Johnse Hatfield. The daughter soon died of tuberculosis as well. The son grew up to join the Navy and died of dysentery in Egypt, leaving Johnse and Nancy with no surviving descendants from their tempestuous union.[13]

It escaped no one's notice that three of the principal Hatfield feudists—Devil Anse, Johnse, and Cap—were alive and free, while several of their comrades were dead or in prison. Johnse managed to elude arrest in West Virginia for six years.

Always fearful of being apprehended and taken to Kentucky on the still-standing indictments for his role in the Pawpaw Murders and the New Year's Night Massacre, Johnse Hatfield fled to Washington State in 1896, where he worked as a lumberman. Rumor credited Ranel McCoy with financing seven detectives to follow him there, based on a tip from Johnse's first wife, now Nancy McCoy Hatfield Phillips, as to his whereabouts.[14] As the detectives closed in on him, he swam a river and fled to British Columbia, where he also cut timber. A friend in Washington sent a lock of his hair home to his family, telling them that he had been killed while felling a tree—in hopes of ending his pursuit by the detectives.[15]

But in 1898 Johnse Hatfield returned to West Virginia and cut virgin poplars and oaks at a remote lumber camp, where he fell in love with the daughter of a neighboring farmer. They married, and her father gave them three hundred acres as a wedding present, which Johnse started logging. It was reportedly a happy marriage that brought the beleaguered Johnse some peace and contentment. But his wife soon died, leaving Johnse with three small children. He married twice more.[16]

The eldest son of Devil Anse Hatfield, Johnse Hatfield was named for Johnson McCoy, a nephew of Sarah McCoy who married a sister of Devil Anse's wife. Even in his later years, Johnse Hatfield retains the dashing looks that made him, when younger, the family Lothario. COURTESY OF WEST VIRGINIA STATE ARCHIVES

Johnse Hatfield had a rival in the lumber business named "Doc" Ellis. One day Johnse was walking along railroad tracks in West Virginia when three armed men appeared before him and three more behind. They escorted him to Kentucky, where Doc Ellis was so thrilled to see him finally in captivity that he shot a rifle over his head and shouted gleefully.[17]

Tried for his role in the Pawpaw Murders and the New Year's Night Massacre, Johnse Hatfield received a life sentence.[18] Six years into it, he witnessed a fellow inmate attack the warden of his prison with a sharpened fork. As the crazed prisoner tried to plunge the fork into the warden's throat, Johnse intervened. The prisoner threw Johnse to the floor, but Johnse cut his attacker's jugular vein with a penknife. He was granted parole as a reward for saving the warden's life.[19]

Johnse Hatfield went on to become a land agent for the Island Creek Coal Company, owned by the Rockefeller family.*[20] Johnse continued to drink heavily, and his good looks started to fade. A cocksure young man, he became quiet and diffident as he aged.[21]

Johnse's nephew Coleman A. says, "In their last years both [Johnse and Cap] realized the mistakes of their youth in the score of years which followed the Civil War, but both realized that they had been victims of the tragic times during the last quarter of the 19th century."[22] It is admittedly a stretch to regard perpetrators of the Pawpaw Murders and the New Year's Night Massacre as victims.

Johnse Hatfield died at age sixty of a heart attack while riding a horse.

‡

Unfortunately, the feud mentality had not died among some of the younger Hatfields. Charges of murder were filed against Cap Hatfield's teenaged brothers Troy and Elias (not to be confused with Devil Anse's

---

* Some sixty years later, John D. "Jay" Rockefeller IV, John D. Rockefeller's great-grandson, settled in West Virginia, a state whose natural resources had contributed to making his great-grandfather the richest American ever ("Richest Americans in History," *Forbes,* August 24, 1998, www.forbes.com/asap/1998/0824/032.html). After serving West Virginians impoverished by rapacious multinational corporations as a VISTA volunteer, Jay Rockefeller was elected governor for two terms. He has served as US senator in West Virginia since 1984.

brother Good Elias or Preacher Anse's brother Black Elias) over a death resulting from a fight. They decided to flee the law, and Cap agreed to take them to Oklahoma. Cap continued on to Colorado, where he worked as a farmhand, eventually returning to West Virginia.[23] While Cap was gone, his second son, Shepherd Hatfield, died of malnutrition.[24]

Upon his return from Oklahoma, Elias Hatfield began working at a saloon in Kentucky just across the Tug Fork from Williamson, West Virginia, a new coal town. On the Fourth of July, 1899, Elias—said to be a good-looking young man with black hair and blue eyes—was posting mail in Williamson when Doc Ellis, the man who had arranged the capture of Elias's older brother Johnse, arrived on a train to participate as a master of holiday ceremonies for the afternoon events. A popular and civic-minded man, Doc belonged to the Masons, the Eagles, and the Odd Fellows. No one knows exactly what happened, but some report that Elias called Doc a son of a bitch.[25]

"I'll show you who's an SOB," Doc Ellis replied, grabbing a rifle and shooting at Elias, whom a friend pushed aside just in time. Elias shot back, the bullet hitting one of Doc Ellis's gold cufflinks and ricocheting upward to break his neck.[26]

But this is the Hatfield version. Others maintain that Doc Ellis, on spotting Elias, retreated into the train car to grab his pistol. Poised for his return, Elias shot him the moment he stepped out of the coach.[27]

While Elias Hatfield was awaiting trial, his brother Cap, caught in the firm grip of the well-earned Hatfield family fear of the gallows, helped him to escape, and they fled once again to Oklahoma. Returning later to West Virginia, Elias was tried and sent to prison but soon received parole.[28]

Twelve years later, in 1911, Elias and Troy, Devil Anse and Levicy's eighth and ninth children, opened a saloon together in a new coal-mining town. A competitor cut prices to lure away their customers, employing an Italian to take orders and make deliveries to the large community of Italian miners.

In a confrontation in a miner's kitchen, the Italian bootlegger shot Elias three times, and Troy six. The brothers, in turn, shot him four times. The Italian died immediately. Elias and Troy reclined on the back porch, discussing their wounds, for the ten minutes it took Elias to die. Troy died twenty minutes later.[29]

✝

In 1882, the then eighteen-year-old Cap Hatfield had had a girlfriend, his first cousin Nancy Elizabeth Smith, the daughter of Devil Anse's sister Emma. Some say her uncle was the notorious Confederate guerrilla leader Rebel Bill Smith.[30] While Cap was pursuing feud-related activities, Nancy married a merchant from Georgia who was having a dispute with his business partner. In September 1882, not long after the Pawpaw Murders, Nancy's husband was shot in ambush while doing chores outside his house. Some claimed his business partner shot him; others, that Cap Hatfield shot him because he was still in love with Nancy.[31]

Cap's grandson Coleman C. indignantly denies this last possibility: "It takes a very small mind to accuse a 15-year-old woman of marrying her husband's killer. Nancy Hatfield did no such thing." He further points out that his grandparents weren't married until more than a year after the murder of Nancy's first husband.[32] Though a year later might still sound suspiciously soon to some small-minders.

In any case, Cap and Nancy Hatfield's marriage seems to have been a happy one. Nancy was said to be a better rider and shooter than Cap. One day Cap, his son Coleman A., and several others tried to shoot a blue heron in flight and missed. Nancy grabbed the gun and blasted it out of the sky.[33] Why anyone would want to shoot a blue heron is, of course, another question.

During the final years of the feud, Nancy taught Cap to read and write. Like Calvin McCoy, whom he had helped to kill, Cap appears to have been very intelligent and to have loved learning. He and Nancy bought books and subscribed to magazines, and he could recite passages from the classics by memory.[34] Employing his new literacy, Cap wrote a letter in 1889 to the governor of Kentucky offering to surrender, though he never followed through on this generous offer.[35]

After the convictions of his comrades for the Pawpaw Murders, Cap Hatfield—still subject to the outstanding indictments—had a hard time putting out crops and tending livestock because he had to be on the lookout constantly for bounty hunters. He fled often to the hills to hide out. No one wanted to hire him for other kinds of work because of his unfortunate reputation—and presumably his sporadic attendance.[36] Nancy said of those years, "It was a horrible nightmare to me. Sometimes for months Cap never spent a night in our house. He and Devil Anse, with others, slept in the nearby woods to guard our homes against surprise attacks."[37] Attacks not unlike the one they themselves had launched on the McCoy cabin, one would imagine.

Cap and Nancy Hatfield moved their family to Matewan, West Virginia, in 1895. Unlike other new company-owned coal-mining towns, Matewan was independent, with its own mayor and police force. It was located, coincidentally, just across the river from the sinkhole in which the three McCoy sons had been tied to pawpaw trees and shot among the putrefying corpses of sheep-killing dogs. Cap built a house and worked at a new sawmill there.

Disillusioned with the Democratic party, to which most children of former Confederates belonged, Cap Hatfield became a Republican, believing that that party offered more hope for a solution to the economic problems of his region. This wasn't a popular decision in a traditionally Democratic area, but his grandson Coleman C. regarded it as Cap's political declaration of independence from his father, Devil Anse.[38]

Unfortunately for Cap Hatfield, his reputation as both a Republican and also a dangerous man had preceded him. But Matewan already had its neighborhood bully: the Democratic postmaster, John E. Rutherford. John's father, Dr. Elliott Rutherford, had been a close friend and supporter of Devil Anse, who had named his fifth child after him. Devil Anse, Good Elias, and Elliott had established a school together, the one run by the sinister Charlie Carpenter with the bulging eyes. The school folded, and the building was later used to incarcerate the McCoy brothers prior to the Pawpaw Murders. Elliott had also lent Devil Anse money with which to pursue the case of illegal timbering against Perry Cline.[39] But they had had a falling out over a shoot-out that Elliott had had with a first cousin of Devil Anse's wife, Levicy. Elliott had shot Levicy's cousin in the spine, crippling him for life.[40] Another son of Elliott was now the mayor of Matewan, and one of Eliott's daughters had married Ranel McCoy's second son, the diffident Floyd McCoy.[41]

John E. Rutherford had been joking around Matewan that he wanted to put Cap Hatfield over in Kentucky—equivalent to saying that he wanted to turn Cap over to Kentucky authorities under the old indictments, which could result in his hanging. Dreading such a possibility, Cap always carried a gun.

As usual, the Hatfields couldn't seem to stay away from Election Days, however poorly those events had always worked out for them.[42] Cap Hatfield and his fourteen-year-old stepson Joe Glenn attended an Election Day in Matewan on November 3, 1896. Upon his arrival, Cap passed a Rutherford-owned store, where John's brother said to him, "I'm surprised you're down here today. I can smell the nigger on you."[43] This was a way of insulting Republicans for their support of emancipation during the Civil War and of Reconstruction following it. It also stemmed from the fact that many freedmen were Republicans.

Not taking the bait, Cap passed by. But at the end of the afternoon, when almost everyone had drunk too much, John Rutherford fired his shotgun twice at Cap, grazing his ear and neck. Cap, in turn, shot John in the side, according to Cap's son Coleman A. Other researchers maintain that bystanders couldn't say who had fired first.[44] Either way, five of Rutherford's friends began shooting at Cap.

John Rutherford's brother-in-law, standing on the steps of the polling site cheering John on, was shot and killed—some say by accident, others say by Cap's stepson Joe Glenn. Cap and Joe fled, chased by Rutherfords. Sheltered by a railroad bridge, Cap and Joe fired at their pursuers until another Rutherford fell dead, just across the river from the site of the Pawpaw Murders.[45]

Cap Hatfield and Joe Glenn hid out in a friend's attic while a posse of twenty-five searched for them down below.[46] The next day they hopped a baggage car that roared through Matewan without stopping. In

Huntington, West Virginia, they turned themselves in and were charged with involuntary manslaughter.[47]

Others say that detectives captured Cap and Joe while they were sleeping in a crevice near a natural rock fort on Grapevine Creek, which had been used as a hiding place during the feud.[48]

Whatever the case, Joe Glenn was sent to reform school,[49] and Cap was incarcerated in the Williamson jail.[50] Learning of a plot to kidnap him upon his release and take him to Kentucky to face trial for the McCoy murders, Cap asked his wife, Nancy, to bring him a drill. (Others say that Cap chopped open his cell wall with a hatchet during one of the many noisy parties he was allowed to host while in jail.[51]) Somehow Cap managed to get out of his cell. He met the ever-patient Nancy on the road out of town, where she gave him a basket containing clothes, money, and a pistol. He escaped to a remote region in the Cumberland Mountains, emerging to rescue his brother Elias from jail after the murder of Doc Ellis and flee with him to Oklahoma.[52]

A few years later, the Hatfield prisoners convicted of the Pawpaw Murders were released from the penitentiary for good behavior.[53] I have found no reports concerning whether they ever met up again with their comrades who had escaped punishment, or of what was said if they did.

In 1908, once again distancing himself from those who wanted to escort him to Kentucky for his crimes, Cap attended law school in Tennessee. Returning to West Virginia after six months, he continued to study law on his own and was later admitted to the bar.[54]

The only case Cap Hatfield reportedly handled was that of his younger brother Willis Hatfield, Devil Anse and Levicy's twelfth child, charged in 1912 with the murder of a West Virginia doctor. Willis, his wife, and baby were living in a West Virginia town, where he worked in a saloon. One day when he had been drinking heavily, he ran out of whiskey and went to see a physician at a local lumber company to ask for a prescription so that he could purchase more at the drugstore. Realizing that its use wasn't medicinal, the doctor refused. Willis cursed him, and the doctor slapped him. So Willis shot him six times, killing him.[55]

Cap Hatfield's grandson Coleman C. reported that "Cap thought that Willis had brought on unnecessary trouble for the rest of the family."[56] It is unknown whether Coleman C. recognized the full irony of this statement, coming as it did from the family's chief troublemaker. Devil Anse Hatfield attended Willis's trial with a rifle on his knees. Willis was charged with voluntary manslaughter and received a sentence of four years in prison. He served his term and afterward lived a quiet life, working as a personnel officer for a coal company.[57]

Cap Hatfield set up a law practice with his son Coleman A. and Coleman's daughter Aileen, the first woman admitted to the bar in Logan County.[58] Cap didn't involve himself in the day-to-day running of the law office. Some claim he spent his time away from the office making moonshine.[59] He went on to become a deputy sheriff, a deputy US marshal, and a private security guard. Ambidextrous, he loved to approach a miscreant with his right hand poised above his holster and then to sucker punch him with his left.[60]

Cap Hatfield died at Johns Hopkins Hospital in Baltimore in 1930 of complications from the old bullet wound that had damaged his intestines when he was fifteen. The scar tissue had become cancerous. As the Greeks used to say, "Though the mills of the gods grind slowly, yet they grind exceeding small."

Joe Glenn, Cap's stepson, who was with him at the Matewan polls when the three Rutherfords were killed, left reform school after several years and later became a respected attorney.

Of Cap Hatfield's children with his wife, Nancy, one became an attorney and judge; another a magistrate; and a third a deputy sheriff.

†

Devil Anse Hatfield's younger brother, Good Elias, the reluctant feudist, was indicted but never arrested or tried for the Pawpaw Murders. Although Devil Anse's grandson Coleman A. Hatfield felt that Good Elias helped to incite the New Year's Night Massacre by insisting that the McCoys were trying to assassinate him and that a counterattack "would have to be did," Good Elias had always done his best to avoid direct participation in the feud. After it ended, Good Elias sought safety by moving away from the feud zone to Logan, West Virginia,[61] just as

Cap Hatfield and his stepson, Joe Glenn, as attorneys. COURTESY OF WEST VIRGINIA STATE ARCHIVES

the governors of Kentucky and West Virginia had always recommended to both families, just as Ranel and Sarah McCoy and their sons Jim and Sam had already done on the other side of the Tug Fork, just as the family of Ava Reed McCoy's husband, Homer, had also already done. In Logan, Good Elias became a councilman, constable, and chief of police.[62]

Good Elias Hatfield finally nailed down respectability for his family through the achievements of his sons, double first cousins to Devil Anse's children, since their fathers were brothers and their mothers, sisters.[63] His son Greenway, shedding an early reputation as a moonshiner,[64] became a deputy US marshal and a three-term sheriff for Mingo County.[65] Sons of Greenway became the postmaster, jailer, and mayor of Williamson, West Virginia.

Good Elias Hatfield's third son became a physician.[66] His second son, Henry D. Hatfield, also earned a medical degree and worked as a surgeon for the Norfolk and Western Railway, later starting two hospitals in West Virginia. After winning election to the West Virginia Senate and then presidency of the state senate, he became governor of West Virginia in 1913 at the age of thirty-seven.[67] Later he became a US senator.[68] His daughter married the president of the United States Steel Corporation.[69]

One of Henry D. Hatfield's goals as governor was to reassert local control over the coalfields and timber stands of West Virginia, largely subjected to absentee ownership since the turn of the twentieth century. This appears to be his only unsuccessful undertaking.

✝

Devil Anse and Levicy Hatfield's third child, Bob, whom Levicy had perhaps persuaded to drop out of the New Year's Night Massacre, and who had shot Bud McCoy in the gun shoulder during the Battle of Grapevine Creek, became a successful merchant and owned a great deal of real estate.[70] Their fifth child, Elliott, became a prominent physician, graduating from City College in Louisville.[71] Their tenth child, Joe, born not long after the Pawpaw Murders, became the first Republican sheriff of Logan County.

Tennis, their thirteenth and final child, born during the year of Ellison Mounts's hanging, succeeded his brother as sheriff of Logan County.

As usual, nothing is recorded about Devil Anse and Levicy Hatfield's four daughters.

It is striking how many of Devil Anse and Levicy Hatfield's sons, grandsons, and nephews, as well as one great-granddaughter, took up careers related to law enforcement following the feud years—almost as though they felt obliged to uphold the laws their elders had flaunted, thus policing the potentially violent sides of their own natures. Eight grandchildren of the midwife Nancy Vance Hatfield also became physicians, as though from a need to heal the wounds their elders had inflicted on the body politic.

Of the two families, Coleman A. Hatfield wrote: "In later years, Hatfields have been known to visit the family graveyard overlooking the old home place of the McCoys and to kneel upon the earth and shed tears for their one-time enemies who lost their lives in that terrible family conflict. . . . The shock of the death of Allifair [sic] was lamented by the Hatfields, as well as the grief-stricken McCoy relatives. There was no intention by either side to wage war against women and children."[72] Such an assessment would have come as news to Sarah McCoy, whose bones Jim Vance's rifle butt had crushed; to Mary Daniels and her mother-in-law, beaten unconscious with a cow's tail by Cap Hatfield and Tom Wallace; to the ghost of Alifair McCoy, murdered in cold blood by Cap Hatfield or Cottontop Mounts when she limped outside to draw well water. Perhaps it was the later generations of Devil Anse Hatfield's grandchildren and great-grandchildren, innocent heirs to the damage inflicted on these women, to whom Coleman A. Hatfield was referring in this passage. His own son said that Coleman A. regarded the feud as "a tragic misfortune for both families."[73]

†

After the imprisonment of his supporters and the deaths of his brother Wall and his nephew Cottontop Mounts, Devil Anse Hatfield settled into a quiet life on his mountainside, his fort standing ready nearby in case bounty hunters tracked him to his lair. After Cottontop's hanging, someone anonymously mailed Devil Anse a piece of the rope.[74] Haunted by the story of the hanging of his great-grandfather Abner Vance by Virginia authorities, Devil Anse was determined not to let himself fall into the hands of Kentucky authorities. Those already convicted for the Pawpaw Murders and the New Year's Night Massacre were among the feudists least guilty of the crimes charged against them. Devil Anse no doubt knew that he, the perceived mastermind, would hang, just as his great-grandfather had, just as his nephew had.

Devil Anse and Levicy Hatfield in their later years, standing in front of their house in Sarah Ann, West Virginia. COURTESY OF WEST VIRGINIA STATE ARCHIVES

Through timber sales and leases on some of his land to coal companies, Devil Anse Hatfield earned a comfortable living. He eventually replaced his log cabin with a large white frame house with a two-story front porch, a design more commonly found in nearby towns than in the countryside.[75] As he had all his life, Devil Anse farmed and hunted, made moonshine, and raised hogs. He hunted bears until he was seventy-five,

Even after the feud had ended, when Devil Anse Hatfield went into town, he always carried a rifle across the pommel of his saddle or held it in his hand as he walked. He was said to be a superb rider and marksman. As his great-grandson recalls, this horse was named Fred. COURTESY OF WEST VIRGINIA STATE ARCHIVES

shooting three in one winter when he was sixty-five.[76] He also kept bees, as had Eph-of-All, Valentine, and Big Eph before him.[77] A neighbor told a reporter that Devil Anse was "universally regarded in this community in a favorable light."[78]

When Devil Anse went into Logan, he always carried a rifle across the pommel of his saddle or held it in his hand as he walked. When he talked with others, he stood with his back to a tree or a wall and scanned the surroundings with wary eyes. If he entered a room, he sat or stood with his back to a wall.[79] The feud had left its mark on him, just as it had on so many others.

Two of Devil Anse Hatfield's brothers, Wall and Ellison, had died from feud-related events. His younger twin brothers had always distanced themselves from his undertakings. Five of his sons—Johnse, Cap, Troy, Elias, and Willis—had been on the lam and in and out of prison for murders they had committed. Devil Anse must have suspected, in the dark of the night, that he hadn't set a very good example for his brothers or his sons. Coleman C. mentions that his great-grandfather was quoted as saying that "he was sorry the troubles began."[80]

The wisdom of old age is often a function of lacking the energy for the nefarious deeds of one's youth. Sometimes, too, it's hard to remember exactly whom one hated and why. A certain peace also comes from knowing that you have outlived your enemies, and Perry Cline and Frank Phillips had already died. In 1911, Devil Anse was seventy-two years old and still kicking.

Three weeks before his sons Elias and Troy were shot to death in their dispute with the Italian bootlegger, Devil Anse Hatfield was "saved" by his old friend and hunting partner Dyke Garrett.[81] Tall, lean, and quick, Garrett was an expert fiddle player. Deaf in one ear, he had been made a chaplain during the Civil War. Forced to participate in the execution of deserters, he began to take his assignment seriously. After the war, while playing his fiddle at a square dance, a lightning bolt knocked the instrument from his hands. This electrifying experience triggered a religious conversion. He was baptized and went on to found a Church of Christ congregation in West Virginia.[82]

Devil Anse Hatfield's extended family gathered on the banks of Island Creek to witness their patriarch's baptism by Reverend Dyke Garrett on September 23, 1911. Observers said that he had a pistol in his pocket. He stands in the front row on the right with his wife, Levicy, beside him. Reverend Garrett with a white beard is sitting on the left. The man sitting on the far right is Henry D. Hatfield, Devil Anse's nephew, who became governor of West Virginia the following year. COURTESY OF WEST VIRGINIA STATE ARCHIVES

Devil Anse Hatfield's extended family gathered on the banks of Island Creek to witness their patriarch's immersion on September 23, 1911.[83] Some claim that Devil Anse had a pistol in his pocket.[84] If God had refused to accept Devil Anse into the fold, there's no telling what might have happened to Him. But apparently all went well, and God prevailed over the Devil. Unfortunately, it came too late to benefit those who had had to endure the living hell of the feud years.

Following his baptism, Devil Anse Hatfield sent his son Cap's attorney stepson, Joe Glenn, to Pikeville to offer the McCoys $10,000 to withdraw their indictments from 1882 and 1888 against the Hatfields. Jim McCoy, now a policeman, still a man of principle, refused the money but assured Joe Glenn that he and his family no longer sought revenge.[85]

143

Devil Anse's great-grandson Coleman C. Hatfield says, "The Hatfield family was devastated by the killing of Ellison and later came to regard the killing of the McCoy brothers with bitter shame."[86] He doesn't specify which Hatfields experienced this tardy bitter shame, but it would probably be safe to assume that they included Devil Anse and Cap since they were the primary sources of information for his book.

In 1921, after several months of illness, Devil Anse had a stroke, losing the ability to move or speak.[87] A week later he died in bed at his house on the mountainside from pneumonia. The *New York Times* announced it to a world that had become as fascinated with Devil Anse as they would soon be with Al Capone.

Around five hundred people attended the 1921 funeral of Devil Anse Hatfield, held in his large white frame house, with its distinctive two-story front porch, in Sarah Ann, West Virginia. COURTESY OF WEST VIRGINIA STATE ARCHIVES

Five hundred people, including Anse's eleven surviving children, almost all of his forty grandchildren, and several great-grandchildren, made the trek to his home in Sarah Ann, West Virginia.[88] They filed past his open casket of golden oak, "his beard, tinged with grey, spread on his chest like the plumage of a large bird."[89] A mountain choir sang ancient hymns and chants.

Devil Anse Hatfield lying in his golden oak casket, surrounded by mourners, in 1921, with his immediate family in the front row. COURTESY OF WEST VIRGINIA STATE ARCHIVES

It was said that Devil Anse Hatfield's deathbed wish was for his sons Cap and Elliott to reconcile. It's unclear why they were estranged, but the story goes that Cap offered his hand to Elliott, and Elliott took it. Both wept.[90]

Cap Hatfield informed Dyke Garrett that he had made his peace with God and wanted to be baptized. Garrett promised to baptize him later in the same stream in which he had baptized Devil Anse a decade earlier. After reaching this agreement with Garrett in front of his father's coffin, Cap raised his hands above his head and declared that he would fight no more, and that if anyone wanted to take his life for his past deeds, he would not resist.[91] He didn't, however, offer to go to Kentucky to face trial.

The day was cold, and rain alternated with snow. Levicy Hatfield, now seventy-five years old, bereaved, and unable to manage the walk to the graveyard, said farewell at home to her husband of over sixty years. The mourners walked to the cemetery along with the casket bearers. The gravesite sat just below a mountain crest overlooking the Guyandotte Valley on one side and the Tug Fork Valley on the other.[92] An umbrella was held over Devil Anse in the open coffin as the onlookers crowded around[93] and listened to prayers led by a former Logan Wildcat.[94] Then the casket was lowered into a steel vault and buried.

A few years after his death, Devil Anse Hatfield's descendants commissioned a life-size monument, carved of Carrara marble, to top his grave. It lists the names of the feud leader, his wife, and their 13 children. It is on the National Register of Historic Places. His widow, Levicy, is standing in the center. COURTESY OF WEST VIRGINIA STATE ARCHIVES

A few years later, Devil Anse's descendants commissioned a life-size standing monument of him, carved of Carrara marble at a cost of $3,000 (equivalent to $36,000 today), to top his grave. The statue, based on photographs, portrays Devil Anse in a frock coat and riding leggings. Mules hauled it up the mountainside to the graveyard. Devil Anse was a phenomenon in death, just as he had been in life.

Listing his name along with those of Levicy and their children, the monument rises some thirteen feet above the feud leader's grave. At its base lie the more humble graves of some who emulated him and served him so loyally during his lifetime—his sons Johnse, Bob, Elliott, Elias, Troy, Joe, Willis, and Tennis, and his nephew-in-law French Ellis.[95]

Cap Hatfield's remains, you will note, are not there. Some maintain that Devil Anse left instructions prohibiting his second son and most loyal deputy from being buried in the family plot, rejecting him in death just as Devil Anse's father, Big Eph, had rejected Devil Anse by leaving him no land in his will. But Cap's grandson states the more likely case that Cap didn't want to be buried alongside the man whose demands had dominated his youth and helped damage his later reputation.[96] He was determined to separate himself from his father in death, as he had not been able to in life. Yet Cap's younger brother Willis maintained that "the whole Hatfield family would have been killed if Cap had not been present to protect them and warn them of dangers."[97]

Levicy died in 1929, also of pneumonia, and joined her husband in the shadow of his towering marble effigy.[98] She had lived her life in his shadow, and her situation was no different in death.

12

OTHER FEUDS

THE HATFIELD-McCOY FEUD TOOK PLACE ALONGSIDE MANY OTHERS IN THE southern Appalachians, and especially in southeastern Kentucky, during the decades following the Civil War. The incidents that sparked them and the episodes that followed are almost incomprehensible. Newspaper accounts are just as inflammatory and as inaccurate as were those for the Hatfield-McCoy feud, and the oral histories are just as contradictory. But it's worth looking at a handful of them to see if a general pattern emerges to explain this epidemic of feuding during those years.[1]

THE BAKER-WHITE FEUD

Early in the nineteenth century, while cattle wars were raging between settlements on the north and south forks of the Kentucky River in Clay County, the Garrard and White families drilled wells into abundant salt deposits in the area. Both families shipped salt throughout the Southeast, making fortunes that they used to build grand houses and send their children away to fancy schools. They emerged as fierce competitors, each lowering prices to outsell the other.

But their real troubles with one another began in 1844 when Susan, a White daughter, married Abner Baker Jr., son of the well-respected court clerk in the county seat of Manchester. Abner Jr. tried his hand at several professions without success and then moved back home, where he was said to be a poor loser at cards. The Whites didn't approve of this volatility, and they were right to worry.

After the wedding, Abner Baker began accusing Susan White of conducting affairs with every man in sight, including the household servants and even her own father. Eventually, Abner shot and killed his sister's husband, Daniel Bates, because he suspected Bates of having cuckolded him.

General Garrard, a friend of Baker's family, arranged a competency hearing at which Abner was declared insane. But Daniel Bates's family, aided by the Whites, refused to accept this ruling and had Baker indicted for the murder of Bates.

At his trial, Baker's lawyers brought in experts who testified that he suffered from monomania concerning his wife Susan's supposed faithlessness. The jury, unconvinced, found him guilty of murder and sentenced him to hang. On the day of the hanging, Baker struggled with his captors as they led him up the steps. When the noose was placed around his neck, he cried out, helpfully, "Go ahead! Let a whore's work be done!"[2]

The Bakers railed at the Whites over this execution of someone so obviously crazy. The Whites railed at the Bakers for trying to prevent justice against Abner for ruining Susan's reputation. They also fumed at their old salt-rival, General Garrard, for siding with the Bakers.

The hanging of another Baker soon added tinder to the smoldering coals of resentment between the two factions. William Baker, a cousin of Abner Baker Sr., was charged with killing a shoemaker, possibly because the shoemaker had propositioned his wife. The killer slung the shoemaker's corpse across an ox and took it to the woods for a clandestine burial. William's wife was cleared of suspicion, but William, despite the

Garrards' help, was found guilty and hanged. Five years later, William's widow confessed on her deathbed to the shoemaker's murder.[3]

The shoemaker had belonged to the large Howard family of Clay County, so now the Howards joined the Whites against the Bakers and the Garrards.

In August 1897, a Howard supporter who was a deputy sheriff met three Bakers on a road outside of town. Suspecting they were headed into Manchester to disrupt a meeting of the White-Howard-Bates alliance, the deputy sheriff demanded to know where they were going. When the Bakers refused to say, someone started shooting. All joined in until their guns were empty. Miraculously, no one was killed, but Anse Baker was wounded, and his horse was killed.

That night the Howard-allied deputy sheriff's house burned down. Anse and Bad Tom Baker were charged with arson, and a Garrard bailed them out. On the day of their trial, a gang of Bakers converged on the courthouse to witness the proceedings. The two men were acquitted, which understandably distressed the Whites and Howards in attendance. The sheriff, a White, argued with a Baker and then pistol-whipped him. As blood streamed down the Baker's face, several Whites emerged from the offices they all occupied as county officials to engage in a brawl with the Bakers. Eventually the Bakers fled the courthouse.

A month later, Bad Tom Baker and his brother were riding on a path alongside a creek when they encountered an itinerant peddler. Drunk, they harassed him, shooting at his feet to make him dance. When he objected, they shot him dead and threw his body into the creek. "Let the turtles have him," Bad Tom Baker said.[4]

The Howards and Bakers both owned timberland on Crane Creek. A month after the peddler's murder, Bad Tom and several other Bakers were felling trees with which to construct a raft to float downriver to a sawmill. Bal Howard, patriarch of the Howard family, along with several kinsmen, was doing the same on the opposite side of the creek. Bal Howard and Bad Tom Baker got into a quarrel over a debt. Bad Tom threw a tool at Bal, and Bal swung a peavey at him. Then Bad Tom whacked Bal with his pistol, and Bal's son shot Bad Tom, the bullet grazing his flesh. The others jumped in to stop the fight—for the time being.

Bad Tom Baker was in his yard the next day when a neighbor stopped by to warn him that Howards were waiting to ambush him if he went to his woodlot. He stayed home, but as he sat on his porch, a bullet zinged past him and lodged in his door frame.

The next day, both families were working on their rafts. The Bakers went home for lunch, while the Howards cast off their raft for its journey downriver. Then the Howards headed home on their horses for lunch, too. As they rounded a bend, a volley of rifle fire killed two of them. Bal Howard was also shot, and his horse bolted and carried him down the road. He fell from his saddle, still alive, and was later retrieved by his relatives.

Big Jim Howard, oldest son of Bal Howard and a one-time schoolteacher, rode toward his father's house to visit his wounded father, only to be shot at from the woods. Trying another route, he was shot at again. He returned to a nearby post office in a rage, trying to figure out how to visit his father without getting killed himself.

Suddenly Baldy George Baker, patriarch of the Baker family, rode into town. Spotting him, Big Jim Howard grabbed his rifle. Baldy George jumped down to take cover behind his horse. Big Jim's bullet went through the horse's neck and lodged in Baldy George's bowels. Carried into a nearby store, he was laid on the counter. Two doctors stitched up his torn intestines, but he died anyway.

Big Jim Howard turned himself in to Deputy Sheriff Will White and was released on his own recognizance. Forty armed guards took position around Bal Howard's house, while anonymous gunmen shot into the yard from the surrounding forest. Since Baldy George Baker had had fifteen sons and Bad Tom Baker had thirteen, the less prolific Howards direly needed these outside reinforcements.[5]

When the Howards arrived at their family cemetery a couple of days later to bury their two murdered kinsmen, bullets whizzed all around them from the woods. Not believing violence possible on such a solemn occasion, the Howard men had foolishly left their guns at home. Carrying their coffins, they retreated to another cemetery several miles away.

Back in Manchester, the Garrards and Bakers demanded that Big Jim Howard stand trial for the murder of Baldy George Baker, and the Whites and Howards demanded that Bad Tom Baker stand trial for the murder of the two Howards and the wounding of Bal Howard. Virtually everyone carried arms all the time, and few dared to venture into the streets at night. Though it seems hardly possible, the men in town were drinking more than ever to quell their stress.

As Deputy Sheriff Will White passed the former courthouse office of Baldy George Baker one morning, he said, "Well, I guess old Baldy George is roasting in hell by now."[6] Regrettably, a Baker son—in the office, cleaning out Baldy George's belongings—overheard this remark and reported it to his brother Bad Tom.

A few days later, when Deputy Sheriff Will White was collecting delinquent taxes, he ran into Bad Tom Baker. Apart from Will's indiscreet remark about Baldy George's spiritual destination, Bad Tom hated Will for having arrested him for burning down Deputy Sheriff Howard's house and for sheltering Big Jim Howard after he killed Baldy George Baker. So Bad Tom killed Deputy White—insisting that White had drawn on him first.

Bad Tom Baker was acquitted of murdering the two Howard kinsmen after witnesses swore he was miles away at the time. Then Big Jim Howard stood trial for the murder of Baldy George Baker. But the case was abandoned because Big Jim had been arrested in the meantime for the assassination of George Goebel, the Democratic governor elect of Kentucky, in a scenario that would require an entire book to explain.[7] Found guilty of murdering the governor elect, Big Jim Howard spent two years in prison before receiving a pardon.

Meanwhile, Bad Tom Baker went to Manchester to stand trial for the murder of Deputy Sheriff Will White. Bad Tom had refused to come unless state militia ensured his safety. He also refused to stay in the local jail. So the militia pitched a tent for him on the courthouse lawn. As Bad Tom stood outside his tent posing for newspaper photographs, someone shot him. The killer was never identified.

At Bad Tom Baker's wake late the next night, as his family sat around his open coffin, there was a scratching at the door. When someone opened it, a large turtle lumbered in and headed for the coffin. It startled those who recalled the murder of the peddler, whom Bad Tom had thrown into the creek saying, "Let the turtles have him." A mourner grabbed the turtle, carried it outside, cut its throat, and threw it back into the creek.[8]

Representatives of the Whites and Garrards negotiated and signed a truce on March 8, 1901.[9] If you count the start of the feud from the cattle wars of 1806, it had lasted ninety-five years. Somewhere between 100 and 150 people died. The murders in Clay County didn't cease in 1901, but the older members of the feuding families appear to have become exhausted by their lifetimes of mindless violence. They turned the feud over to younger, even dumber, hands, in which it sputtered along for another three decades.

The feud inexplicably ceased in 1936 after the shooting of a son of Bad Tom Baker by an unknown assailant as Baker drove a Garrard into Manchester. Big Jim Howard had, meanwhile, become a traveling shoe salesman who carried a pistol in a shoulder holster. As he bent over one day, the pistol fell to the ground and shot a bullet into his back. He recovered, however, and went on to live a long and otherwise peaceful life, never responding to the question of whether or not he had actually assassinated the governor elect.

THE STRONG-LITTLE FEUD

During the Civil War, Capt. William Strong was a leader in the Union Home Guard of Breathitt County, Kentucky, clashing with several other Home Guards over the division of spoils from bushwhacking raids on civilians. After the war, Captain Strong continued his role as guerrilla chief, holding courts-martial in the middle of the night and condemning opponents to execution by his lieutenants.[10] Fellow Home Guards who had opposed his decisions concerning the bushwhacking spoils were murdered in this fashion.

In 1878, an attorney named Burnett was elected county judge with the support of Captain Strong—and in spite of opposition from the Little family, who favored another candidate. Burnett soon made the gruesome discovery that Jason Little's dead wife lay buried beneath the Little house, and he ordered her dug up. The Littles responded that she would be dug up over their dead bodies. Once disinterred, she was found to be pregnant, her body riddled with bullet wounds patched with beeswax.[11] Burnett sent Jason Little to the Lexington jail to await trial.

A deputy sheriff who was a cousin of Jason Little got a court order for his return to Jackson, the Breathitt County seat. Learning of his deputy's intentions, Sheriff Hagins hurried to Lexington and retrieved Jason himself.

Back in Jackson, Captain Strong's group, who wanted Little hanged for murdering his pregnant wife, occupied a log building near the courthouse. Among his seventeen supporters was his top killer, Hen Kilburn, who had named his rifle The Death of Many. Also in Captain Strong's party were a former slave named Nigger Dick Strong and two mulatto brothers named William and Daniel Freeman.

The Littles arrived in Jackson, too, with their strongman, Big John Aikman, who detested Captain Strong. Both groups lounged just down the street from one another. Daniel Freeman made the unfortunate mistake of walking up to Big John Aikman, however, and asking him what he wanted.

"I'll take a dead nigger," Big John replied, shooting Daniel in the back as he turned to run. William rushed to help Daniel and was also shot.[12]

The Strongs retreated to their log building. The Littles took over the courthouse. Everyone else left town.

The Strongs and Littles shot at each other all afternoon. Someone finally dared to go into the street to rescue the two wounded Freemans. Daniel soon died, but William, shot in the back and thigh, recovered.

At nightfall, the Littles left for a barbecue at someone's house in the country. Deputy Sheriff Little arrived at the barbecue and announced that he had been unable to rescue Jason Little, who was now en route to the Jackson jail with Sheriff Hagins.

A group of fifty Littles stationed themselves in town to intercept Sheriff Hagins—but Hagins took a side road and locked Little into a jail cell before his relatives realized that he had arrived. As Burnett and Hagins walked from the jail to their boardinghouse, a Little supporter shot and killed Burnett.

Meanwhile, other Littles set about breaking down the door of the jail to free their kinsman. One of Little's cousins pleaded with his relatives not to take the law into their own hands, so someone shot and killed him. Everyone else withdrew: Captain Strong's men to their log house, the Littles to the courthouse, Sheriff Hagins to a hotel. They all started shooting, not knowing at whom or why, until the liquor ran out. Then everyone sobered up and went home.

Jason Little stood trial for the murder of his pregnant wife and was sentenced to life in prison. He was pardoned after five years.

The governor ordered Big John Aikman apprehended and tried for several murders. He received a twenty-year sentence but was pardoned after just one. Prison pardons were common in those years, in return for election support from prisoners' kinsmen. "A life sentence was often little more than an extended vacation away from home," as John Ed Pearce puts it.[13]

About a hundred people died in the Strong-Little feud, with nothing much having been accomplished.[14]

By the early 1880s, Captain Strong had aged and mellowed, and was known now as "Uncle Bill." But he was still conducting his deadly midnight courts-martial. During one, he assigned his top gun, Hen Kilburn, to kill a respected local farmer. Kilburn hid in the bushes with The Death of Many and shot the farmer as he rode into town.

Unfortunately, Kilburn had failed to take into account that this farmer belonged to the Ku Klux Klan. Hen was arrested and thrown into jail, along with a black friend who had brought him food while he was in hiding. As midnight approached, hundreds of Klan members surrounded the jail. They forcibly removed the jailer when he refused to give them the keys to Kilburn's cell. Then they chopped down the door with axes and dragged Kilburn and the black man to nooses hanging from the courthouse doorway. The bodies remained there until the next morning, by order of a message posted on the courthouse door by the Klan.[15]

His chief henchman dead, Captain Strong realized that his days of power had ended, so he mostly stayed quietly at home, dandling his grandchildren. One day, with a grandson behind him, he rode his mule to a store, where he bought a few items and chatted for a while. As grandfather and grandson rode home, Big John Aikman and two others ambushed them. They killed Uncle Bill and his mule—but they spared his young grandson, who lay screaming in the road as they emerged from the bushes to riddle Uncle Bill's body with more bullets.[16]

THE MARTIN-TOLLIVER FEUD

A store owner in Morehead, Kentucky, and a clerk for Rowan County, John Martin lost his store over gambling debts. When he falsified records in an 1878 election, he lost his clerkship as well. He went to live at the home of George Underwood, whose sons had been Union Home Guards during the Civil War. A neighbor named Holbrook accused Martin and an Underwood son of stealing some horses, but Underwood denied it.

George Underwood was shot through the shoulder in his yard one afternoon. When one of his sons emerged from hiding to help him, the son was shot through a lung and died. That night, a dozen Holbrooks arrived at the Underwood house, their faces blackened to conceal their identities. They demanded to search the house for John Martin, the horse thief. Not finding him, they shot old man Underwood a second time, killing him as he sat beside his dead son, holding his granddaughter's hand. Martin escaped, survived, and went on to become a moonshiner with a major role in the next feud to ignite in Rowan County.

After a dance in a Morehead, Kentucky, hotel in 1884, two years after the Pawpaw Murders, Lucy Trumbo got tired and went up to her room. Unfortunately, she went into the room of an itinerant timber merchant by mistake. When he returned to find her lying on his bed, he tried to profit from the situation. She screamed and fled.[17]

At yet another drunken election day, Lucy's husband demanded a public apology from the timber merchant. The merchant refused, saying he had only done what any man would have done upon finding an attractive woman in his bed. A fight erupted. When the town marshal tried to stop it, someone hit him in the head with a rock.

During this fight, Floyd Tolliver knocked down John Martin (of the previous Underwood-Holbrook feud). Martin brandished his pistol, as did Floyd Tolliver. After the dust settled, Martin and another man were

Craig Tolliver had learned to fire a gun at an early age, after watching his father killed in bed during a robbery. He later vowed vengeance against John Martin, who had killed his brother Floyd. FROM *DAYS OF ANGER, DAYS OF TEARS*, COURTESY OF JUANITA BLAIR AND FRED BROWN

wounded, and a friend of Martin had died. Since no one could figure out who had shot whom, Martin, Tolliver, and the sheriff were all indicted. While awaiting trial, Martin and Tolliver, both drunk, ran into each other at the Morehead hotel. Tolliver drew his gun, but Martin shot him first, with his gun still in his pocket, which ruined his jacket but killed Tolliver.[18]

Floyd's brother Craig Tolliver vowed vengeance, so the judge moved John Martin to a jail in Winchester, Kentucky. Six feet tall, with blue eyes, brown hair, a full mustache, and sometimes a goatee, Craig Tolliver had learned to fire a gun at an early age, after watching his father be killed in bed during a break-in, the robbers seizing a large sum of money the Tolliver father had received from the sale of his farm in North Carolina prior to moving to Kentucky.[19]

Acting on his vow of vengeance against Martin, Craig Tolliver sent two of his henchmen to the Winchester jail with a forged order instructing the jailer to turn Martin over to them for transport back to the Morehead jail. Martin begged the jailer not to release him, but he did anyway.

John Martin's wife, who had just visited her husband in the Winchester jail, was on the train back to Morehead. Without her knowledge, Craig Tolliver's fake deputies put her shackled husband on the same train—but in a different car. As the train pulled into a station just outside Morehead, Craig Tolliver and ten henchmen entered John Martin's car. Martin tried to run but was shot and fell to the floor. Hearing the commotion, Martin's wife ran to her husband's car and found him bleeding in the aisle. She took him back to Morehead, where he died the next morning.[20]

Craig Tolliver and his supporters were Democrats, and the Martins and their backers, Republicans. Craig got himself elected town marshal. Republican sheriff Cook Humphrey and some Martin supporters exchanged harsh words with a couple of Tolliver men in a hotel one day, the two groups shooting at each other until their ammunition ran out. Tolliver reinforcements arrived and shot up the town until the Humphrey contingent fled. Then the Tollivers patrolled the streets, brandishing rifles, while the townspeople cowered behind barricaded doors.

Many citizens understandably moved out of Morehead, some to nearby towns, others out West. Lawyers, businessmen, and county officials asked the governor of Kentucky to intervene. He summoned the two groups—the Republicans led by Cook Humphrey and the Democrats represented by Craig Tolliver—to Louisville to work out a truce. Both sides agreed to cease hostilities and received amnesty.[21] Craig Tolliver was reelected town marshal.

Later, Humphrey and a friend were staying at a Martin house inhabited by only women and girls, the men and boys having fled to Kansas after death threats from Craig Tolliver. Tolliver and his henchmen surrounded the home and demanded that the visitors surrender. When they declined, Tolliver crept into the house and up the stairs, where he encountered Cook Humphrey, who shot him in the face with a shotgun. Tolliver survived but was badly scarred for the rest of his short life.

A Martin daughter fled the house and careened into Craig Tolliver in the yard, his face covered with blood. He told her he would kill her if she went to Morehead for reinforcements. Ignoring his threat, she ran toward town. Craig shot at her but missed. When she reached the town seeking help, a Tolliver deputy promptly jailed her.

Back at the Martins', meanwhile, Tolliver threatened to burn down the house if Humphrey and his friend didn't surrender. The two dashed out the back door, jumped a fence, and raced across a cornfield. The friend was shot down as he ran, but Humphrey made it to the far woods and escaped.

Frustrated, Tolliver burned down the Martin house anyway. Another Martin daughter fled the flames and also ran to Morehead for help, where she quickly joined her sister in jail. The remaining Martin women spent the night under a tree by the burnt-out carcass of their home.[22]

When 150 state militia arrived in Morehead, the Martin girls were released, and Craig Tolliver and his supporters were arrested. But one of the magistrates, a Tolliver supporter, announced that there was no cause for a trial, so the Tolliver faction was released.

Craig Tolliver later bought the Morehead hotel at a bargain price from a Martin supporter who had made the mistake of clashing with one of Craig's brothers. The law required a liquor license for the hotel, but Tolliver, who had also opened a dry goods store, couldn't be bothered to get one.

Cook Humphrey, no longer sheriff, still paraded around Morehead with a band of men. Tolliver gave the new sheriff a warrant for Humphrey's arrest. When the sheriff delivered it to Humphrey, he jeered at the sheriff. Once again, everyone started shooting. The sheriff and his son were wounded, and one young Martin man was killed.

The state militia came back, and a truce was negotiated in which Craig Tolliver and Cook Humphrey signed oaths to leave the county and never return, except for funerals, in exchange for dropping the charges against them.

Humphrey kept his word and moved out West. Tolliver went to Cincinnati until the indictments against him were dropped. Then he returned to Morehead and installed himself as county judge. The charges against him were reinstated, but most of the town officials were Tolliver men, so no one pursued them.

Tolliver's saloon, running without a liquor license, also operated as a brothel.[23] Whenever anyone complained, Tolliver notified him of the date selected for his funeral, and the plaintiff usually decided to leave town before said date. The Tollivers routinely shot up the town at night, so other downtown businesses dried up. More than half the citizens moved away. The Martin woman whose house Tolliver had burned sent a poisoned turkey to a Tolliver ally.[24]

Several men surnamed Logan were indicted for planning an attack against two Tolliver supporters and were sent to the Lexington jail for their own protection. Two of these Logans, Jack and Billy, were released on bail, while their father remained in jail. Believing that they would testify for their father, whom Tolliver wanted convicted, he issued warrants for the boys and sent a posse to their house to rearrest them. Jack Logan was eighteen and studying to become a minister. Billy Logan, twenty-five, had tuberculosis.

The Tolliver posse shot out the windows of the Logan family home. The boys retreated upstairs, and Tolliver and another deputy followed them. Jack Logan shot the deputy with a shotgun, injuring but not killing him.

Then the posse set the house on fire. A deputy entered the burning building and assured the boys that if they came out, Tolliver would spare their lives. They exited with hands raised. The posse tied them up and took them to a nearby spring, where they executed them, severely battering their bodies to render them unidentifiable. On the ride back to town, Tolliver made everyone swear to confirm the story that the boys had been armed and resisting arrest.[25]

Boone Logan went to the burnt-out house in hopes of retrieving his cousins' corpses. Tolliver told him that if he attended the boys' funeral, he would be killed. He suggested that Boone leave the area, promising to hire Boone's wife as a maid so that she could support their children.

Boone Logan and a couple of other outraged citizens started meeting in secret. Even though Tollivers patrolled all the roads out of town, the Logan sleeper cell managed to hop a train to Frankfort, where they met with the governor and described the dreadful situation. The governor sympathized but pointed out that he had already sent troops to Morehead three times and had spent $100,000 of taxpayer money—with no resolution to the conflict. Each time the troops left, violence resumed. Passing the buck, he said it was up to the citizens of Morehead to liberate their town from the thugs who had taken over.[26]

Boone Logan traveled to Cincinnati, where he bought fifty Winchesters and two thousand rounds of ammunition. Back in Morehead, he rounded up over a hundred men equally fed up with the Tollivers. He distributed the firearms, and the men encircled the town. The sheriff delivered to Tolliver's hotel warrants against thirteen Tolliver supporters for the murder of the young Logan brothers. The Logan posse closed in, and Boone called for Craig to surrender.

Tolliver and his men started firing and dashed out of the hotel. Over the course of two hours, using fifteen hundred rounds of ammunition, Logan's men shot almost all the Tolliver backers present, hunting down and killing even the wounded. Legend has it that Craig Tolliver, for reasons known only to him, had vowed not to die with his boots on. He removed them and was promptly shot in the head in his sock feet.

Tolliver's fourteen-year-old brother, Cal, stood in front of the hotel, shooting a pistol in each hand, their twelve-year-old brother, Cate, beside him. When Craig fell dead, Cal grabbed his watch and wallet and crawled under a house, taking a bullet in his buttocks as he did so. He and Cate were the only Tolliver combatants spared that day.[27]

A stray bullet started a fire in the hotel, and a cask of moonshine exploded, spreading the fire to other buildings in town.[28]

The Tolliver corpses were delivered in a wagon to Craig Tolliver's wife, said to be a mild-mannered woman who was devoted to her husband. Like Mafia wives, she seemed to have no idea what he did for a living. The other bodies were laid out by the courthouse for relatives to retrieve.[29]

Boone Logan called a town meeting and announced that he had been following the governor's orders by executing the Tollivers and that free and fair elections would soon commence. The remaining Tolliver supporters indicted two of the Logan posse for murdering Craig Tolliver, but the jury of their deeply grateful peers found them not guilty.

The final body count for the three-year bloodbath clocked in at twenty killed and sixteen wounded.[30]

The Turner-Howard Feud

The Turner-Howard feud began in 1887—just before the Hatfield-McCoy New Year's Night Massacre—in a town originally, and ironically, named Mount Pleasant, later known as Harlan Courthouse. Hostilities erupted when Wix Howard and Little Bob Turner were playing poker. Little Bob was drunk. While he napped, Wix set his hair on fire.[31]

When they met in the street the next day, Little Bob Turner shot Wix Howard in the arm to repay him for his prank. So Wix fired his shotgun into Little Bob's chest, killing him instantly. Wix was acquitted of the murder on grounds of self-defense and had no further role in the feud about to flare up between his family and that of Little Bob Turner.[32]

Wix Howard's aunt Alice made whiskey, selling it at her store in Harlan. Little George Turner demanded that she stop selling it to his father, who drank too much. Aunt Alice told Little George that they should tell his father not to buy it. Then Little George "spoke badly to Mama," as her son Wilse Howard later put it.

The following week on a rural road, Wilse Howard ran into Will Turner, known as "the bulldog of the Turners."[33] They insulted and shot at each other because Wilse was mad that Will's brother Little George Turner had insulted his mother, and Will Turner was mad that Wilse's cousin Wix Howard had set Will's brother Little Bob Turner's hair on fire and then killed him. That night the family bulldog, Will Turner, led a gang in an attack on the Howard home in which Will Turner was wounded. He left town in order to heal.[34]

While Bulldog Will Turner was gone, a well-meaning citizen tried to negotiate a truce between the two families. But the Turner matriarch replied, "I'd rather have my boys brought home on blankets."[35]

Once Bulldog Will Turner got home, his wound healed, he proposed that the Howards meet the Turners at the Harlan courthouse in order to "decide by the arbitraiment [sic] of blade and bullet who has the better right to rule the county."[36]

The Howards agreed. At dawn on the appointed day, the Howards took up strategic positions in and around the courthouse. Not realizing that the Howards had already arrived for the rendezvous, the Turners were strolling toward the courthouse after breakfast when hell broke loose.

Bulldog Will Turner was shot in the stomach. His friends carried him onto the porch at his house. As he lay there screaming, his mother, who had already expressed a preference for having her sons brought home on blankets, marched out and said, "Stop that! Die like a man like your brother [Little Bob Turner] did!" He soon died, in obedient silence.[37]

Meanwhile, back at the courthouse, a few more men were shot, none seriously. The Howards came out and smoked cigarettes, as though after a bout of lovemaking in a French art house film. Then they mounted their horses and went home, having established for the time being who was boss of the county.

Not content to let this verdict of bullets stand, Little George Turner started stalking Wilse Howard, and Wilse responded in kind. Wilse found Little George drinking from a spring and shot him. Little George returned fire, and they emptied their guns into one another, until Wilse Howard was wounded in the thigh and part of Little George Turner's head had been partly blown off. Wilse Howard holed up in a cave while his thigh healed.[38]

Governor Buckner, who had already intervened in the Hatfield-McCoy feud, sent state militia troops to Harlan to protect jurors and witnesses as ordinary courthouse business was conducted. After the troops departed, Wilse Howard and some twenty followers shot three Turner backers.

Judge Wilson Lewis, related to the Turners and wanting to take over Aunt Alice Howard's whiskey trade, assembled a posse and went to the Howards' house to demand the surrender of the Howards who had shot the Turners. In reply, the Howards killed three of Judge Lewis's deputies, wounding three more.

Wilse Howard and his uncle decided that it was a good time to see America. Once out West, they took part in several gunfights and spent some time in jails and brothels. After killing a deaf-mute in Missouri, Wilse Howard jumped bail and, for reasons unknown, went back home to Harlan Courthouse.[39] Judge Lewis raised another posse to welcome him. As the posse tried to burn down Wilse's house, two of them were shot, and the rest fled.

Wilse Howard escaped to the West again, this time to California, where he robbed a stagecoach and went to prison under an assumed name, possibly as a ploy to escape prosecution in Missouri for killing the deaf-mute. Someone in prison recognized his face from a WANTED poster, and a detective who had been tracking him was summoned.[40]

Wilse Howard was taken to Missouri. His bootlegging mother, Alice Howard, and his sister came to St. Louis to be with him during the trial. He was found guilty of killing the deaf-mute. He admitted to killing five men, though not the deaf-mute. Researchers have assigned him a body count closer to seventeen. His mother, Alice Howard, clung to him and wept as he boarded the train that carried him to the gallows. Wilse Howard was hanged in 1894.

The Turner-Howard feud had lasted some seven years, the death toll estimated to run between twenty-five and fifty.

THE FRENCH-EVERSOLE WAR

A merchant and attorney in Hazard, Kentucky, Fulton French became an agent for a large coal consortium and began buying up land and mineral rights from local landowners. Also a merchant and attorney,

Joseph Eversole descended from one of the first settlers in the area and felt that French was fleecing the mountain people on behalf of the English syndicate he represented.[41] Both men armed themselves and their cohorts and hired gunmen.

Eversole was at his farm in 1887 when he learned that a band of French supporters had gathered on the road to Hazard, planning to attack the town. When the French gang reached Hazard, they were disappointed to find no one barring their way. They took over the courthouse and ordered all Eversole supporters to clear out, which they promptly did.

Eversole and seventeen of his men proceeded to Hazard and attacked the French faction, fighting them until dark, with no casualties on either side. The two groups clashed sporadically for several months after that, with deaths on both sides,[42] until they all grew bored.

Fulton French and Joseph Eversole were running out of money to support their private armies, in any case. Their dry goods stores were suffering because many citizens had left town, and those in the countryside were afraid to come into town to do their shopping. So the two men drew up a truce, agreeing to hand over their weapons to two judges. Few who knew them believed they would.

They were right not to. French accused Eversole of retrieving his guns when his judge wasn't looking. Eversole accused French of never relinquishing his in the first place.[43]

To lead his team, Fulton French signed up Bad Tom Smith, a big-boned epileptic widely known for rescuing friends under attack by hitting one gunman over the head with a rock, grabbing his gun, and shooting the other two attackers. Before the French-Eversole feud, Smith had robbed a man of his watch. The man took him to court, where Smith was fined. A few nights later the house of the man's mother burned to the ground.

Bad Tom Smith had also stolen a horse belonging to Joseph Eversole's brother-in-law. After Eversole took him to court over it, Bad Tom threatened to kill the judge, jurors, witnesses, and attorneys. Ever after, he regarded Joseph Eversole as his enemy. But he told a reporter that his loyalty to Fulton French stemmed from the fact that Eversole, having heard a rumor that he was a French adherent, knocked him down with the butt of a gun and kicked him into the street, whereas Fulton French had always treated him with kindness.

Smith and another French gunslinger became best friends and committed several murders together. But one day at Bad Tom's house, they started drinking and ended up arguing, so Bad Tom killed his best friend.[44]

In the spring of 1888, Joseph Eversole and two others were riding down a country road. As they rounded a bend, rifle fire from the woods struck Eversole and Nick Combs eight times apiece. The third man reported that, as he fled, he saw Bad Tom Smith and another man emerge from the woods, shoot the bodies several more times, and go through their pockets. Nick Combs regained consciousness long enough to ask Bad Tom why he had shot him. By way of reply, Bad Tom shot him in the head.[45]

Eversole supporters came out from Hazard to retrieve the bodies. Fifty armed men guarded the funerals.

John Campbell took the place of the murdered Joseph Eversole as head of the Eversole faction. He posted sentries around town and instructed them to shoot anyone who tried to enter without knowing the secret password. Unfortunately, Campbell himself entered town one night, and the sentry, who had been asleep, got so confused about the secret password that he shot and killed Campbell.

Shade Combs next assumed command of the Eversoles. His plan was to end the feud by assassinating Fulton French. But he had to deal first with Bad Tom Smith, who had warned Combs to leave the area or his family would be killed and his house burned down. Combs and two henchmen tried to ambush Smith, but he ambushed them instead, killing one of Combs's men.

Shade Combs raced home to protect his family. When he ventured into his yard to play with his children one day, a bullet from the woods killed him. Bad Tom Smith rode past the yard minutes later, smiling at Combs's wife.[46]

Governor Buckner (again) sent in the state militia, this time to organize a company of local militia to maintain the peace in Hazard. But when the outsiders left, hostilities resumed because all the Hazard militiamen were feudists.

Grand juries handed down multiple indictments against Bad Tom Smith, but no one dared to enforce them. Bad Tom warned several town officials who supported the Eversoles to move away from Hazard, and they did.

At a meeting of the circuit court, both the French and Eversole factions brought about thirty men into town. They started shooting away at one another. The Eversoles seized the courthouse, and the Frenches the jail. The shooting continued for eighteen hours until the Eversoles ran out of ammunition. Two men were killed, and the courthouse was pocked with bullet holes. A few months later someone burned it down.[47]

Governor Buckner again sent troops, who rounded up gunmen on both sides, including Fulton French and Bad Tom Smith. Bad Tom was taken to another venue, tried, found guilty, sentenced to life in prison—and then released on appeal. Fulton French was tried, acquitted, and moved away from Hazard.

After his release from prison, Bad Tom Smith moved to another county, where he took up with a woman who ran a boardinghouse on Quicksand Creek. He began drinking heavily and killed a doctor.

Bad Tom was arrested, tried, and sentenced to hang. He started to saw his way out of jail, but another prisoner snitched on him. A circuit-riding Methodist minister helped him write his memoirs, to be sold for twenty-five cents a copy at his hanging. The sheriff had a crisis, though, because he didn't have rope thick enough for a noose. When he telegraphed to Louisville for thicker rope, no one there had any either.

On the eve of Bad Tom Smith's hanging, people crowded into the jail to sing hymns and pray for him. Reporters copied down his every utterance. His estranged wife brought their three children for a farewell. His girlfriend, who ran the boardinghouse on Quicksand Creek, was unable to comfort him because she was also in jail as an accessory to the doctor's murder. The stress of it all triggered an epileptic seizure for Bad Tom.

The next morning Bad Tom Smith's brother and sister walked with him to the gallows, near the spot where Hen Kilburn had been lynched. The crowd of three thousand fell silent, except for a few crying babies. Bad Tom explained to assembled reporters that he had, in fact, shot the doctor, but only because his girlfriend had told him that the doctor had twice tried to kill him while he was passed out from drinking. She had promised to take the blame because she believed no one would prosecute her.

"It was whiskey and bad women that brought me here," Bad Tom concluded, "and I want to tell you boys to let them alone." Then he admitted to five other murders, not saying whether bad women were also involved in those deaths.

He urged the crowd not to do as he had done. He asked those who intended not to follow his example to raise their hands. Everyone raised a hand, and Bad Tom proclaimed himself pleased. He prayed out loud, asking God for forgiveness. Several preachers on the scaffold joined him. Then he led the huge crowd in singing, "Guide Me, Oh Great Jehovah."

Bad Tom Smith dropped to his knees and prayed again for mercy. The sheriff tried to lure him to the noose, but Bad Tom begged for another hymn. The ministers returned to the scaffold and joined him in singing "Near the Cross."

The crowd fell silent. The sheriff bound Bad Tom Smith's arms and legs with leather straps and drew a hood over his head. "Save me, oh God, save me!" he cried out. The deputy pulled the lever at 1:45 p.m. on June 28, 1895. Many women in the audience fainted.

Thus ended the seven-year feud that had taken the lives of some seventy-four people.[48]

†

So what conclusions can we draw from these feuds? They certainly demonstrate that the Hatfield-McCoy feud was neither the longest nor the deadliest by a long shot—so to speak. They took place in towns as well as in the countryside. Some feudists were doctors and lawyers, merchants and businessmen, while others were subsistence farmers, herders, and loggers.

Stolen animals triggered hostilities in several feuds—cattle and horses, in addition to Ranel McCoy's hog. Economic competition also played a role: in the salt trade, whiskey-making, timber-cutting, merchandising, doctoring, and lawyering.

Old Civil War antagonisms played a part in some, but not all, of the feuds. Most who supported the Union became Republicans, and most Confederates became Democrats, so it could be argued that postwar politics merely extended wartime animosities. Political offices were often used for partisan advantage rather than for public service. Prison terms were so mild, and paroles and pardons so readily available, as not to act as a deterrent.

Too much liquor and too many guns held center stage in all the feuds. Insulted honor often acted as a factor, as it did for Little Bob Turner, for instance, when his hair was set on fire. Stupidity also played a major role in most feuds.

Bad Tom Smith, an epileptic, was the villain in the French-Eversole feud. So was the mentally impaired albino Cottontop Mounts in the Hatfield-McCoy feud. Bad Jim Vance, another Hatfield villain, suffered from a condition that made his eyes oscillate uncontrollably. Cap Hatfield carried a hideous wound that emptied the contents of his stomach into his lap. All four men had probably been teased and bullied about their conditions and reacted by becoming bullies themselves. But not all of the many bullies in these feuds had such understandable excuses for their bad behavior.

Each feud had its godfather with a role equivalent to that of Devil Anse Hatfield: Captain Strong, Craig Tolliver, Wilse Howard, Fulton French. Each feud also featured people behaving admirably during horrific circumstances: young Sheriff Hagins, Boone Logan, Sarah McCoy.

Sam Hill, a representative of Governor Buckner, investigated the Craig Tolliver feud. His report laid blame on corrupt county officials, "want of moral sentiment," domination and intimidation of the law-abiding segment of the population by the criminally inclined, and alcohol.[49] That sentence alone probably sums up the causes for all the feuds as succinctly as possible.

But why did these factors, also in operation elsewhere in America, overwhelm the forces of moderation that prevailed elsewhere, resulting in this epidemic of feuding in the southern Appalachians during the last decades of the nineteenth century? And why did the Hatfield McCoy feud, of all these and the many others not described here, become so iconic, such that most contemporary Americans have heard of it, yet not of the others?

The most important factor to come into play is the role of the media. Regional newspapers covered the events of most feuds, and papers with a broader readership, such as the *New York Times, New York World, Cincinnati Enquirer,* and *Pittsburgh Times,* covered the major feuds. But—and this is key—the Hatfield-McCoy feud was the only one about which an entire book was published for a mainstream readership: T. C. Crawford's *An American Vendetta: A Story of Barbarism in the United States.* Written by a reporter based in New York City, it reached a wide audience and spawned spin-offs in the form of novels and silent movies. With that one little book, Crawford almost single-handedly shaped the enduring stereotype of the depraved mountaineer.[50] Ninety-two silent movies were later filmed, based on this stereotype of feuding hillbillies. Their wide distribution and enormous popularity assured that the stereotype became deeply embedded in the American psyche.

What set the Hatfield-McCoy feud apart from all the others was its built-in plotline. The other feuds appear, on the surface, if not also below it, to be chaotic collections of ludicrous episodes. But the Hatfield-McCoy story possesses an inherent structure: Harmon McCoy's murder derives from Civil War antagonisms, always a compelling topic for Americans, and especially so in the years immediately following that war. Next comes the Hog Trial, with its potential for comic relief. Then we have the Johnse-Roseanna love affair, a favorite of those with a taste for doomed romances. The Election Day Brawl, the Pawpaw Murders, and the New Year's Night Massacre provide an escalating triple climax. The Supreme Court case regarding the right of private Kentuckians to haul West Virginians to their state for trial captured the attention of the entire nation with its implications concerning the rights of individuals against the needs of a civil society. It also provided a variation on the question of states' rights, which had triggered the Civil War. The hanging of Cottontop Mounts closes the feud with a denouement to satisfy those with a need to see justice prevail—or at least a scapegoat punished.

All these events, taken together, partake of a cause-and-effect relationship that other feuds lack. The saga also includes a compelling coda: Devil Anse's baptism, when Dyke Garrett lowers the elderly brigand into Island Creek. Americans love no plot more than that of a sinner redeemed.

Perhaps the strongest appeal of the Hatfield-McCoy feud, though, was a largely unconscious one. Most other feuds took place, at least partly, in towns. Many participants were middle class or higher: doctors, lawyers, businessmen, merchants, judges, hotel operators, former military officers, county officials, schoolteachers. The idea that upstanding men could participate in such criminal behavior no doubt shocked respectable citizens in other parts of the country. One way in which to deny that they themselves might also be capable of such acts was to focus instead on a feud conducted largely in the wilderness by men who, unlike themselves, were illiterate farmers, herders, lumbermen, and moonshiners. What else could you expect from such shiftless rural savages who lacked the many civilizing advantages of city life? Like Greek tragedy, which has survived the centuries, the Hatfield-McCoy feud became a screen onto which other Americans could project and disavow their own capacity for such irrational violence.

This was also the age of Darwinian survival of the fittest. The grotesque atrocities of the feudists were an exaggerated parody of the ruthless behavior widely admired at that time in robber barons and in those who waged major wars against minor banana republics. Critics could sputter with outrage over the savage excesses of the Hatfield-McCoy feud while secretly thrilling to the feudists' displays of untrammeled manliness that loudly proclaimed their evolutionary fitness. The Hatfields and the McCoys presaged Teddy Roosevelt and the Rough Riders.

13

The Corsica of America

Many different theories attempt to explain the Hatfield-McCoy feud, and most apply equally well to all the feuds in the southern Appalachians in the closing decades of the nineteenth century. The Hatfield-McCoy feud, as we have seen, was merely one manifestation of a region-wide aberration.

One of the most obvious explanations is that the geography of the Cumberland Plateau preserved an inherited frontier culture. Both the Hatfield and the McCoy feudists descended from the original European settlers in the Tug Fork Valley, who formed their own militias for protection against Native attacks. In the beginning years of settlement, there were no towns or courthouses, judges or jails. Justice was meted out locally. The jury was one's neighbors, and the verdict was usually eye-for-an-eye retaliation. (There were also frontiers, militias, and attacking Native tribes in the Northern states, but a feud culture didn't develop there. On the other hand, no one was burned for being a witch on the Cumberland Plateau.)

The fledgling legal system in the Tug Fork region during the first half of the nineteenth century largely yielded to the chaos of the Civil War years. Courthouses and records were burned. Guerrilla bands and bushwhackers ruled the day and dispensed "justice" in accordance with partisan beliefs or personal needs. Devil Anse Hatfield was merely continuing in this wartime tradition by executing the McCoy sons in the pawpaw patch after their murder of his younger brother Ellison. Most of the later murders in the feud resulted from Devil Anse's attempts to thwart the McCoys in their determination to subject his followers and himself to the Kentucky court system.

. When the McCoys appealed to the Kentucky governor in Frankfort for assistance in bringing their Hatfield prisoners to trial, the traditional face-to-face methods of the Tug Fork Valley for dealing with such crimes no longer applied. The Hatfields felt overwhelmed by outside forces they didn't understand and couldn't control. This fed their paranoia about being hauled to Kentucky for trial by hostile strangers.[1]

Devil Anse Hatfield preserved a sinister template in his mind: His great-grandfather Abner Vance had been hanged because he had wrought his own version of frontier justice on a man who had harmed his daughter and humiliated Abner himself. Devil Anse dreaded a similar outcome for himself, as did his sons Johnse and Cap, who had no doubt heard the story of Abner's hanging throughout their childhoods. For the unfortunate Cottontop Mounts, this grisly childhood tale proved a self-fulfilling prophecy.

The Tug Fork Valley hovered midway between a traditional justice system of self-generated retaliation and a modern one. Many citizens interpreted democracy to mean individual autonomy—rather than majority rule combined with institutionalized respect for the rights of individuals and minorities. Although courts and their officials wielded a certain amount of power, most saw their role as one of extending that power to those who could dominate them. Votes were bought and sold, and elected officials often served those who had delivered the votes. (So what else is new?) The concept of blind justice was unfamiliar. When a jury pronounced a verdict unacceptable to one faction, that faction sometimes regressed to the traditional frontier system of personal retribution.

†

The enduring ramifications of Civil War hostilities cast a long shadow over feud participants. It's almost impossible to sort out Ranel McCoy's role or lack of one during the Civil War, so it's hard to say whether he sided with the Confederates and Devil Anse Hatfield or with the Unionists and Col. John Dils, or first one and then the other, or neither. This much we know: Ranel's brother Harmon McCoy enlisted as a Union Home Guard and soldier. Jim Vance killed him either simply for being a Union soldier or for acts he had committed, or intended to commit, against Confederate comrades of Devil Anse, and possibly against Devil Anse himself. His murder fed McCoy animosity toward the Hatfield clan. Twelve of Harmon McCoy's sons and nephews and one son-in-law, once they were old enough to fight, ranked among Ranel McCoy's most ardent adherents. Five died in the struggle that was, at least in part, an attempt to avenge the killing of Harmon, who was the father to one of the murdered and uncle to four more.

$$\dagger$$

Recent genetic and genealogical research has established that some early settlers in the southern Appalachians were racially mixed—all combinations of European, African, Native American, South Asian, and Middle Eastern. People with darker complexions were trying to escape the racial prejudices of more settled regions to the east and south that would have branded them as African, whatever their actual descent, and would have subjected them to seizure and sale as slaves. One of my own ancestors in the region was said to be Portuguese Indian.[2] This research flies in the face of much prior scholarship that portrays the population of the southern Appalachians as "the purest Anglo Saxon stock in all the United States . . . kept free from the tide of foreign immigrants."[3]

Daniel Sharfstein's study *The Invisible Line: Three American Families and the Secret Journey from Black to White* carefully documents the life of one such man, Jordan Spencer, who settled in Kentucky some fifty miles northwest of the Tug Fork. His origins were hazy. He had lived farther south in Clay County in the household of a "free person of color" named

George Freeman and was perhaps his son or brother, possibly a former slave freed by the same master who had freed George Freeman.

Jordan Spencer married a white woman, and his neighbors largely accepted him as white, despite the fact that the red dye he used on his dark, wavy hair bled down his face when he sweated. Sharfstein makes the point that his neighbors allowed Spencer to maintain the obvious fiction that he was white because many of them also had darker complexions than their "white" neighbors.[4] In fact, many would be reclassified as mulattoes or Indians by census takers when racial categorization became more stratified in the decades following the Civil War.[5]

In colonial days, throughout the eastern portion of what became the United States, invading soldiers, explorers, traders, settlers, and servants of various ethnic origins, the vast majority males, mated freely or forcibly with Native women and with indentured European women. Some of their descendants, depending upon their physical appearances, passed as white, African, or Native American and joined those communities. But many whose appearances were too ambiguous for acceptance by existing communities, or who had no wish to abandon their friends and families, clustered together and moved to unproductive land that European settlers didn't want, usually swamps or ridgetops, where they kept to themselves, often shunned and stigmatized by their white neighbors for having what appeared to be African ancestry. From farther east and south, dark-skinned racial refugees—escaped slaves and free dark-complexioned people who feared enslavement—joined these communities as the years went by.

Some of these people were labeled "free people of color" in the last decades of the nineteenth century and weren't allowed to vote, to marry white people, to attend white schools, or to testify against white people in court. Brewton Berry, in his book *Almost White,* maintains that some two hundred of these groups—with names like the Redbones, Brass Ankles, Moors, Turks—existed well into the twentieth century throughout the eastern United States.[6]

The Melungeons of East Tennessee and southwest Virginia were one such "little race," as a prominent sociologist labels these communities.[7] Splinter groups left the Melungeon settlements to migrate across the

Cumberland Plateau, through Kentucky to Ohio and points north and west, leaving behind pockets of relatives along the way.[8] These people, accustomed to prejudice and rejection, were braced for confrontations and prepared to fight for their right to live in freedom.

In the Tug Fork Valley itself, Tom Wallace, a farmhand who was hired by Devil Anse Hatfield's son Cap and who helped Cap whip Mary Daniels with a cow's tail, was said to be "half Hatfield and half Indian."[9] Devil Anse's nephew, the murdered Ellison's son Elliot, was nicknamed "Indian." Devil Anse's close friend Mose Christian claimed Shawnee ancestry.[10] Several Hatfields were described as "swarthy"—Black Elias,[11] Good Elias,[12] and Levicy.[13] Johnse was said to have a dark complexion.[14]

Among the McCoy ranks, Frank Phillips was also described as "dark-complexioned."[15] Truda McCoy remarked that many McCoys were olive-skinned, often with dark or auburn hair. In the earliest years of settlement, the population of the Tug Fork Valley had included the remnants of Native tribes who had previously occupied the area, and it would be unrealistic to think that some mixing didn't occur among the former and current inhabitants. The descendants from such unions would possibly have absorbed cultural traditions from their Native relatives, including eye-for-an-eye justice.

All the Tug Forkers lived on farms, so complexions that appeared so dark to urban reporters may have been nothing more than the result of lives lived outdoors. But it is also likely that some inhabitants of the Tug Fork Valley questioned their own racial identities. Belligerent facades allowed racially ambiguous people to fend off challenges to their right to enjoy the same freedoms as their white neighbors. But the price of these freedoms was the various personality disorders that can result from not knowing who you are—or from knowing and concealing it.

Ranel McCoy's forebears are believed to have been Lowland Scots, perhaps mixed with Highland Celts.[16] Lowland Scots were themselves a mixture of Picts, Gaels, Norsemen, Angles, Saxons, Normans, and Romans from all corners of their empire, including Africa. Roman troops stationed at Hadrian's Wall and the Antonine Wall on what is now the English-Scottish border mixed with local women, and some remained in the area when they retired or when the troubled empire recalled its legions to defend the mainland. As a result, some born and bred Englishmen have African Y chromosomes,[17] as do two of my cousins in the Appalachians who always believed themselves to be of British heritage.* Devil Anse Hatfield's Y chromosome falls into the same haplogroup as that of Napoleon. One researcher proposes that it was brought to the British borderlands by Roman troops from the Balkans.[18]

Such Scotch-Irish people, immigrants and the descendants of immigrants from the borderlands between England and Scotland and from Ulster in Ireland, make up by far the largest population group that settled the mountains of Kentucky and Virginia, Tennessee and North Carolina. Both English armies from the south and Scottish armies from the north regularly attacked these Border Reivers, as they had been called in Britain. Their crops and homes had been destroyed time after time, their herds seized or slaughtered, their women raped, their families murdered. In response, they banded together in extended kinship groups and wrought havoc on one another, rustling from and blackmailing the borderland families to whom they were not related or otherwise allied.

A quarter of a million of these people immigrated to America in the eighteenth century, searching for an alternative to the high rents, low wages, heavy taxes, short leases, and deadly famine that most had endured in their homeland. Many traveled down the Shenandoah Valley from the seaports in Philadelphia to follow the rivers and passes into the Allegheny and Cumberland Mountains, the Blue Ridge and the Smokies. The original Hatfields are thought to have immigrated from the English borderlands,[19] and the McCoys from the Scottish borderlands.[20]

This overall migration pattern resulted in a volatile mix of touchy people in the mountains of Kentucky and southwestern Virginia, which the Tug Fork bisected. Most of the men hunted for game and therefore had knives and guns, and knew how to use them. Most participated in

---

* Other possible explanations for the existence of African haplogroups in the British borderlands are early migrations out of Africa and the Middle East, as well as African slaves brought to Britain before slavery was abolished there at the end of the eighteenth century, in addition to their free descendants after abolition.

militias designed to provide defense against Native attacks and knew how to fight. Many had chips on their shoulders and trigger-quick tempers.

David Fischer, in his brilliant study *Albion's Seed*, describes cultural features of this American backcountry that derive directly from the British borderlands, such as place names, vocabulary and accents, wedding and funeral customs, cooking and clothing styles, architecture, and attitudes toward work, sex, sports, and religion.[21] He contends, not that these cultural dispositions were somehow genetic (which of course they couldn't be), but rather that these folkways, as he calls them, developed in the British borderlands over the course of centuries in response to the atmosphere of threat and insecurity that reigned there.

The folkways came to America with those who immigrated from the British borderlands. Because the conditions of danger and threat in the backcountry mirrored those in the borderlands, the transplanted folkways took root and flourished in the new locale. Interestingly, the Tug Fork Valley became a borderland itself during the Civil War, caught between Union and Confederate armies, both sides assaulting the residents and stealing their supplies and livestock—the exact same scenario as in the British borderlands with regard to the English and Scottish armies.

One of these folkways especially relevant to the feud concerns the borderland system of "tanistry."[22] Because the British borderlands were so strife ridden, the people trying to live there needed strong leaders to organize their protection. A tradition evolved in which the eldest and toughest male within the span of four living generations emerged to head each extended family. He received great respect and deference because he represented the entire family's bulwark against destruction and death. Men who challenged his leadership and lost the contest were treated with contempt and cast out, or barely tolerated. In ancient days they had been killed.

Devil Anse Hatfield was such a figure for the Tug Fork Valley. His forebears had defended it against Native attacks. His father was widely known as the strongman of the valley and had served as a justice of the peace for many years. Devil Anse himself had defended the valley against Federal troops and guerrillas during the Civil War. In the years that followed, he provided jobs and land for many residents on his timber crews.

Ranel McCoy, filing suits against Devil Anse Hatfield and his supporters after the Civil War and pursuing indictments against them after the Pawpaw Murders, was tweaking the tail of a panther. Because he didn't challenge Devil Anse more directly, even after Devil Anse had killed three of his sons, Ranel took on the role, at a subconscious level at least, of one of the defeated old men in the still-lingering borderland system of tanistry. People feared and respected Devil Anse, but they felt a certain amount of impatience with Ranel McCoy, however justified his litany of complaints. In the end, Devil Anse tried to kill off his failed rival in the New Year's night attack on his cabin—but this time he, also, failed.

Psychologists Richard Nisbett and Dov Cohen maintain that immigrants from the British borderlands were primarily herders and that herding cultures all over the world display high levels of violence.[23] In Corsica, for instance, the rocky mountainous birthplace of Napoleon, where sheep, goats, and hogs have been raised for centuries, an estimated thirty thousand people, a quarter of the population, died in the heyday of vendettas between 1683 and 1715.[24] A herd is easily stolen, so a herder's livelihood depends upon his ability to defend his livestock. Affronts to his reputation for strength, toughness, cunning, and violence must be squelched immediately and forcefully. An unanswered insult announces that its target is weak and can be bullied out of his animals.[25]

These herders from the British borderlands settled primarily in the southern highlands, such as the Cumberland Plateau of Kentucky, where the Tug Fork Valley is located, a mountainous terrain that favors herding over farming. We have already seen the role played in the feud by a wandering hog and in other feuds by stolen horses and cattle. One possible explanation for the idiom "to get one's goat," meaning to anger someone, is that it stems from herding cultures. To steal someone's goat would deprive him of its milk and meat, and would no doubt trigger furious retaliation.

Such engrained cultural traits can persist indefinitely, maintain Nisbett and Cohen, even after the herds that inspired them no longer exist. In various experiments on young men from both the northern and southern United States, they found that, when insulted, those from the South exhibited elevated levels of the stress hormone cortisol and of testosterone, the hormone mediating aggression. The young men from the North tended to defuse with humor or indifference situations that those from the South interpreted as humiliating, the Northerners experiencing no such elevation of their cortisol or testosterone levels.[26]

Between 1865 and 1915, the Cumberland Plateau had a homicide rate more than ten times the national homicide rate today and twice as high as that of our most violent cities.[27] In those rural regions, even as recently as 1996, the homicide rate among white males registered over four times higher than that for the same group in rural New England, the Middle Atlantic states, and the nonindustrial western Midwest.[28] Accordingly, Nisbett and Cohen label the social system of the American backcountry a "culture of honor."[29] Their findings lend statistical support to the name given the region in 1878 by the *New York Times*: "the Corsica of America."[30]

According to the rules of conduct in a culture of honor, the McCoys, by not retaliating in kind to the Hatfields' murder of Harmon McCoy and the later murders of Ranel's three sons, were signaling weakness and setting themselves up for further attacks.[31] As the eminent sociologist of the South, John Shelton Reed (my older brother) says, "Sometimes people are violent, even when they don't want to be, because there will be penalties (disgrace is a very effective one) for *not* being violent."[32]

By honoring the Christian-based wishes of his wife, Sarah, to turn the other cheek, Ranel McCoy broke another rule of conduct in cultures of honor, in which women are expected to be silent and submissive helpmeets to their warrior husbands and sons. It would have been a difficult myth to sustain in the Tug Fork Valley since the women were doing most of the work to keep their households and farms functioning while their menfolk were out sowing terror and havoc.

Some of the McCoy women, as we've seen, displayed an assertiveness that undercuts this code of submission expected from warrior wives. Fed up with his abusive and neglectful treatment, Peggy McCoy divorced her husband,

Daniel, after fifty years of unhappy marriage. Sarah McCoy restrained Ranel's fury against the Hatfields at various points during the feud. Against the wishes of her father, Roseanna McCoy took Johnse Hatfield as her lover. Nancy McCoy later henpecked Johnse and then abandoned him in favor of Bad Frank Phillips. On the Hatfield side, Levicy Chafin Hatfield perhaps persuaded her son Bob to quit the patrol that committed the New Year's Night Massacre, and Devil Anse's mother, Nancy Vance Hatfield, kept some of her sons from joining the feud in the first place.

Many other warrior wives of the Cumberland Plateau may never have been as submissive as their husbands would have preferred. One Hatfield woman said, "You couldn't kill one of them with a hammer. . . . You didn't have to be around them very long until you found out who crowed and who laid the eggs."[33] These women left their female descendants a legacy of fierceness that prevails even today: 58 percent of all American homicides in which a wife kills her husband occur in the South.[34] Recently I saw written on a women's bathroom wall in a gas station near Cumberland Gap, "Always fight back, and never let them take you alive!"

┼

Some have proposed the lack of schools and churches in the Tug Fork Valley as a factor in the feud. But there were churches for those who wanted to attend. Preacher Anse Hatfield ran the Old Pond Creek Baptist Church on the Kentucky side of the river. Ellison Hatfield and his family attended a Baptist church on the West Virginia side. Dyke Garrett, who eventually baptized Devil Anse, had a Church of Christ congregation in the valley.

Ranel and Sarah McCoy were said to be devout Christians, and they certainly behaved that way more than most in the feud. But Devil Anse Hatfield, before his baptism, had no interest in church. "I belong to no Church," he was quoted as saying, "unless you say that I belong to the one great Church of the world. If you like you can say that it is the devil's Church that I belong to."[35] Many in the southern Appalachians at that time associated churches with stifling rules and oppressive hierarchy, such as their ancestors had suffered in Britain. They felt that a personal experience of the divine was what mattered and not the real estate or authority figures involved in organized religion. With their intense relationships to nature, many may have felt no need for other spiritual outlets.

But a lack of schooling did likely contribute to the feud mentality. During the 1880s and '90s, there were four schools in the Tug Fork Valley.[36] But in such rural areas only about a quarter of the children attended on a regular basis, and the school term lasted just three months each year, in the quiet winter season after crops had been harvested and the livestock slaughtered and butchered. The winter weather in the mountains would have prevented many children from attending regularly even during those three months.

Devil Anse and Elias Hatfield and Elliott Rutherford set up a school in their West Virginia neighborhood around 1870. Charlie Carpenter, who composed the document authorizing vigilante justice against the McCoy sons before the Pawpaw Murders, had taught in this school. But it had been abandoned, and the McCoy sons were imprisoned there while waiting to learn if Ellison Hatfield would live or die. Devil Anse was illiterate, as was his son Cap, who learned to read and write from his wife, Nancy, in his twenties. But perhaps Charlie Carpenter's role in the Pawpaw Murders proves that education doesn't necessarily provide an inoculation against cruelty and violence.

✝

In the closing decades of the nineteenth century in the southern Appalachians, as elsewhere in America, there were no radios, movies, television, telephones, or theaters; there was little access to books or magazines for the few who could read; and people didn't travel for pleasure as we do today. Playing music, clog dancing, singing ballads and hymns, and telling tall tales were the primary forms of entertainment. But there is little mention in the feud literature of those activities having occurred in the Tug Fork Valley.

So, like participants in modern-day reality shows, feudists composed real-life soap operas for their own entertainment, in which they were the stars—at least in their own eyes. They acted out deadly impulses that people in more sophisticated cultures might have been able to experience and exorcise through various art forms with no loss of life or limbs. Elsewhere in the southern Appalachians, such impulses were being expressed and digested by way of the gory ballads of love and war brought by early settlers from Britain, such as "Lord Thomas and Fair Eleanor" and "The Banks of the Yarrow."

✝

In 2007, Revi Matthew, an endocrinologist at Vanderbilt University in Nashville, Tennessee, published research indicating that some contemporary McCoys suffer from a disease called Von Hippel–Lindau syndrome (VHL). Tumors occur in the eyes, ears, pancreas, kidney, brain, or spine, causing blindness, deafness, dizziness, kidney cancer, or brain damage. He reported that three-quarters of the McCoys with VHL whom he tested had tumors on their adrenal glands, increasing their production of adrenaline. Symptoms of this version of the syndrome include high blood pressure, racing heartbeat, severe headaches, facial flushing, nausea, vomiting, and violent outbursts. One McCoy child with this disease had been diagnosed at school as having ADHD.[37]

VHL is autosomal dominant, meaning that the syndrome can manifest in those who receive a mutated gene from only one parent. Given the amount of cousin marriage among the McCoys of the Tug Fork Valley, it's possible that many suffered from VHL. The irrational behavior of some McCoy males—Ranel's repeated lawsuits, Tolbert's knife attack on Ellison Hatfield, Squirrel Hunting Sam's and Paris's murder of Bill Staton—might suggest such adrenaline surges. Ron McCoy, who helped organize a reunion in 2000 for both Hatfield and McCoy descendants, acknowledged in response to this medical discovery, "The McCoy temperament is legendary."[38] However, he rightly maintains that many other issues also played a part in the conduct of the feud.

However, the McCoy cases of VHL don't explain the equivalently enraged behavior of the Hatfields, unless we conclude that there had been so much intermarriage between the clans that both families suffered from this syndrome. Nor does this genetic explanation begin to account for the hysterics of feudists unrelated to the McCoys, such as Bad Frank Phillips, Craig Tolliver, Bad Tom Smith, and many more. Also, much McCoy anger seems justified, given the murders and arson that they suffered at the hands of the Hatfields.

✝

Altina Waller, in her book *Feud,* offers one of the most convincing explanations for the feud. She concludes that local hostilities were a reaction to a region-wide shift under way since the close of the Civil War, with Northern industries moving into the defeated South to replace a rural farming, timbering, and herding economy with an industrialized one based on large-scale coal and timber extraction, the profits of which flowed to absentee capitalists. Though the feud participants themselves didn't realize it, of course, they were acting out their despair at the impending loss of their traditional culture and personal autonomy.[39]

In the first half of the feud, Devil Anse Hatfield channeled his neighbors' resentment because his small-scale timber business was successful, in contrast to those of Perry Cline and Daniel McCoy. Devil Anse also ruthlessly acquired Perry Cline's land, flying in the face of the pioneer ethic of community, in which residents were expected to help one another rather than to compete with and crush their neighbors. In that sense, Devil Anse himself was an early mountain capitalist, with a payroll and employees.

By the second half of the feud, though, the modernizers in Pikeville—Colonel Dils, Perry Cline, and others—joined Ranel McCoy's heretofore ineffectual campaign against Devil Anse Hatfield. Colonel Dils was never an overt antagonist of Devil Anse during the feud years, but there is little doubt that he was pulling strings behind the scenes, and he certainly had motives for wanting to engineer Devil Anse's downfall, given his many wartime clashes with the former Confederate guerrilla leader.

Modernizers in both Pikeville, Kentucky, and Logan, West Virginia, wanted to attract national and international corporations that would bring in railroad lines so as to harvest the area's timber and coal reserves, using the labor of the local people to fill their own pockets. The feudists quickly became stumbling blocks in the path of progress because these capitalists wouldn't commit their resources to an area inhabited by what they saw as "white savages."

For many, Devil Anse, with his small-scale timber business, employing friends and family on his own land, was a champion of local autonomy in the face of the huge and remote coal, timber, and railroad consortiums that were sharpening their knives over the region. In the beginning, Devil Anse would have felt for these absentee capitalists in Northern and European cities the same contempt he had felt during the Civil War for the plantation owners in the Virginia Tidewater who counted on soldiers much poorer than themselves to protect their property. "A rich man's war and a poor man's fight" was the rallying cry of those appalled that subsistence farmers who owned no slaves were fighting and dying to preserve slavery for wealthy planters.

The Pikeville modernizers championed Ranel McCoy because they wanted an end to the feud so that big industry could claim the area. But those same Pikeville businessmen, several with family ties to the McCoys, must also have felt compassion for Ranel, who had become a sad shadow of a man, endlessly repeating the story of the New Year's Night Massacre to passengers as he piloted his ferryboat on the Levisa Fork, a lamenting Charon who wouldn't shut up.

†

Then there was the younger generation, which produced the fiercest feudists of all—Hatfield's Hellhounds and McCoy's sons and nephews. Hailed as heroes, Eph-of-All Hatfield's peers early in the nineteenth century settled the Tug Fork Valley and fought off native attackers. After midcentury, Devil Anse's peers fought heroically in the Civil War, even if those who fought for the Confederacy lost the struggle. But the generation

185

of Devil Anse's and Ranel's children had no equivalently heroic deeds they could perform.

Large farms required large families to work them, but those farms in the Tug Fork Valley had been split up among the many heirs time after time, growing smaller and smaller with each passing generation. Many young men from families that had once owned huge tracts of land now owned no land at all, having to work as laborers or loggers on other people's land.[40] Downwardly mobile, they needed manly deeds to perform to make them appear as heroic as their fathers, grandfathers, and great-grandfathers.

Because of the easy availability of moonshine, they drank too much. Because they drank too much, they got into fights over trivial matters involving challenges to their fragile sense of self-worth. Because they all carried knives and guns for hunting and for display, their fights often turned into bloodbaths.

But beneath all this seemingly incomprehensible violence lay anxiety. Their culture of freedom and autonomy was becoming extinct—and they knew it. When you have no land of your own, you have no domain over which you are sole ruler. You are no longer the master of your own fate. The world as they knew it was crashing to an end. Home distilling—a centuries-old technique for preserving excess produce, passed down the generations—became a federal offense in 1862 in what appeared to many mountaineers as an attack upon their culture. In the early 1880s, about the time of the Pawpaw Murders, hundreds of revenue agents flooded the southern Appalachians, destroying stills and arresting those who operated them. These agents bribed neighbors for information and sent out spies disguised as peddlers, surveyors, and cattle and timber merchants. They engaged in shoot-outs with moonshiners and fueled the atmosphere of suspicion and mayhem that ruled this hill country.[41] Both Devil Anse and Johnse Hatfield were indicted at different times on charges of dealing in illegal liquor.

In 1887, in response to the dwindling supply of wildlife due to overhunting, West Virginia adopted its first fish and game laws.[42] Timbering and the silting of lakes and streams with topsoil eroded from clear-cut forest floors were also destroying the habitats of fish, birds, and wild animals. Without the income from whiskey and pelts, and without the sustenance provided by wild game and fish, the households of the Tug Fork were facing a burgeoning economic crisis—and the stress that loss of livelihood entails.

Outsiders were building a railroad up the valley. If the young men were to have a role in the emerging economy of large-scale lumbering and coal mining, they had to change their entire way of life, morphing into wage laborers who went to work at a certain time every day, all year round, always performing the same tedious and often dangerous tasks. Such a life was unthinkable for young men accustomed to relaxing when they wanted and to working at a variety of jobs, according to the weather, the season, and their own whims.

Feuding gave them a chance to do something heroic. They could ride out in gangs and right what their leaders told them were wrongs. They could showcase their courage and their skills with weapons and horses. They became a generation of hillbullies—and they were proud of it.

Recent psychological studies have suggested that those who are inconsistent and unpredictable in their behavior command other people's attention more than those who behave in a steady and reliable fashion. This is not news to those who have ever attended kindergarten. This watchfulness has survival value. You must observe those who are unpredictable to see what they are going to do next and to make certain that it doesn't harm you or your loved ones. This is one reason for the appeal of the bad boy.[43] The bad boys of the Tug Fork Valley attracted attention. Much of this attention was fearful, but some of it was admiration from people wanting or needing protection.

Pushed too far, the bad boy ethos verges on psychopathology, and some of the Hatfield behavior does appear sadistic. Whipping women, young or old, with the tail of a butchered cow certainly falls into that category. So does shooting a young woman handicapped from polio as she attempts to draw well water to quench the flames destroying her house, or beating an elderly woman with a rifle butt when she rushes to comfort a dying child.

Coleman C. Hatfield claims that Devil Anse Hatfield "got a charge from scaring people silly. . . . Anse's own grandchildren were often his prey when he decided to tell scary stories."[44] His younger brothers called him "the boogerman."[45] His favorite source of amusement after he killed a bear was to throw its skin around himself and terrify his children and grandchildren.[46] This behavior is on a par with tickling children unmercifully and then claiming that it's all in fun.

Truda McCoy maintains that Devil Anse Hatfield promised Sarah McCoy to bring her three sons who had killed his brother back to Kentucky alive.[47] That he brought them to Kentucky alive, as promised, and then promptly shot them, would strike many as sadistic. So would Cap Hatfield's promise to Jeff McCoy that he would let him live if he could swim the Tug Fork, followed by his shooting Jeff as he clambered up the Kentucky bank.[48] These are the actions of men who might have tortured small animals when they were boys, as Truda McCoy claims Cap Hatfield did.[49]

†

Normal everyday life in the Tug Fork Valley—if there was ever such a thing during the feud years—was no doubt tedious. Barring natural or man-made disasters, the routines of a household and a farm are the same, day in and day out, year after year. Thread is spun, cloth is woven, clothes are sewn and washed, floors are swept, fires are fed and banked, food is gathered, preserved, cooked. Seeds are planted, weeds are hoed, crops are harvested and stored for winter. Animals are fed and bred and slaughtered, and their meat preserved. It's backbreaking, mind-numbing work.

To relieve the stresses of this tedium and the labor it required, women supplied themselves with the calming properties of their own progesterone while pregnant, with pain-soothing endorphins during childbirth, and with bond-inducing oxytocin while nursing. They were either pregnant or nursing constantly, and many died in childbirth, often very young.

Boredom didn't pose as much of a problem for the women as it did for their sons and husbands. As Blaise Pascal put it in seventeenth-century France, "Man finds nothing so intolerable as to be in a state of complete rest, without passions, without occupation, without diversion, without

· effort. Then he feels his nullity, loneliness, inadequacy, dependence, helplessness, emptiness."[50] The male equivalents of the female feel-good hormones were adrenaline, cortisol, and testosterone. Devil Anse's generation acquired regular and generous infusions of all three during the terror, arousal, and aggression of Civil War raids and battles. After the war ended, they needed new ways to trigger those chemical highs. The violence of the feud, stimulated by the inhibition-reducing effects of alcohol, gave them their fix.

The McCoy men who had VHL already produced too much of their own adrenaline. Not knowing this to be the case, though, they needed to manufacture conflicts to explain and justify their extant inner rage.

Three of the most ruthless participants in the feud were chronic outsiders. Cottontop Mounts, the illegitimate son of Ellison Hatfield, was a mentally handicapped albino always seeking acceptance from his biological father. Jim Vance, most vicious of the feudists, had a condition called lateral nystagmus, which caused his eyes to oscillate uncontrollably.[51] Like Cottontop, he too was illegitimate. Tom Wallace, who worked for Cap Hatfield, was known as "half Hatfield and half Indian." In their eagerness to belong to the Hatfield clan, these men performed whatever terrible deeds Devil Anse and his band asked of them.*

Some have blamed the feud on the way in which boys were raised in the Southern mountains. Their games were boisterous, rough, and competitive, and they were rarely scolded for anger or rudeness. A favorite pastime was a game—if you could call it that—known as rocking: waiting in ambush along a path and assaulting an enemy with volleys of rocks.[52] Fights sometimes involved biting off ears or noses and gouging out eyes.[53] Boys were encouraged to react fiercely to any possible slight, and they

---

· * Anyone who has attended middle school will recognize this syndrome.

often grew up to become arrogant, quarrelsome young men. The girls, as in many warrior cultures, were reared to serve the men and boys and to submit to them.

I have a photo from this era that shows mountain men and boys sitting at a table laden with food, eating heartily while the women and girls stand behind their chairs, poised to refill their plates. The women and girls ate the men's leftovers. If you consider the football culture that now prevails in the Southern mountains, with squads of devoted young women cheering on the combatants, you will see the warrior ethos alive and well. It has assumed a new exterior, but the internal dynamics remain the same.

Reared in Appalachia, I can attest to the fact that children there are raised to be respectful to their elders and kind to those younger than themselves. This is the theory, anyway, if not always the practice. So two episodes of the feud that particularly surprised me were Devil Anse Hatfield's seizure of Perry Cline's land and his killing of Ranel McCoy's children, all of whom were much younger than he. The most shocking event of all was Devil Anse's attempts to kill Ranel McCoy, fourteen years his elder. And despite the fact that the Hatfields had called Sarah McCoy "Aunt Sally" before the feud,[54] a couple of them beat her nearly to death during the New Year's Night Massacre.

A psychotherapist might say that Devil Anse Hatfield was acting out his Oedipal fury at receiving no land from his father, while all his brothers did. Instead, he confiscated the land of young Perry Cline, his longtime next-door neighbor and a surrogate younger sibling. He then tried to kill Ranel McCoy, a surrogate father. He succeeded in killing some of Ranel's children, more surrogate siblings. The events of the feud that Devil Anse masterminded also resulted in the deaths of two of his own brothers, whom he may have subconsciously wanted to destroy because his father loved them, but not him.

To push this psychotherapeutic explanation to its outer limits, many men on both sides of the feud appear to have had father issues. Jim Vance and Cottontop Mounts were illegitimate. Big Eph Hatfield disapproved of Devil Anse—rightfully so, it turns out—and left him no land. Both

Johnse and Cap Hatfield squirmed under the thumb of their father. Johnse was unable to defy him in order to marry Roseanna McCoy and unable to limit his participation in the feud in order to keep his marriage to Nancy McCoy intact. Cap performed atrocious acts in his eagerness to please his father. Their brother Bob appears torn between the demands of his father to participate in feud events and the pleas of his mother not to.

On the McCoy side, Perry Cline lost his father at age nine, leaving him vulnerable to the machinations of Devil Anse Hatfield. Frank Phillips never met his father, who was killed in the Civil War, and he spent much of his time trying to live up to his father's reputation for bravery. Harmon McCoy's sons lost him to murder when they were very young. Ranel and Harmon McCoy's father, Daniel, failed in his traditional responsibilities by giving them no land when they started families of their own. Ranel McCoy failed his own sons similarly. Daniel left a legacy of shiftlessness, and Ranel of litigiousness.

Observers have wondered why feud participants felt such rage over matters that often seem so trivial to outsiders.[55] I sometimes picture all these sad young men, and some not so young, fighting their shadowbox battles for or against phantom fathers, acting out their longing for fathers who had died or never claimed them, their hatred of fathers who had failed or rejected them—and slaughtering one another in the process.

†

Any one explanation for the feud, taken on its own, doesn't do justice to the extent or the gravity of the events. But taken as a whole, their collective weight seems valid: too many guns, too much moonshine, too little regard for human life, an inflated sense of personal pride, an exaggerated need to experience hormonal highs through violence, inchoate rage spawned by largely subconscious inner conflicts. British borderland folkways and the remnants of a frontier culture still exerted their influence. Civil War antagonisms and the habit of guerrilla justice lingered on. Without regular schooling, feudists hadn't learned how to subdue destructive emotions with rationality. Without churches, many had no sense of moral values that transcended personal or family whims. The warrior ethos conditioned into young boys taught them to disparage or disregard advocates for peaceful solutions to clashes. Young men with no land of their own were raging against the approaching exploitation of their labor and extinction of their way of life occasioned by the arrival of the large-scale timber and coal consortiums.

The Hatfield-McCoy feud was a perfect storm. It resulted in many deaths. But this was a man-made disaster, not a freak of nature. Given some measure of sobriety, humility, rationality, and compassion, most of these deaths could have been avoided.

†

The greatest horror to me is the plight of the women whose menfolk enacted the feud. Harmon McCoy's wife, Patty, was seven months pregnant when she dragged his bloody corpse home through the snow. Roseanna McCoy was pregnant when she rode bareback to West Virginia to warn Devil Anse Hatfield of his son's capture by her father and brothers. Ellison Hatfield's wife, Sarah, was pregnant when the three McCoy sons killed him. Devil Anse's wife, Levicy, gave birth a month after the Battle of Grapevine Creek. Enduring childbirth is stressful enough in a peaceful environment, but these women were giving birth on a battlefield.

Then there were all the wives left alone with so many children to rear and no husbands to help them. Cap Hatfield's wife, Nancy, tried and failed to take care of their five children when Cap was on the lam out West. Their oldest son, Coleman, describes his heartbreaking struggle to run their farm by himself when he was just nine years old. He managed to acquire only a year and a few months of schooling in between planting, plowing, and harvesting. Despite his mother's and his own best efforts, his brother Shepherd died of malnutrition.

Harmon McCoy's wife, Patty Cline, found herself widowed with six small children to raise; Ellison Hatfield's wife, Sarah Staton, with ten.[56] Ranel and Sarah McCoy, themselves approaching sixty, took in their murdered son Tolbert McCoy's two children. The burdens borne by these women and children whose husbands and fathers died such violent deaths must also rank among the collateral damage caused by the feud.

Though none of the women perpetrated feud violence, some fell victim to it.* Sarah McCoy was brutally beaten and Alifair McCoy killed during the New Year's Night Massacre. Adelaide McCoy went insane after that night if a newspaper report is to be believed (which some doubt). Roseanna McCoy died of depression. Nancy and Mary McCoy (or Mary and her aged mother-in-law) were beaten unconscious with a cow's tail.

The role of women in the feud was to mop up after their menfolk's messes. Sarah McCoy tried repeatedly to calm Ranel's wrath, and she often succeeded—to the probable detriment of her later-murdered children. Sarah McCoy and her daughter-in-law pleaded unsuccessfully with Devil Anse for Tolbert's and his brothers' lives after their murder of Ellison Hatfield. Roseanna McCoy rode across the river to warn Devil Anse that her brothers might kill his son.

Levicy Hatfield tried to keep at least one son out of feud events. Judging from the disapproval of Devil Anse Hatfield's twin brothers, their mother, Nancy Vance, must have exerted a restraining influence on some of her other sons. Ellison Hatfield's wife nursed him after the Election Day Brawl, though she wasn't able to save his life. Cap Hatfield's wife, Nancy, taught him to read and write, and wrote letters for Devil Anse in his ham-handed attempts to broker a peace with Perry Cline after Jeff McCoy's murder.

When the women of the feud weren't enduring or cleaning up after the violence, they enabled it. They seem to have felt that boys will be boys, and girls must put up with it. They loved men who didn't deserve it. They gave birth to sons who grew up to become murderers. They kept farms and households functioning, washed the bloodstains out of shirts, and mended the bullet holes, while their men plotted and schemed, threatened and blustered, cantered and killed.

If only the feudists had spent as much money and effort on acquiring contraception (which was, in fact, available in other regions of the United States at this time) as they did on acquiring guns, ammunition, and

---

* None of the Hatfield women, however, experienced any harm from McCoy men.

moonshine, a different scenario might have evolved. With fewer children, their farms could have remained intact instead of being constantly subdivided into ever-smaller plots. Those angry young hillbullies would have had secure livelihoods and perhaps wouldn't have felt such a compulsion to charge around the countryside on horseback, expressing their fury by creating such terror and misery for others.

14

THE INNER HILLBILLY

CHARLES HOWELL OF THE *PITTSBURGH TIMES* WAS ONE OF THE FIRST TO start shaping Devil Anse Hatfield's image as a wild and crazy savage for a national audience. His report from Pikeville following the New Year's Night Massacre in 1888 portrayed Devil Anse as a ruthless tyrant intent on demolishing the McCoys for no reason at all, even though Howell never met the man. He called the feud "a succession of cowardly murders by day and assassinations and houseburnings by night. All of the murders have been cruel, heartless and almost without the shadow of a provocation."[1]

John Ed Pearce, in his book about several of the Kentucky feuds, would probably agree with this portrayal of the Hatfield-McCoy feud. "Devil Anse, Jim Vance, Johnse, and most of the other Hatfields," he says, "were little more than thugs. I cannot find grounds for admiring Devil Anse, who not only engineered the two instances of brutal murder but lacked the backbone to commit them himself and sent his underlings out to do the slaughtering."[2] But Pearce sees both sides as "basically backward, mean-tempered people."[3] But others maintain that the feud and the feudists were more complicated and more likeable than this.

When T. C. Crawford's book *An American Vendetta: A Story of Barbarism in the United States* appeared in 1888, he presented a more favorable but equally stereotypical portrait of Devil Anse Hatfield as a Stonewall Jackson of the Cumberlands.[4] A Confederate veterans' magazine in 1900 stated admiringly that "Devil Anse always goes with a Winchester, a sack around his neck full of cartridges, a pair of Smith and Wesson's, and, I am told, that a pair of good Damascus blades luxuriate constantly from his boot legs. . . . When you hear that Devil Anse has been shot, it will not be in the back; he will have several piled around him."[5] Maintaining this bloodthirsty public image must have placed a great strain on Devil Anse since he shed it after he emerged from Island Creek as a dripping wet Christian, living a quiet and peaceful life* until his death in his bed at home from old age.

Crawford also commented on the respect that Devil Anse received from his family and the high regard in which his neighbors held him, concluding that the Civil War had destroyed the community mechanisms for maintaining order, so that group retaliation became the only recourse available in the face of criminal activity.[6] These two versions of Devil Anse coexisted, depending upon whether an informant sympathized with the Kentuckians or the West Virginians. Devil Anse was simultaneously a vicious lunatic and a revered elder statesman thrust into a position of leadership by the needs of his community.

There was a third Devil Anse as well, a rival to Paul Bunyan, with his woodsman skills and his feats of hunting, shooting, and riding. He was said to still be able to shoot a squirrel from the top of the tallest tree in his seventies.[7] He raised as pets bear cubs whose mothers he had killed. Sometimes young lawyers or politicians trekked up to his house to see the living legend for themselves, like visiting Mount Rushmore. Devil Anse got a kick out of sending them on a chore into his yard, where they encountered a friendly bear and fled in terror.[8]

A favorite tale that the patriarch told his grandchildren concerned the day he brought home four deer with one bullet. As a doe and a half-grown buck rested on the ground in a meadow, he shot one, the bullet passing through it to kill the other as well. When he cut the doe open to gut her, he found that she was carrying nearly full-term twin fawns, which he raised on bottles.[9]

* Apart from his participation in and promotion of a movie about the feud, about which, more later.

The most famous image of the feud, this 1897 photograph of part of Devil Anse Hatfield's extended family, depicts him sitting with a rifle on the left, while his second in command, Cap Hatfield, sits with a rifle on the right. Around them, standing and sitting, are Devil Anse's younger children and grandchildren, none of whom participated in the feud, and his hunting dog, Yellow Watch. To the right stands W. D. Borden, a local store clerk who commissioned the photo. The photographer whom Borden hired asked the men and boys to brandish their guns, which they did, unknowingly stigmatizing the Hatfield side of the feud for the rest of their lives and beyond. COURTESY OF WEST VIRGINIA STATE ARCHIVES

Another story concerns Devil Anse Hatfield's testifying at a trial for the murder of an itinerant peddler. He described tracking down the murderers, their bloodstained clothing, and the stolen booty by following clues like leaves pierced with boot nails and blobs of tobacco juice spit onto the path.[10]

Other admiring anecdotes involve Devil Anse's adopting an ill and disconsolate young orphan who passed the old man's house in a wagon train bound for the West. The orphan grew up to be one of Devil Anse's most loyal feudists,[11] perhaps hiding Cap Hatfield and Joe Glenn in his attic from a posse after their murder of the three Rutherfords on the Matewan Election Day. Another story in Devil Anse's hagiography, which stretches the limits of even the kindest credulity, reports that he organized his henchmen to hoe weeds from the corn patches of widows and the disabled,[12] which would be equivalent to Al Capone's thugs laying down their tommy guns to wash windows in a Chicago old folks' home.

Buffalo Bill Cody brought his *Wild West Show* to eastern Kentucky in 1893. One reporter maintains that Devil Anse Hatfield emerged from the audience to match Buffalo Bill's marksmanship shot for shot.[13] But Devil Anse was avoiding Kentucky during those years from fear of the indictments against him there. The myths had already begun to write themselves.

In 1897, seven years after the feud had ended, a clerk at a local store arranged for an itinerant photographer to take pictures of some members of the Hatfield family. The photographer asked the men and boys to brandish their guns. Understandably naive about the extent of media manipulation, they grabbed their rifles and pistols and displayed them "like jewelry" (as one writer has said of Afghan men and their firearms[14]). Two of these photos soon gained notoriety all over the world, stigmatizing the Hatfield feudists for the rest of their lives and beyond.

The public was especially shocked by a little boy in one of these photos—Cap Hatfield's son Coleman A., the eventual Hatfield feud chronicler—who clutched a pistol as though it were a teddy bear, and by the apparently dimwitted pride with which all the men flaunted their weapons. The great irony is that only two of them—Devil Anse and Cap—had actually fought in the feud. But psychologists say that children respond to the expectations of those around them, so three of Devil Anse's younger nonfeudist sons in these photos eventually killed people, and two were killed in turn.

Devil Anse and Levicy Hatfield with seven of their children, a hired hand, and a store clerk, posed to look like desperados. Of the eleven, only Devil Anse and Cap Hatfield actually fought in the feud, which had been over for seven years by the 1897 date of this famous photo. 1: Ock Damron, a hired hand. 2: Elias Hatfield, son of Devil Anse. 3: Troy Hatfield. 4: Rose Hatfield. 5: Joe Hatfield. 6: Cap Hatfield. 7: W. D. Borden, a store clerk. 8: Tennis Hatfield. 9: Devil Anse Hatfield. 10: Levicy Chafin Hatfield. 11: Willie Hatfield. COURTESY OF WEST VIRGINIA STATE ARCHIVES

One of Devil Anse's obituaries states that he was persuaded to go on the vaudeville stage in much the same manner as Sitting Bull had joined Buffalo Bill Cody's *Wild West Show.* But he was reminded, or he remembered, just in time that if he ventured away from his home and his log fort, the outstanding indictments against him might be served.[15]

Emmett Dalton, of the infamous Dalton Gang, convinced Devil Anse Hatfield to star in a silent movie in 1915, to be shown at theaters along with a movie called *The Last Stand of the Dalton Boys,* which concerned

Devil Anse Hatfield playing the part of a rugged mountaineer with rifle and cartridge belts. This photo is believed to be a publicity shot taken to promote Devil Anse's silent movie about the feud, made with Emmett Dalton of the Dalton Gang.

the Dalton Gang's attempt to outdo Jesse James by robbing two banks in broad daylight while wearing false beards. Their ploy failed: Four of the gang were killed, and Emmett Dalton went to prison for fourteen years. Dalton claimed that both the Hatfields and the McCoys starred in the feud movie and that he inspected their guns before the sham battles along the Tug Fork to make sure that no former feudist had slipped real bullets into his gun so as to rekindle the feud. Dalton said that when he showed the film to the participating feudists, they were "tickled as children" to watch this screen version of their activities.[16] In reality, no McCoys participated.[17]

The movie ran for a time in southern West Virginia. Truda McCoy claimed that Devil Anse and Levicy took along a moonshine still to screenings and demonstrated its operation to movie audiences. She also claimed that the theater owner in Pikeville decided not to show the movie there out of respect for the feelings of the McCoys.[18]

Some of Devil Anse Hatfield's friends eventually pointed out to him that neither the Hatfields nor the McCoys had robbed strangers for money. They insisted that it was unseemly for their activities to be equated to the depredations of the Dalton Gang.[19] Anse agreed and withdrew from the project. But the damage had been done, leaving behind yet another photo believed to have been taken as a publicity still—of Devil Anse, rifle in hand, wearing double cartridge belts. The aging Devil Anse was quickly becoming a caricature of himself.

†

Unfortunately, the reporting of the feud tended to tar all inhabitants of the southern Appalachians with the same brush. Some of the adjectives most frequently used in articles about the region were: *backward, barbarous, dissolute, idle, primitive, revolting, savage, uncivilized, violent,* and *wild.*[20]

Between 1905 and 1928 ninety-two silent movies were filmed for national distribution that featured feuding mountaineers exhibiting all those damning qualities and more.[21] One writer describes the shift that occurred during this period in how other Americans perceived Appalachian people: "Images of the mountaineer as pathetic and romantic gave way before a new set of images of the mountaineers as feudists and desperadoes, criminals and social deviants."[22] Whereas Southern mountain people had been portrayed prior to the feud era as "our contemporary ancestors,"[23] afterward they became crazed outsiders. With their feuding and their moonshining, they had ventured beyond what had become the new American pale. The media at the time stressed the European origins of their violence, among the Highland clans of Scotland—from which most in the Southern backcountry hadn't, in fact, descended.

An adjective frequently found in reviews and synopses of the scripts of these silent movies about Appalachian feudists is "virile."[24] Once again, while audiences gasped in horror at the outrageous behavior of the fictional feudists, they admired their ruthless aggression. As one writer puts it, "Those forces, which were shaping a new American business and political elite—and hence American mass culture . . . found the idea of man's 'wolf-law' nature a useful indulgence, a justification for annihilating one's rivals, or minor nations."[25]

But in the final reel of each silent film, the feudists were usually arrested, and their women were whisked from the mountains to a richer life in the cities of America.[26] So, after a brief flirtation with anarchy, urban audiences emerged from the darkness of the movie theaters knowing that they were different from, and superior to, these vicious outlaws prowling the Southern mountains.

Coal formed the foundation of the industrial revolution in Europe and America in the nineteenth century because it powered steam engines and fueled the manufacture of steel. Anthracite fields near the East Coast were nearly exhausted, so the bituminous seams in the southern Appalachians looked very attractive to industrialists.[27] William MacCorkle, elected governor of West Virginia in 1892, maintained that the abundance of raw materials in West Virginia would assure that the state would become a major manufacturing center, bringing abundance and harmony to its citizens.[28]

Unfortunately, the arrival of industry in the Tug Fork Valley didn't provide the panacea that Governor MacCorkle blissfully predicted for the people who lived there. Many local residents sold their farms and timberlands to these large corporations or sold the rights to the minerals beneath them, for prices ranging from twenty-five cents to three dollars per acre. Some sold entire mountains for a mule, a horse, or a rifle, like the Lenape who supposedly exchanged the island of Manhattan for some beads.[29]

Some mountaineers made such deals not by choice but because overlapping land grants and unreliable eighteenth-century surveys put many existing land titles in West Virginia into jeopardy. Nonresident agents challenged traditional proprietors, who lacked the resources to fight these challenges in court. Some preferred to sell their land for pennies on the dollar rather than to face the confusing and expensive maze of legalities required to uphold their own claims.[30]

Others exchanged their mineral rights for quitclaim deeds that assured them of ownership of the land on which their families had already been living for generations. Unfortunately, these deeds granted the owners of the mineral rights access to the minerals by any and all means necessary for their extraction. At the time the deeds were signed, this provision meant a tunnel in a hillside and space for a tipple and a railroad spur. Later, in the twentieth century, this same provision allowed for strip-mining, mountaintop removal, and complete destruction of the land that the original owners had sought to preserve by signing away the mineral rights in the first place.[31]

Unable to rely any longer on farming, herding, hunting, and riding their rafts of logs downriver to the sawmills for their sustenance, many Tug Fork Valley residents became wage laborers. Those who took up mining soon discovered that they were required to work twelve-hour days, six days a week[32]—an incomprehensible schedule for people accustomed to working their own land at their own pace according to the demands of the weather and the seasons.

Coal seams often lay in remote coves, so mining companies had to build entire towns for their workers, in which the companies owned the houses, schools, churches, and stores.[33] Wages usually came in the form of scrip that had to be spent at company stores, where prices were manipulated artificially according to the requirements of the companies' profit margins.[34] The valleys they mined were sometimes so narrow that there was room for only a creek, a road, a railroad track, and a row or two of buildings, with walls of rock rising up on either side and blocking out the sun by midafternoon. The houses "squatted on the mountainside like 'great drab beetles with their stilt legs braced against the slope.' "[35]

West Virginia in 1900 had the largest percentage of native-born coal miners in the nation, but there weren't enough of them, so miners came from eastern and southern Europe, as did blacks from farther south.[36] Within a decade, West Virginia had the highest percentage of foreign-born workers south of the Mason-Dixon Line.[37] Whereas once the Tug Fork Valley had hosted very few people, most related to one another and most of them subsistence farmers and loggers, now people from all over the country and all over the world called the valley home. But they knew only the inhabitants of their own isolated coal towns and depended entirely upon the whims of absentee owners for their shelter and sustenance.[38]

The last decade of the nineteenth century and the first two of the twentieth were an age of industrial violence. Major strikes occurred all over the United States. In the Lawrence, Massachusetts, textile strike, for example, twenty-three thousand workers left their looms, demanding higher wages and safer working conditions.[39]

But in West Virginia the coal companies were in bed with state and county governments to prevent any form of regulation.[40] Those who used to win elections in the Tug Fork Valley were the best orators and those who enjoyed the support of extended kinship groups. They often bought votes with free liquor, as the West Virginia Hatfields did in Kentucky, where they themselves couldn't vote. Replacing this system was one dominated by industrialists who bought support with private patronage.[41]

Hand-loading coal required miners to lie on their backs and undercut coal seams with picks, to augur holes with drills braced against their chests, to pack these holes with explosives, to light the fuses, and then to run like hell.[42] West Virginian coal miners were more likely to lose their lives on the job than soldiers fighting in World War I.[43] They could die from explosions, roof falls, poisonous gases, or the lingering suffocation of black lung disease.[44] Unions, which negotiated for safety regulations and higher wages, were allowed in most states, but not in West Virginia due to the influence of the coal operators. As a result, cheaper, nonunion coal from West Virginia flooded the national market and forced a reduction in price for union coal mined elsewhere.[45]

The United Mine Workers of America (UMWA) moved in and unionized the mine at Paint Creek, some seventy-five miles from the Tug Fork Valley. But the mine at nearby Cabin Creek remained without a union. So in 1912 the Paint Creek owners outlawed the union there and hired the Baldwin-Felts Detective Agency to root out any miners who objected. A hundred Baldwin-Felts guards, some former criminals, moved in with machine guns and evicted the miners' families from company houses, beating up and killing several miners in the process and kicking one pregnant woman, who later lost the child.[46]

The ousted miners moved to a tent colony during an unusually harsh winter. Strikebreakers roared past the colony in an armored train called the Bull Moose Special and fired machine guns into the tents.

The coal operators brought in scabs, whose trains the union miners attacked. Martial law was declared, and Mother Jones, a UMWA organizer, was arrested and sentenced to twenty years in prison for reading the Declaration of Independence from the statehouse steps in Charleston.[47]

At this point Henry D. Hatfield, Devil Anse Hatfield's nephew and the son of Good Elias, became governor of West Virginia. A practicing physician, he went to Paint Creek carrying his doctor bag. While helping the miners' families with their health problems, he earned their trust. He brought union leaders to Charleston, put them in a room with the coal operators, and insisted that they reach a deal to end the strike. They did so—but the deal didn't include the right for miners to unionize.

In 1912, Woodrow Wilson became the first Democratic president of the country in twenty years. A friend of labor, he established the Federal Trade Commission, instituted a federal income tax, and introduced some

Henry D. Hatfield, Devil Anse Hatfield's nephew and the son of Good Elias, became governor of West Virginia and tried to mediate the conflict between union leaders and coal companies. COURTESY OF THE LIBRARY OF CONGRESS

pro-union legislation regulating wages and working conditions, and protecting existing unions during mergers.[48]

Some four million American soldiers mobilized for World War I, and the country needed those who stayed at home to cooperate in the war effort. Industry made many concessions to keep the war workers happy, and union membership soared from two million to five million. But during the recession following the war, wages fell, layoffs ensued, and regulations protecting both wages and working conditions came under attack.[49]

Meanwhile, the UMWA was trying once again to unionize the coal mines in and around the Tug Fork Valley, so as to stabilize coal prices at union rates all around the country. Many miners in Mingo County, a new county formed along the Tug Fork from part of Logan County, West Virginia, favored the union. Its main town was Matewan, where Cap Hatfield had lived following the Battle of Grapevine Creek, until the shoot-out in which he and Joe Glenn had killed the three Rutherfords.

Matewan chief of police Sid Hatfield had worked in a mine and sympathized with the miners' plight. Although he claimed to be related to Devil Anse Hatfield and was raised by a Hatfield family on Blackberry Creek in Kentucky, he was actually an orphan whom they had adopted.[50] However, he gave Devil Anse a run for his money when it came to constructing a legend about himself.

On May 19, 1920, a dozen Baldwin-Felts detectives arrived in Matewan by train.[51] They traveled half a mile out of town to the coal camp of Red Jacket on Stone Mountain, where all the miners had joined the UMWA. As a result, several miners had been fired, blacklisted, and ordered to vacate their company houses. Since they had refused to leave, the detectives evicted them, throwing one woman's furniture into the road in the rain. (The detectives claimed she had asked for their help in moving.)

Sid Hatfield and the town mayor, Cabell C. Testerman, standing in front of Testerman's jewelry store, confronted the detectives. One of them produced a warrant for Hatfield's arrest for interfering with their own arrest of a union organizer. Testerman studied it and pronounced it a fraud.

Gunfire immediately erupted among the detectives, Sid Hatfield, and several deputized miners stationed around the town. One researcher says the detective with the warrant started this barrage by firing five times at Mayor Testerman, followed by Sid Hatfield's shooting the detective in the head.[52]

When the dust settled, seven Baldwin-Felts agents lay dead, including two brothers of Tom Felts, the agency owner. Two miners were also dead. Mayor Testerman himself was badly wounded and soon died. Two detectives swam the Tug Fork and escaped into the wilds of Kentucky, as did a third detective, who was wounded as he crossed a bridge over the river. Two others hopped a train that arrived in the station during the melee. The bodies of the dead detectives lay in the street for two hours until the sheriff arrived and ordered the miners still lurking in the streets to help him load them into the baggage car of a passing train for transport to an undertaker in a nearby town.

Sid Hatfield and twenty-two miners were indicted for the murders. Greenway Hatfield, son of Good Elias and nephew of Devil Anse, was in charge of helping select the jury.[53]

Eleven days later, detectives spotted Sid Hatfield and Testerman's widow, Jessie, entering a hotel room in Huntington, West Virginia. The couple was arrested and jailed for "improper relations." But they were released the next day when they showed the judge their marriage license dated the previous day. The judge agreed to cancel their fine if they married that same day, which they did. Rumors then swirled that Sid had shot Mayor Testerman in order to marry his wife.[54] Nevertheless, miners all over the country regarded Sid Hatfield as a hero, a symbol of hope that it was possible to prevail over the injustices of mine owners and their hired guns.

The ousted Red Jacket miners and those evicted from other coal towns settled into tent colonies along the Tug Fork and conducted raids and attacks on nonunion mines in the area. State police moved into one such colony and shot and arrested some miners, ripping up their tents and demolishing their belongings.

It isn't hard to imagine how these Tug Fork–native miners must have felt living in tents on land they had once owned or roamed. Now the hills where they had hunted were stripped of timber, punctured with mine shafts and railroad tracks, and bled of coal.

In 1870, two-thirds of West Virginia still had its virgin timber. By 1910 this figure had been reduced by four-fifths. By 1920 no virgin forests at all were left.[55] Pastures and second-growth forests replaced them in the lowlands. But on the high plateaus and mountainsides, debris left from clear-cutting often caught fire from lightning or sparks spewed by passing locomotives or by mining equipment. The fires burned through the fertile humus down to the rocky subsoil, leaving blackened wastelands incapable of growing anything for many years.[56]

Mine shafts honeycombed these denuded hills, in which the Tug Fork miners spent their daylight hours in the dark, on their backs, chopping at coal seams with picks. The valleys were piled high with rock waste left from the extraction of coal. Rivers where they had once fished ran red from sludge created by cleaning the coal. Streams silted up from topsoil that washed off the bare hillsides. Acidic-smelling dust filled the air.

In days gone by, the families of many of these blacklisted miners had produced all they needed from their own land. Now the miners depended on manufactured goods bought from stores with scrip that could only be earned by working in the mines. Jobs that had seemed to promise lives of plenty had yielded, instead, devastation of their forests and streams, and the danger of death or dismemberment. Like Esau, they had sold their birthright for a pot of beans. When they had tried to join the union so as to demand higher wages and safer working conditions, even the pot of beans had been taken away from them. They now had nothing.

The following winter, Sid Hatfield and the miners indicted for the Matewan Massacre were found not guilty. For all the subsequent rejoicing, the situation still looked bleak for the UMWA. Of the nonunion mines, 80 percent had reopened with scabs and former miners who had capitulated to the owners' terms. Blacklisted miners continued to attack these mines. Martial law was again declared, but pro-unionists continued their guerrilla activities up and down the Tug Fork, as had their fathers and grandfathers during the Civil War and the feud years.[57] The feud had ended, but these later generations finally had their chance to perform heroic deeds.

A participant in the Matewan Massacre, in which coal company detectives killed the Matewan mayor, Sid Hatfield (right) was gunned down later on the steps of the Welch, West Virginia, courthouse along with friend Ed Chambers (left). Both died on the spot while the wife of one repeatedly beat an attacker over the head with her umbrella. COURTESY OF WEST VIRGINIA STATE ARCHIVES

Tom Felts, however, was gunning for Sid Hatfield for the deaths of his detective brothers. He managed to get Sid charged with dynamiting a tipple at a mine in another county, which required Sid to leave Mingo County for a trial in Welch, West Virginia. Sid, a friend, and their wives were ascending the courthouse steps in Welch when six Baldwin-Felts detectives riddled the men with a volley of bullets.[58] Both died on the steps while one of their wives repeatedly beat an attacker over the head with her umbrella.[59]

The miners of West Virginia rose up in rebellion, supported by miners all over the nation. Mother Jones was quoted as saying, "There is never peace in West Virginia because there is never justice."[60] Miners demonstrated at the capitol in Charleston, presenting a petition of demands, which were rejected.[61]

Then, somewhere between five thousand and fifteen thousand armed miners began a fifty-mile march across southern West Virginia to Mingo County.[62] They intended to free the miners arrested for guerrilla activities, to end martial law, and to organize the nonunion mines. Some dressed in uniforms left over from their World War I service. Others wore overalls with red kerchiefs around their necks. It was the largest armed insurrection in America since the Civil War.[63]

Don Chafin, a cousin of Devil Anse Hatfield's wife, Levicy, was sheriff of Logan County, which stood in the miners' route to Mingo County. Coal operators in 1920 paid Chafin, under the table, the equivalent of $300,000 to support their goals.[64] He deputized a force of two thousand to three thousand men. Armed with machine guns, they stationed themselves in trenches along the top of Blair Mountain, on the border of Logan County. Chafin also hired a private plane to drop shrapnel bombs on the protesting miners.[65]

The War Department in Washington threatened to send federal troops to end this confrontation. In response, the UMWA told the marchers to go home. Some did. But when Chafin's army of deputies started pursuing and arresting marchers, many homebound miners returned, and the battle resumed in earnest for several more days.

Gen. Billy Mitchell, a military air tactician who kept himself busy bombing derelict ships in the Atlantic, sent fifteen to twenty single-engine planes to West Virginia, along with two or three large bombers.[66] Several crashed or were lost en route.[67] It was the first time the US government had ever deployed military aircraft against its own citizens. Some planes performed aerial surveillance on the miners.

When federal soldiers finally arrived to break up the fracas, they stationed themselves half behind the miners and half behind Chafin's men, demanding that they stop fighting. Many of the miners had fought in World War I and didn't want to fire on their fellow soldiers, so they withdrew.[68]

Both sides claimed victory, the miners because they hadn't stopped fighting due to Don Chafin's might, but, rather, due to their loyalty to Uncle Sam. Some miners rode a streetcar through Charleston and were cheered as victors. But the real victory went to the mine operators. Within a few years, union membership in West Virginia had plummeted from fifty thousand to ten thousand—and wages from seven dollars for an eight-hour day to two dollars for a twelve-hour day.[69] Almost a thousand miners from the Blair Mountain March were indicted for murder and for treason against the state of West Virginia. Some were acquitted, but others went to prison for several years.

Bill Blizzard, leader of the march, was also tried for treason. In a courtroom jammed with witnesses, reporters, lawyers, and union members, Blizzard was acquitted and was carried out on supporters' shoulders.[70]

But an unknown number of miners and guards alike had died on Blair Mountain, and many more had been wounded.[71] The large corporations had originally refused to enter the Tug Fork Valley due to the supposed savagery of the people who lived there. But the system the corporations had set in place instead turned out to be far more savage and lethal than anything enacted by the Hatfields and the McCoys.

✝

Devil Anse died just before twenty-eight-year-old Sid Hatfield went to trial for the Matewan Massacre. No mention is made anywhere of how Devil Anse regarded Sid Hatfield or the union battles. He himself had been the poster boy for freedom, autonomy, and self-reliance, and one might expect him to have resented the machinations of the large corporations and absentee owners, just as he had resented the wealthy Tidewater planters during the Civil War.

But Don Chafin, his wife's cousin, was leading the antiunion forces. His sons Johnse and Cap worked as guards for coal operators, and his son Willis was a personnel officer for a coal corporation. His children and relatives had sided with the coal industry and were benefitting from it. So it's hard to say where Devil Anse's loyalties might have lain. Perhaps he felt indifferent. He was an old man who had fought his own battles. The Tug Fork Valley had become a different place from what he had known as a young man, when he and his men had thundered across the river on horseback in the dead of night, pursuing their missions of vengeance. He might have regarded the union battles as having little to do with him, no matter how much the pro-union guerrilla activities along the Tug Fork resembled the campaigns of his youth.

Unfortunately, those new battles along the Tug Fork *did* have a lot to do with Devil Anse Hatfield—or rather, with how his behavior had been portrayed in the national media. Because other Americans had come to regard the residents of the southern Appalachians as brutal savages, they felt little concern that those savages were now being starved and maimed, their once-sparkling rivers murky with toxins, their towering primeval forests reduced to stumps.

A similar process had robbed Native Americans of their land in the western states in the last decades of the nineteenth century. The national press widely portrayed them as vicious barbarians, which made it acceptable to other Americans that they be corralled on reservations and reduced to poverty, while their ancestral lands yielded profits for outsiders. Blacks have suffered a similar program of systematic dehumanization throughout their history in America, painted as violent and unintelligent in order to justify their subjugation, first as slaves and later as freedmen.

The hillbilly stereotype spawned by the Hatfield-McCoy feud—of an uncouth bearded bumpkin in a slouch hat and overalls, holding a rifle in one hand and a jug of moonshine in the other—in part justified the exploitation of coal miners and lumbermen in the southern Appalachians and the destruction of their environment. It masked and made a mockery of the real issue of who would control and benefit from the enormous natural resources of the region.

This stereotype of the venal hillbilly served several other functions as well. The Civil War had ended when the feud began. More than six hundred thousand soldiers died, and many more were maimed for life, to say nothing of the civilian toll. As Americans attempted to put these staggering statistics behind them and resume life as a supposedly civilized society, they projected their own participation in such brutality onto the powerless rural people in the Southern mountains—a perfect example of the pot calling the kettle black.

Nor had all the atrocities happened in the past. At the same time that feuds were playing out in the southern Appalachians, lynching reached its height in the plantation South, as did strikes and riots in the industrialized North. The regional stereotype of the savage mountaineer remained in force during the Spanish-American War, with its nearly 20,000 deaths, and throughout World War I, with its 10 million civilian deaths and 9.7 million military deaths. It remained strong despite the estimated five hundred deaths engineered by Al Capone in Chicago.

The hillbilly stereotype absorbed the shadow sides of those who held it. As Altina Waller puts it, underneath the stereotyping lurked "the terrible fear of the dark or 'savage' side of their own natures that might gain the upper hand if allowed the freedom that mountaineers enjoyed."[72]

This stereotype remains strong even today, over a century after the end of the feud. My own generation grew up laughing at the stupidities of the hillbillies in the funny pages and on television. Many of us shuddered over the gruesome scene in James Dickey's *Deliverance* in which a degenerate mountaineer rapes a man from the city.

Meanwhile, the brain drain has continued. Many counties in Appalachia have declining and aging populations. Almost a quarter of all Americans have college degrees, but fewer than 18 percent of Appalachians do.[73]

Many Appalachian forests have been clear-cut, so logging jobs, once plentiful in the region, are now scarce. The ownership of farmland had been limited by the large purchases by railroad, timber, and coal consortiums, and by confiscations by the federal government for national parks and Tennessee Valley Authority dams and lakes. Much land that remains is unusable for farming because it is too steep, or because the topsoil has eroded due to clear-cutting or has been buried by strip-mining and mountaintop removal.

Requiring only half as many laborers, mountaintop removal is largely replacing the old method of underground mining. Explosives expose coal seams located as much as four hundred feet below the surface. The explosions and the rocks they blast into the sky damage nearby homes. The toxic dust harms some inhabitants' lungs, many already suffering from the black lung disease acquired in underground mines. Called the "overburden," trees, soil, and rocks, often saturated with heavy-metal content, are scraped off coal seams into surrounding valleys. Sometimes this overburden buries the headwaters of streams, destroying water supplies for humans and habitats for fish and wild animals. The toxic runoff pollutes drinking water far downstream.[74]

The rate of birth defects in babies born near mountaintop removal sites is 42 percent higher than that of babies born elsewhere in Appalachia, and the cancer rate for those near such sites is 14.4 percent versus 9.4 percent for other Appalachians.[75] The speculation is that the contaminants released into the air and water by the blasting and the runoff impair fetal development. The Coal River Mountain Watch maintains that mountaintop removal is causing a "wholesale poisoning of Appalachia."[76]

Several thousand pro-union miners fought on Blair Mountain against Don Chafin's army of three thousand antiunion deputies in 1921. It's a site of major historic significance for the American labor movement. Yet Alpha Natural Resources plans to remove a portion of Blair Mountain[77] and ship it to markets in India, Turkey, and Egypt.[78]

Strip-mining and mountaintop removal have destroyed five hundred mountains in Appalachia so far.[79] That coal corporations can freely subject citizens of the region to the demolition of the mountains in which their families have lived for generations further testifies to the damage done by the stereotypes spawned by the Hatfield-McCoy feud. Once all the peaks have been leveled and shipped to India, once the region has become merely an extension of the Great Plains, there will be no more towering mountains and no more ornery mountaineers to impede the grand march of Progress.

15

Man Toys

I grew up in a wide river valley in East Tennessee, the Smoky Mountains and the Blue Ridge on one side, the Cumberland Plateau on the other. My town, Kingsport, was founded in 1916 as a base for Northern industry. The main employer is the Tennessee Eastman Chemical Corporation. When I was a child, the town also hosted a large printing company, a paper mill, a glass plant, a couple of textile mills, a brickyard, and a defense contractor. Factories, some now closed, spread down the banks of the Holston River, alongside the tracks of the Carolina, Clinchfield, and Ohio railroad, on which coal arrived from the mountains all around us to fuel their activities. The factories discharged wastewater into the river and smoke into the air, which still has a sweet-and-sour odor to it. The parents of many of my schoolmates had moved to Kingsport from area farms to work in these factories. The managers, often from the North or from Southern cities, were friends of my parents and grandparents.

We were the New South—though we thought we were the Old South. The unions at the printing company, the largest press under one roof in the world at that time, went on strike for four years during the 1960s. While strikers were shooting up the homes of their supervisors and tear gas was floating on the mountain air, my friends and I were waltzing at the country club in elbow-length kid gloves and strapless gowns with hoop skirts, trying to convince ourselves that we were Southern belles.

My father and his parents had been born in Virginia. In the minds of many Virginians, this chance occurrence is like winning the lottery. My grandmother portrayed herself as a descendant of Tidewater aristocrats and Confederate Cavaliers. She helped found the Virginia Club. At their meetings, members gave papers on famous Virginians and expressed pity for those of us born in Tennessee.

In reality, my grandparents had grown up in a coal-mining area in southwestern Virginia—not to be confused with northern Virginia, a suburb of Washington, DC, or with the eastern Tidewater and its former plantations.* My grandmother came from a town named Darwin, where her father had farmed. My grandfather came from Skeet Rock in a district called South of the Mountain, at the foot of the Cumberlands that separate Virginia from Kentucky. His father was also a farmer. Their towns were about twenty-five miles, as the crow flies, from Pikeville, Kentucky, and thirty-five miles from the Tug Fork Valley, epicenter of the Hatfield-McCoy feud.

My grandfather William Henry Reed was born in 1882, the year of the Pawpaw Murders. Both his parents died when he was ten. He went to live with a married sister, but after a few years he ran away to Kentucky, traveling on foot the twenty-five miles to the house of his eldest brother, Madison, a teacher in Johns Creek, Kentucky—where McCoy champion Frank Phillips had grown up—just over the ridge from the Tug Fork Valley. Madison gave my grandfather rides to school on the back of his horse.

Later my grandfather moved in with another older brother, Robert, the carpenter and Dunkard preacher who was Ava McCoy's father. He boarded at a private high school in Inez, about twenty miles along crooked mountain paths from Blackberry Fork, where Ranel McCoy had lived until his cabin burned down during the New Year's Night Massacre in 1888. Robert always sent my grandfather a horse to ride home for the holidays.

....

* Northern Virginia and the Tidewater are the arrogant stepsisters to the Cinderella southwest.

While teaching in Darwin, Virginia, as a young man, my grandfather encountered my grandmother, a second cousin he had never met. She, too, became a teacher. When they married, they decided he should pursue his dream of attending medical school. After a year at the University of Louisville, they moved to Richmond, where she worked at a cosmetics counter in a department store to support them while he completed his studies at the Medical College of Virginia. In the summers, he worked as a logger for the Yellow Poplar Lumber Company, one of the international consortiums denuding Appalachian forests, paying $1.50 per tree, some of them eight feet across and two hundred feet tall.[1]

During his final year of medical school, my grandfather served as chief medical officer at the Confederate Veterans Home. My grandparents returned to Clintwood, Virginia, near where both had grown up, and my grandfather conducted a medical practice via house calls on horseback. In 1919, four years after my father's birth, they moved to Kingsport, Tennessee, where my grandfather opened a hospital.

My grandparents maintained minimal contact with their fourteen brothers and sisters and many cousins, nieces, and nephews in southwest Virginia. My father took us children there only once. I remember a huge slate dump outside a coal mine in which we unearthed some wonderful fossils of ancient plants. I also remember meeting some of my father's cousins at the white-framed house of his aunt Cora.

As a Girl Scout, I used to backpack in the Smoky Mountains, and I felt very much at home in their towering embrace. But the Cumberland Mountains from which my grandparents had emerged seemed dark and forbidding. As an adult, I made several trips there to meet relatives and to do genealogical research. But I was never at ease as I drove the winding roads through that dark and bloody ground—even before I knew that name for it.

My mother, who grew up in the Finger Lakes region of New York State, always said that the southern Appalachians were so steep compared to the rolling hills around the Finger Lakes that she felt hemmed in by them. It bothered her not to be able to see the far horizon or to spot someone coming along the road up ahead. But this wasn't the problem for me. I felt comfortable in the Smokies and the Blue Ridge, just not in the Cumberlands. I didn't understand why until much later.

My grandparents talked about their reasons for leaving southwest Virginia and moving to Kingsport. They spoke of the pernicious effects of easily available moonshine. A first cousin of my father died in his twenties from lead poisoning acquired from moonshine made in stills with lead seams.

My father often talked about a visit to southwest Virginia as a boy to stay with an uncle named Cas Artrip. Uncle Cas grabbed a jug of moonshine as they departed for a fishing trip. "Fishing" that day involved sitting on the bank of a stream while Uncle Cas got progressively drunker. My father boyishly informed him that moonshine was against the law. "Son," he replied, "over here I am the law." At the end of the afternoon, Uncle Cas tossed a stick of dynamite into the creek, and my father collected the fish that the explosion tossed onto the banks of the stream.

My grandparents also discussed the too-plentiful supply of weapons in the region they had left behind. Many men routinely carried guns and knives for hunting but also for fighting. My grandfather described an incident at a Sunday school meeting at which a local bully, Tom Stuart, drunk of course, chased my grandfather's cousin with a knife because of a prior political dispute. My grandfather ended up having to fight Tom to save his cousin's life. He threw Tom down and choked him before onlookers pulled him off. After that he, too, carried a pistol, and he had several more near encounters with Tom Stuart. He later heard rumors that Tom had sobered up, found Jesus, and become a preacher.

Several years after that, when my grandfather was coming home on his horse from a house call in the mountains, he passed a gathering similar to the Election Days that had proved so disastrous for the Hatfields and the McCoys. In his memoirs he wrote, "Fifty or a hundred people would gather, drink moonshine whiskey, trade horses, and engage in fights—and too often there would be gunplay and someone killed."[2]

As he sat on his horse watching, my grandfather spotted a man racing toward him on his horse. The reins hung loose around the horse's neck. In one hand the rider held a pistol, which he was firing into the air. The other hand was holding a bottle of whiskey. It was Tom Stuart, who, having found Jesus, had evidently lost Him again. Stuart hadn't yet recognized my grandfather, but my grandfather took no chances, wheeling his horse around and galloping off in the opposite direction.

Soon after this encounter, my grandparents and my four-year-old father moved to Kingsport. I don't know whether there was any connection between Tom Stuart and this move. No one ever said.

I witnessed this ethos of overwrought machismo firsthand when I was a teenager. As a candy striper volunteering at the hospital where my doctor father worked, I saw the results of many "accidents" involving knives and guns. I heard more such stories at the dinner table when my father discussed the patients he treated at the emergency room each day. Once or twice a week, I watched boys fighting at the bus stop at school. No one ever knew why they were fighting. Almost everyone but me seemed to enjoy it, both those fighting and those watching. The world, or at least my part of it, was starting to feel like a pretty crazy place.

My grandparents also decided to leave their birthplace because of the quality of the medical care there—ironic since my grandfather was himself a doctor. But he talked about his anxiety over not having colleagues with whom to discuss difficult cases, and over not having modern equipment and supplies when he had to treat patients in their remote cabins.

Both my grandfather's parents had died young of treatable conditions—his mother of gallstones and his father of pneumonia. His mother's physician, an herb doctor named Marshall "The Red Fox" Taylor, carried two pistols, one on each hip.[3] He wore a cartridge belt draped over his shoulder and a rifle slung across his back, much as Devil Anse did in surviving photographs. Taylor also wore shoes that he had made himself, with heels nailed to the toes so that anyone trying to track him would think he was walking in the opposite direction.

Dr. Taylor was hanged in Virginia in 1893, just down the road from where my grandparents' families lived, for his role in the Killing Rocks Massacre. He and two accomplices shot three members of the Mullins family as they drove a cart loaded with barrels of moonshine through Pound Gap toward Pikeville. Then they robbed the Mullins family of $1,000.

The Red Fox, wearing a white suit, preached an hour and a half sermon from the upstairs window of the courthouse prior to his hanging. He asked his family to keep him unburied for three days so that he could rise from the dead. (He didn't.)

My grandmother's mother also died of pneumonia, when my grandmother was thirteen. But her attending physician, though equally ineffectual, wasn't nearly so colorful. My grandparents lost a son prior to my father's birth during a difficult delivery that more up-to-date medical facilities could have remedied.

There were other reasons for their departure from the Cumberlands that I learned about much later—rumors of ancestors who were Native Americans and Union guerrillas, which didn't fit well with my grandmother's notions of herself as a descendant of Confederate Cavaliers.

But all I knew as a child was that southwest Virginia was a place my grandparents had left, and didn't talk about very much, and didn't like to visit, and didn't want me to visit. It sounded like a land of drunkenness, violence, and whacked-out physicians.

A tale my father often told didn't alleviate that impression. It involved a feud among some of his Reed ancestors and some ancestors of Shannon Allen, my father's surgical associate. Dr. Allen and my father maintained that several Allen brothers had killed five Reeds during a courthouse shoot-out in Hillsville, Virginia, early in the twentieth century. The idea seemed to amuse them. It appalled me.

Years later I researched this feud, trying to find out if the version I had heard from my father and Dr. Allen were true.[4] I discovered that there were indeed many Reeds in the Hillsville area. I also learned that the patriarch of the Allen clan, Floyd Allen, Shannon Allen's ancestor, was easily insulted and quick-tempered. His family owned large tracts of land and a general store. They were also moonshiners and bootleggers. Nevertheless, members of the Allen family held many local offices, such as sheriff and deputy. (Sound familiar?)

Floyd Allen had shot several people: a man in North Carolina, a cousin, a brother in a dispute over their father's estate. Once he shot a man who was trying to buy his brother's farm because he himself wanted to buy it at a lower price. For this shooting he was sentenced to a hundred-dollar fine and an hour in jail. The governor suspended his jail time.

After being appointed police officer for his county, Floyd attacked a buggy carrying two of his nephews to jail. They had been arrested for fighting during a church service with a young man whose girlfriend one had kissed the previous evening at a corn-shucking bee. One was manacled to the buggy's side rail, the other tied in back with rope. With the butt of his pistol, Floyd beat unconscious the deputy escorting his nephews. Then he rolled the deputy into a ditch and freed his kinsmen. "I just can't bear to see anyone drug around," he later explained to the judge.

At his trial for beating the deputy, almost everyone was armed: the many Allens among the spectators; the court officials, who were expecting trouble; and Floyd himself. When Floyd was sentenced to a year in the penitentiary, he stood up and announced, "I just tell you, I ain't a'going."

Then all hell broke loose. No one knows who started shooting first. The Allens later claimed it was the court officials. The court officials insisted it was the Allens. The spectators had a number of conflicting opinions, but they all saw Floyd shooting a pistol. The Allens fled the courthouse, brandishing their own pistols and twelve-gauge shotguns.

When it was all over, fifty bullets had lodged in the wood of the courtroom and five people lay dead: judge, sheriff, attorney, juror, and witness—none named Reed. It's one of the few episodes in American history in which a convicted criminal has attempted to avoid his sentence by killing the judge. Seven people had also been wounded: court clerk, juror, deputy, two spectators, and two Allens. One of these Allens was Floyd, who was so badly injured that he couldn't escape, so he checked himself into a hotel across the street. When deputies arrived to arrest him, he tried to cut his own throat with a pocketknife rather than face prison.

Posses of Baldwin-Felts detectives and local deputies eventually rounded up all the Allen suspects, discovering several illegal stills in the process. Floyd and his son were tried for the murder of the Commonwealth's attorney and sentenced to death by electrocution. When he heard the verdict, Floyd wept.

Floyd Allen was electrocuted on March 28, 1913, at 1:20 p.m., and his son Claud eleven minutes later. When Floyd's body was examined following his death, the medical staff found scars from thirteen bullet wounds, including five administered by his own family.

The story of the courtroom shooting, which had haunted my youth, had really occurred. Shannon Allen's ancestors had, indeed, instigated it. Five people died, but none was my ancestor. This was my first experience of witnessing how real events in the not-so-distant past transform into legend—a lesson that served me well while researching the feud between the Hatfields and the McCoys.

The civil rights movement was under way when I left the South to attend college near Boston. Many there hated white Southerners for the mayhem in the Deep South, and it was hard to blame them. From afar my homeland looked like a pretty dismal place. But gradually I began to realize that the issues in what had been the plantation South differed somewhat from those in the mountains where I had grown up. I also began to realize that, however much Kingsport wanted to regard itself as a bastion of the Old South, it was actually located smack dab in the middle of Appalachia. We weren't Southerners; we were hillbillies.

Struggling to digest my true identity, I began to research my ancestors. I wanted to know who they really were, finally investigating my grandmother's Tidewater propaganda about Confederate Cavaliers. I learned that most had left the Tidewater behind in the eighteenth century and that many had supported the Union during the Civil War. It's impossible to describe the psychic shock experienced by someone who has always identified with the Lost Cause of the Confederacy, upon learning that her ancestors were actually Union guerrillas.

Grandfather Reed's family were Dunkards, a nickname for the Church of the Brethren, a German Anabaptist sect with similarities to Mennonites. Dunkards opposed slavery, but they were pacifists—not a comfortable stance during the Civil War. When Virginia seceded from the Union, the Reeds moved to Martin County, Kentucky, home to many Dunkards, in hopes of escaping the ravaging bands of both Union and Confederate bushwhackers infesting their South of the Mountain neighborhood.

My grandfather Reed's maternal grandfather stayed behind in South of the Mountain—only to be taken prisoner by Confederates, who slaughtered one of his cows. My grandmother's grandmother also stayed behind. When she heard that Confederate troops were approaching, she piled rocks in all her handmade quilts and sank them in a stream. The soldiers found them anyway and rode away with the sodden quilts draped across their horses to dry.[5]

My grandmother's family—Vanovers, Howells, Swindalls, and Phippses—mostly supported the Union. Alf Killen, a notorious Union guerrilla leader, was a Vanover in-law (my grandmother's great-aunt's husband's brother, to be exact), rumored to be the son of a half-Cherokee mother. Loosely affiliated with Col. John Dils's 39th Kentucky Mounted Infantry, his band operated out of Pike County, Kentucky. He was said to be somewhat deranged because of having been forced to fight for a Confederate Virginia State Line unit when his sympathies lay with the Union. I have often wondered if Alf Killen might have known Devil Anse Hatfield, who also served with the Virginia State Line.[6]

Joel "Dusty Pants" Long, Alf Killen's head henchman (and my grandmother's great-aunt's husband), carried a cane dagger and was said to have been called Dusty Pants because he fled from dangerous situations so quickly that he left behind a cloud of dust. One night while on a mission, he was so cold that he chased some wild hogs out of their rut so that he could sleep among the leaves warmed by their bodies. When he woke up the next morning, the razorbacks had returned and were sleeping snuggled up all around him.[7]

When the war began, John Wesley Swindall—my grandmother's grandfather and also my grandfather's great-uncle—moved his family from South of the Mountain to the Big Sandy River just north of the Tug Fork Valley in Kentucky. Then he joined Company K of Colonel Dils's mounted infantry as a sergeant.

One day, Alf Killen learned that some two hundred Confederate soldiers were camped on the Crane's Nest River near my grandmother's hometown of Darwin, Virginia, and they were looting the homes of Union soldiers and supporters. Alf summoned his cohorts: his brother Bob Killen (married to another of my grandmother's great-aunts), Dusty Pants Long, John Wesley Swindall, several Vanovers in Dils's mounted infantry, my grandmother's great-uncle Eli Vanover, a couple of Phipps cousins, one of my grandmother's great-grandfathers, and perhaps three dozen other Union sympathizers. They intended to ambush the Rebel bushwhackers, but some snitch disclosed their plans to the Confederates, who ambushed them instead. Eight Union partisans died, including Bob Killen, and Eli Vanover's arm bone was shattered.[8]

Toward the end of the war, Col. John Dils, dishonorably discharged from the Union army for fraud, was rumored to have joined Alf Killen's guerrilla band. Killen was eventually killed in the Battle of Big Mud Creek in Floyd County, Kentucky. Improvising on his nickname, Dusty Pants Long was said to have escaped from this battle by donning a woman's dress and sunbonnet and running like hell.

During my research on the Hatfields and the McCoys, I realized that the situation for my ancestors in southwestern Virginia during the Civil War was identical to that in the Tug Fork Valley, with bushwhackers, deserters, draft dodgers, and escaped prisoners of all allegiances, or none, assaulting and robbing civilians at will.

The missing link, Col. John Dils connected my ancestors from South of the Mountain to the Hatfields and the McCoys in the Tug Fork Valley. My Unionist forebears might have known their commander, Colonel Dils, as well as Harmon McCoy, Billy Phillips, and the other Pike County Unionists, and they might have fought against Devil Anse Hatfield, Jim Vance, and the Logan Wildcats.

My grandparents never mentioned the Civil War. Their families' roles in it certainly didn't support my grandmother's notion of herself as a daughter of the Confederacy. My grandparents never mentioned the Hatfield-McCoy feud either, even though my grandfather was eight when Cottontop Mounts was hanged, and my grandmother four. Pikeville, where the hanging occurred, lay just across Pound Gap from South of the Mountain. People from all over the region attended the hanging. It was a major occasion—the first public hanging in Kentucky in forty years, and the last. It's possible that my grandparents were taken there for the event, or that their relatives or neighbors attended.

A few years after the hanging, my grandfather lived with his brother Madison at Johns Creek, home of Bad Frank Phillips and several others who had joined the McCoy posses toward the feud's end. People surely talked about it in my grandfather's presence. But both my grandparents died before the topic interested me, so, sadly, I never asked them what they knew or didn't know about the feud.

As I was researching this book, I discovered even more links from my family to the feudists. Jim Vance, Devil Anse Hatfield's uncle, had stolen horses for Gen. Vincent Witcher's Confederate raiders during the Civil War in Russell County, Virginia. My grandparents' families lived in what was then Russell County. One of Vance's victims was one of his cousins, Wilburn Lockhart. After the war, Lockhart planned a retaliatory ambush on Vance while the latter was plowing a field. Vance learned of the plot and summoned a couple of friends. They ambushed Lockhart's hit men instead, killing one named Harmon Artrip. My father's moonshining, dynamite-fishing uncle Cas Artrip was a second cousin of Harmon Artrip. After murdering returned Union solider Harmon McCoy, Jim Vance had murdered a distant ancestor of mine. The Hatfield-McCoy feud had suddenly come home to roost.

As I investigated the other Kentucky feuds, I was also startled to discover that the infamous Craig Tolliver, of the Martin-Tolliver feud of Rowan County, Kentucky, the thug who inexplicably didn't want to die with his boots on, was a second cousin once-removed to my grandmother's grandfather John Wesley Swindall, a Union sergeant and himself a woods-colt son of Solomon Tolliver. Both Craig Tolliver and John Wesley Swindall had been born in Ashe County, North Carolina. Craig moved with his parents to Rowan County, where robbers murdered his father and stole the money from the sale of his Ashe County farm. John Wesley Swindall moved with his mother to South of the Mountain in Virginia. I will never know if their families knew one another in Ashe County, but it is possible. It is even likely.

The understanding came to me slowly—as had Ava McCoy's understanding of her fear of thundering horse hooves in the night. My fear of the Cumberlands, a visceral one, had been passed down to me from my grandparents by a process of osmosis. You inherit your ancestors' genes, but you also inherit, after birth, the psychic fallout from traumas they endured during their lifetimes. Like the forebears of Ava McCoy's husband Homer, who fled the Tug Fork Valley to escape the Hatfield-McCoy feud violence, like the thousands of others who fled that and other Kentucky feuds, my grandparents had left southwest Virginia in hopes of freeing us, their descendants, from the toxic influence of endemic violence. But it hadn't entirely worked. The irrational, nameless fear remained, buried deep in my psyche, expressed by only a vague unease whenever I was traveling in those mountains that my grandparents had abandoned nearly a century earlier.

After college I lived for many years in Vermont, which was settled by a different group of British immigrants than those in the Southern backcountry. They descended from Puritans from eastern England, small-scale farmers and craftsmen who lived in orderly villages centered around a green usually encircled by a school, a church, a town hall, and a general store. Their urban development expressed the high esteem in which they held education, religion, commerce, community, and the rule of law. Herders tend to live in more isolated rural homesteads, surrounded by their animals and their pastures, over which they keep suspicious watch. Because the wealth and sustenance of farmers reside in their land, which isn't portable, they are generally peaceable people. They have to get along with their neighbors—unlike herders, who must defend their livestock from their neighbors, and who can more readily leave an area when they experience or generate strife.

As the years ticked by, I started spending more and more time back in Tennessee. I got a teaching job at a university there. The region's history and my family's genealogy also began to interest me. I kept a condo in Vermont but commuted regularly to Tennessee for long periods of time.

Like shifts in the barometric pressure, I noted the differences. Tennessee ranks second in violent crimes among all the states; Vermont is number 48.

Kentucky, West Virginia, and Tennessee rank 11, 12, and 13 respectively in gun fatalities. Arriving in Tennessee, my muscles involuntarily clenched. The air itself seemed heavier, as when storm clouds are amassing on the far horizon on a sweltering summer afternoon. I found myself double-checking house and car doors to make sure they were locked, and the home security system to be certain it was set. I glanced all around me in parking lots late at night.

I learned that a very intelligent man whom I love and respect sometimes packs a pistol. I also learned that one of my cousins carries a Glock 26. I started studying friends and neighbors for telltale bulges in their clothing that might indicate a holster. When staying alone at my family's isolated cabin, I sometimes placed on my bedside table a pearl-handled Lady Smith and Wesson pistol borrowed from a friend. The part of me that had become a Vermonter thought this the first step toward madness—but the part of me that was still my grandparents' granddaughter considered it necessary for a restful night's sleep.

Gradually, it dawned on me that within my psyche lurks a subterranean dread that irrational violence will break out at any moment, when I least expect it and for reasons I won't understand. Seemingly friendly people will transform into ogres who want to harm me. By the same token, I, as a distant descendant of the crazed Craig Tolliver, may just as well be the one to unleash the mayhem. Some reasons for this dread are known only to my therapist and me. But one of the most important is the atmosphere in which I grew up, with the results of such violence all around me in the stories brought home from the emergency room by my father and grandfather, to say nothing of the fistfights I witnessed at the school bus stop and the victims of violence I assisted as a candy striper at the hospital.

The threat of violence my grandparents experienced in southwest Virginia, which drove them to Tennessee, existed still—in Tennessee. The alarm it had engendered in them existed still—in me. Whatever may have caused the feuds, the feudists have left their descendants in the southern Appalachians a legacy of anxiety that still haunts those hills and valleys a century later.

✝

When I was in the second grade, in 1952, a man in a town outside of Kingsport went into a general store. His wife's cousin was sitting on a barrel. The cousin's daughter sat in a chair beside her, holding her eighteen-month-old son. The man's wife had recently left him, moving back home to her parents, the Blairs, because he had forced her hand onto a hot stovetop to reprimand her for some domestic failing.

After entering the store and spotting the two Blair women and the baby, the man calmly pulled out a pistol and shot the women. The baby fell to the floor, screaming. The older woman died right away, the younger woman soon thereafter. The man explained to the horrified bystanders that he had shot them in order "to worry the Blairs."

The man was taken to jail. Sheriff Blair, a relative of the two murdered women, agreed to open the killer's cell to a mob of four dozen local men. They planned to drag the killer behind a car until dead. When this posse arrived, though, a phalanx of highway patrolmen had taken charge. They fired shotguns into the crowd to disperse them. The killer was declared insane and sent to the hospital wing of the state penitentiary for the rest of his life, where he entertained himself by creating superb architectural drawings.

As recently as 2011, I was driving through the Cumberland Plateau, minding my own business and enjoying the colorful autumn leaves. Suddenly, looming over me, framed by orange and scarlet foliage, appeared a giant billboard advertising an indoor firing range. At the top stood a huge cutout of a pistol, pointed upward at an angle. The barrel resembled an erect phallus, the trigger guard outlining a testicle. Printed in giant black letters were the words MAN TOYS!

Pulling over and studying the sign, I felt the same Pavlovian stab of nausea that I feel whenever I see a swastika or a Confederate battle flag. There seemed no way to avoid the recognition that, as the Bible says, the sins of the fathers are visited "on the children and on the grandchildren to the third and fourth generations."[9]

The automatic mental process of stereotyping developed because it had survival value. Early humans had to decide very quickly whether a stranger posed a threat, and those decisions usually derived from past experiences. Someone whose appearance resembled that of a previous attacker was also regarded as dangerous. A few defining physical characteristics served as a kind of psychic shorthand. The problem is that physical appearances don't offer a reliable gauge to inner intentions. A tramp can be a millionaire in disguise. Stereotypes present only one facet of the complex gem that is each individual.

Stereotypes also serve another function. Those in a position of power often stereotype those who lack power as inferior and therefore deserving of exploitation. As already mentioned, this is what has happened at varying times to blacks, Native Americans, Appalachians, and all women everywhere.

But people don't only stereotype others; they also stereotype themselves. We humans don't automatically know who we are. It takes time and experience to figure that out. Young people typically try on the roles their culture offers them to see if one will fit, like an off-the-rack Halloween costume. A few people have the courage to try on multiple costumes and cast aside those that don't appeal to them. Stripped, they are then free to find their true identities from within. But most take the easier route of sticking with a prepackaged identity. This is what many young men who became feudists did, copying the examples of their fathers who had been guerrilla fighters during the Civil War, of their grandfathers and great-grandfathers who had fought natives during the settlement era, and of their more remote ancestors who had been Border Reivers.

This is what some young men in the Southern mountains are doing still, donning the hillbilly stereotype bequeathed them by their male ancestors, mistaking cruelty for justice and stupidity for heroism. This stereotype has somehow managed to replicate itself down the generations, even though most of us no longer have herds to protect and no longer face attacks from vengeful natives or from ravaging guerrillas.

But just as a few young men in Appalachia have adopted this swaggering legacy of misplaced machismo from their forefathers, I myself have also inherited the stereotype handed down by the women of the feuds. Those passive bystanders loyally kept the home fires burning, watching their sons and husbands butcher one another and then cleaning up after them. Like them, I have accepted, excused, and even laughed at the obnoxious behavior of modern-day hillbullies, as though jokes were talismans that could ward off their attacks.

Even before they can read books, children read the facial expressions, body language, and tones of voice of their elders. They absorb the loves and hatreds, hopes and fears of the adults around them without knowing it. Obsolete stereotypes that have kept us prisoners of the atrocities in which our ancestors participated—as perpetrators, victims, anxious bystanders, refugees—infest both the hillbullies and me.

The Cumberland Mountains used to be incredibly beautiful. They probably will be again, once the coal corporations have buried the streams, poisoned the drinking water, shipped all the mountaintops to India, and gone back home to count their profits. Those who now live in the Cumberlands are mostly wonderful people with a proud tradition of brave pioneering forebears. A few who aren't so wonderful have a chance of becoming so if they can shed the shackles forged by the violence of their ancestors. Around eighty Hatfield-McCoy feudists, far less than 1 percent of the population of Pike and Logan counties at that time, managed to terrorize thousands of peaceful, law-abiding people.[10] Hopefully, this will never be allowed to happen again.

I have finally realized that to fear the hellhounds of today is to feed this outmoded stereotype. At some point the mouse being batted about by a marauding cat must rise up on its hind legs and defy its tormentor— even if the cat then just bites off its head for a tasty snack. Although I still set my security system, I returned the pearl-handled Lady Smith and Wesson to my friend. Like a horse whisperer, I now calm my own inherited terror of hellhounds who attack in the night with self-assurances that such episodes are ancient history that need alarm me no longer.

I have also recently bought a bridge in Brooklyn. . . .

Epilogue

The Hatfield-McCoy Industry

IN KEEPING WITH THE AMERICAN WAY—OF TURNING PRISTINE FIRST-GROWTH forests into furniture and majestic coal-filled mountains into rubble— the mind-numbing horror of the Hatfield-McCoy feud has itself become an industry.

In 1949, Metro Goldwyn Mayer released a film called *Roseanna McCoy,* starring Joan Evans as Roseanna and Farley Granger as Johnse Hatfield. Picture *West Side Story* set in the Southern mountains with an ending in which the two lovebirds canter off into the sunset astraddle one horse—rather than with Johnse's marriage to Roseanna's cousin Nancy, the death of their illegitimate baby daughter, and the death of Roseanna from depression, as actually happened.

A second movie was made for television in 1975, starring Jack Palance (of *Shane* and *City Slickers* fame) as Devil Anse. Palance's Devil Anse comes across as a lovable old coot who adores his wife and children, and who tries to restrain his followers from their deadly antics. The plot tampers with the chronology of feud events to make the incomprehensible comprehensible. For instance, the hanging of Cottontop Mounts and the death in prison of Wall Hatfield, which ended the feud, occur earlier in the movie to account for some of the Hatfield animosity toward the McCoys. The most egregious episode of the entire feud, the New Year's Night Massacre, becomes a scene in which the McCoys attack the Hatfield homestead in the dead of night instead of the other way around.

In this version of the feud's termination, Devil Anse Hatfield and Ranel McCoy sneak through the wilderness, tracking each other like beasts of prey, periodically shooting one another in non–life threatening areas. They finally bond over their mutual decision not to shoot a buck, thus, presumably, renouncing further shooting of human beings as well.

Several cartoon series have also featured plots based on the Hatfield-McCoy feud, including *Looney Tunes, The Huckleberry Hound Show, The Flintstones,* and *Scooby-Doo.* Why anyone considered such historical violence amusing fare for children is a topic for another book.

Dr. Leonard McCoy, the irascible physician on *Star Trek,* is depicted as being descended from the feuding McCoy family of Kentucky.

One of the country's longest-running TV game shows, *Family Feud,* took its name from a nod to this epic struggle. In 1979, descendants from both the Hatfield and the McCoy families appeared on the show, carrying antique rifles and dressed in period costume—*Little House on the Prairie* dresses for the women and frock coats for the men. A bewildered pig munched feed at the front of the stage. Both families smiled good-naturedly about their ancestral history of mutual hatred. Fortunately, the contest proved a draw.

Theater West Virginia performs a musical about the feud in an outdoor amphitheater several nights a week every summer. Because Devil Anse Hatfield was a West Virginian and one of his nephews, Henry D. Hatfield, became governor of the state, this version of the feud has been sanitized. It ends with a revival in which Devil Anse and two of his sons are baptized and, in Devil Anse's imagination, unite with the McCoys to sing a gospel song about the glory of God's forgiveness—rather than with the imprisonment and hanging of Hatfields that actually ended the feud.

There is also a Hatfield-McCoy dinner theater in Pigeon Forge, Tennessee, gateway to the Smoky Mountains (where the feud didn't take place) with two shows nightly. A building constructed especially for this event resembles two giant cartoon hillbilly shacks. Inside, spectators sit at tables eating fried chicken with all the fixin's while onstage a cheerful comic plot with almost no connection to actual feud events features some of the most admirable achievements of Appalachian culture: singing, the playing of musical instruments, and clog dancing. Many in the audience are, of course, Hatfield or McCoy descendants, who are seated on opposite sides of the theater. They cheer as though at a football game at any mention by the actors of their respective surnames.

An ATV trail, inexplicably christened the Hatfield-McCoy Trail, winds around five mountains in southern West Virginia. It attracts dirt-bikers and ATV riders from all over America, Europe, Australia, and New Zealand. The precipitous trails through the dense forests do give a sense of the world the feud participants must have inhabited as they cut timber and hunted game (and one another).

The tourist office in Pikeville, Kentucky, offers an audio CD guiding motorists from site to site around feud country to the accompaniment of feud-related songs composed and sung by Jimmy Wolford, a country singer descended from Ranel McCoy. Explanatory roadside markers identify various points of interest on the driving tour.

⸸

The Hatfields and McCoys of today seem at peace with their ancestral heritage. My McCoy cousins say that the feud was mentioned only in jokes as they were growing up and that they themselves never felt animosity toward any Hatfields. In 2000, Bo and Ron McCoy and Sonya Hatfield organized a joint Hatfield-McCoy reunion that drew five thousand descendants of the two families from all over the nation.[1] This reunion has been repeated every year since. Bus tours take attendees to the various massacre sites. Marathoners—around 450 in 2011—race along roads that wind through feud territory. They cross the finish line in Williamson, West Virginia, where Devil Anse Hatfield and Ranel McCoy impersonators congratulate them. A tug-of-war across the Tug Fork, featuring as combatants ten T-shirted descendants from each family, provides a climax to the reunion.

The only blip of rancor to appear on this screen of harmony is a lawsuit brought by Bo and Ron McCoy in 2002 against John Vance, a descendant of the notorious Bad Jim. John Vance had closed the access road to the cemetery containing the graves of the five McCoy children killed during the Pawpaw Murders and the New Year's Night Massacre. In the end, the descendants of Ranel McCoy, though not the general public, were awarded access across Vance's property to the cemetery.[2]

In 2003, perhaps in response to hard feelings generated by the cemetery conflict, Reo Hatfield and Bo and Ron McCoy organized an official truce between the two families—even though hostilities on both sides had largely faded over the ensuing decades to bemused disbelief at the strife promulgated by their forebears. Reo stated that, in the wake of 9/11, Hatfield and McCoy descendants wanted to illustrate that Americans could overcome their differences and band together in the face of adversity.[3] And it appears that they have.

⁓ ACKNOWLEDGMENTS ⁓

Special thanks to the following people: Debra Basham, of the West Virginia State Archives, for her help in tracking down feud photos; David Carriere and Laurie Kenney, for their work in drawing this book to the attention of interested readers; Ina Danko, for her cheerful company on research trips, some of them pretty strange, and for her pithy observations on life in Appalachia; James Jayo, for the idea for this book and for his sharp editorial eye; Meredith Dias, for shepherding this project from manuscript to finished book; Jan Hanford, for designing and managing my webpage featuring this book; my agent Martha Kaplan, for her usual good advice and guidance; Sheryl Kober and Justin Marciano for the design and layout of the text, Diana Nuhn for the cover design, and Sally Neale for the family tree; Ava and Doug McCoy, for sharing their family history and memories with me; and my late grandparents William Henry and Elizabeth Vanover Reed, for their courage and resourcefulness. I also thank all the authors of previous books about this feud for their tireless research and engrossing writing.

Appendix

"Green Are the Woods"
by Abner Vance

Green grows the woods where Sandy flows,
And peace along its rills;
In the valley the black bear lies secure,
The red buck roves the hills.

But Vance no more shall Sandy behold,
Nor drink of its crystal wave;
The partial Judge pronounced his doom—
To the hunter a felon's grave.

The Judge called me "incarnate fiend,"
For Elliott's life I saved;
I couldn't agree to Elliott's guilt,
Humanity belongs to the brave.

That friendship I to others have shown,
Has never been shown to me;
Humanity, I say, belongs to the brave,
And I hope it belongs to me

'Twas by the advice of McFarland
Judge Johnson did me call;
I was taken from my native home,
And placed in yon stone wall.

My persecutors have gained their quest
Their promise to make good;
They often swore they'd never rest
Till they had my life's blood.

Daniel Horton, Bob, and Bill,
A lie against me swore.
In order to take my life away,
That I should be no more.

But they and I together must meet
Where all things are made known;
And if I shed a human's blood,
There'll mercy me be shown.

Bright shines the sun on Clinch's hills,
And soft the west wind blows;
The valleys are covered o'er with bloom
Perfumed by the fragrant rose.

But Vance no more Sandy shall behold
Nor smell the sweet perfume;
This day his eyes will close in death,
His body laid in the tomb.

Farewell my friends, my children dear,
To you I bid farewell;
The love I have for your precious souls,
No mortal tongue can tell.

Farewell to you my loving wife,
To you I bid adieu;
And if I reach fair Canaan's shore
I'll wait and watch for you.

—Composed in jail and sung by Abner Vance, while
standing on his coffin, at his hanging in Abingdon,
Virginia; reproduced in L. D. Hatfield's *The True
Story of the Hatfield and McCoy Feud*, pp. 14–15

≈ ENDNOTES ≈

Introduction

1 T. C. Crawford, *An American Vendetta: A Story of Barbarism in the United States,* ed. Eldean Wellman (Verdunville, WV: Eldean Wellman, 2004), 52. Originally published in 1888.

2 Diane K. McLaughlin, Daniel T. Lichter, and Stephen A. Matthews, *Demographic Diversity and Economic Change in Appalachia* (University Park, PA: Population Research Institute, 1999), www.arc.gov/images/reports/demographic/demographics.pdf.

3 Crawford, *An American Vendetta,* 2.

4 Ibid., 37.

5 *Courier-Journal* (Louisville, KY), February 12, 1888, as quoted in Otis K. Rice, *The Hatfields and the McCoys* (Lexington: University Press of Kentucky, 1982), 83.

6 Coleman C. Hatfield and Robert Y. Spence. *The Tale of the Devil: The Biography of Devil Anse Hatfield* (Chapmanville, WV: Woodland Press, 2007), 130.

7 Ibid., 15.

Chapter 1: The Path to Pikeville

1 This description of Harmon McCoy derives from photo #038435 of him from the West Virginia State Archives.

2 This description of Jim Vance derives from photo #133105 from the West Virginia State Archives. Virgil Carrington Jones, *The Hatfields and the McCoys* (Chapel Hill: University of North Carolina Press, 1948), 4. Jones says that Vance had a long black beard to his waist, but the feudists no doubt varied their facial hair throughout their lives, according to the fashions of the times and their own personal preferences.

3 Hatfield and Spence, *Tale of the Devil,* 82. Some say his surname was Francis, others that he was called "Captain Bill."

4 Ibid., 63–64.

5 Ibid., 82–84.

6 Robert Baker, "39th Kentucky Mounted Infantry, US Volunteers 80." http://hiramjustus.hubpages.com/hub/39th-Kentucky-Mounted-Infantry-US-Volunteers.

7 This reconstruction of Harmon McCoy's murder derives from accounts in the following sources: Hatfield and Spence, *Tale of the Devil,* 84–86; Philip Hatfield, *The Other Feud: William Anderson "Devil Anse" Hatfield in the Civil War* (Lexington, KY: Philip Hatfield, 2010), 63–64; Truda Williams McCoy, *The McCoys: Their Story as Told to the Author by Eye Witnesses and Descendants* (Pikeville, KY: Preservation Council Press, 1976), 3–11; Otis K. Rice, *The Hatfields and the McCoys,* 13–14. These accounts differ in some of their details. For instance, Hatfield and Spence's version states that Jim

Vance and Jim Wheeler Wilson followed Patty McCoy's tracks home from the cave and that the two men circled around behind the cave and captured Harmon McCoy as he sat by a campfire outside it. They bound him with ropes and were marching him away as a prisoner when he began to argue with them, maintaining that he never threatened to kill Devil Anse. Jim Wilson started "flirting" with his pistol in its holster. Thinking Wilson was about to draw his gun to shoot him, Harmon tried to twist away from his captors, so Wilson shot him in the head.

Chapter 2: Dark and Bloody Ground

1   Erika Celeste, *Secrets of the Valley: Prehistory of the Kanawha* (Huntington, WV: Paradise Film Institute, n/d), DVD.

2   John Alexander Williams, *Appalachia: A History* (Chapel Hill: University of North Carolina Press, 2002), 60.

3   George R. Stewart, *Names on the Land* (Boston: Houghton Mifflin Company, 1967), 140.

4   John Alexander Williams, *West Virginia: A History* (New York: W. W. Norton and Co., 1984), 96–97.

5   "The State Nicknames," The Commonwealth of Kentucky intro page, www.netstate. com/states/intro/ky_intro.htm.

6   Richard E. Nisbett and Dov Cohen, *Culture of Honor: The Psychology of Violence in the South* (Boulder, CO: Westview Press, 1996), 4–5.

7   Crawford, *An American Vendetta,* 42.

8   Coleman C. Hatfield and F. Keith Davis, *The Feuding Hatfields and McCoys* (Chapmanville, WV: Woodland Press, 2008), 72.

9   "The Matewan Floodwall," adapted from the "Matewan Action Plan," Town of Matewan, WV, website. www.matewan.com/Town/floodwall.htm.

10   Henry D. Shapiro, *Appalachia on Our Mind: The Southern Mountains and Mountaineers in the American Consciousness, 1870–1920* (Chapel Hill: University of North Carolina Press, 1978), 81.

11   Hatfield and Spence, *Tale of the Devil,* 34.

12   Rice, *Hatfields and the McCoys,* 3.

13   Hatfield and Spence, *Tale of the Devil,* 52.

14   Ibid., 18.

15   Rice, *Hatfields and the McCoys,* 3.

16   Hatfield and Spence, *Tale of the Devil,* 55–56.

17   Ibid., 18.

18   Ibid.

19   Ibid., 20–23.

20   Ibid., 23.

21   Ibid., 37–39.

22   Joan Schroeder, "Mary Draper Ingles' Return to Virginia's New River Valley," *Blue Ridge Country,* March 1, 1998. http://blueridgecountry.com/archive/mary-draper-ingles.html.

23   Lisa Ratliff, "A Story of Jenny Wiley," adapted from Arville Wheeler, *White Squaw: The True Story of Jennie Wiley* (Ashland, KY: Jesse Stuart Foundation, 2000). www .jeanhounshellpeppers.com/Jenny_Wiley_Story.htm.

24   Altina L. Waller, *Feud: Hatfields, McCoys, and Social Change in Appalachia, 1860–1900* (Chapel Hill: University of North Carolina Press, 1988), 265–66.

25   Hatfield and Spence, *Tale of the Devil,* 51.

26   L. D. Hatfield, *The True Story of the Hatfield and McCoy Feud* (LaVergne, TN: Kessinger Publishing, 1945), 12.

27   Hatfield and Spence, *Tale of the Devil,* 50–52.

28   Jones, *Hatfields and the McCoys,* 32.

29   Waller, *Feud,* 37.

30   Hatfield and Spence, *Tale of the Devil,* 193.

31   Crawford, *An American Vendetta,* 23–24.

32   Hatfield and Spence, *Tale of the Devil,* 24.

33   Crawford, *An American Vendetta,* 50.

34   Ibid., 16, 50.

35   Rice, *Hatfields and the McCoys,* 4.

36   Waller, *Feud,* 54–57.

37   Ibid., 59.

38   Ibid., 158.

39   Ibid., 59.

40   McCoy, *The McCoys,* 3.

41   Crawford, *An American Vendetta,* 18.

42   Waller, *Feud,* 17, 30, 60; McCoy, *The McCoys,* 5; Hatfield and Spence, *Tale of the Devil,* 82; Rice, *Hatfields and the McCoys,* 11.

43   Philip Hatfield, *The Other Feud,* 72.

44   Waller, *Feud,* 57.

45   Ibid., 61.

46   Rice, *Hatfields and the McCoys,* 31.

47   Jones, *Hatfields and the McCoys,* 3.

48   McCoy, *The McCoys,* 19, 91.

49   Rice, *Hatfields and the McCoys,* 19.

50   Hatfield and Spence, *Tale of the Devil,* 106.

51   Ibid., 61.

52   Waller, *Feud,* 94.

53   Ibid., 253–54. See list of Hatfield supporters.

54   Ibid., 255–56. See list of McCoy and Cline supporters.

55   Ibid., 17.

56   Crawford, *An American Vendetta,* 40.

Chapter 3: Border States

1   Daniel E. Sutherland, *A Savage Conflict: The Decisive Role of Guerrillas in the American Civil War* (Chapel Hill: University of North Carolina Press, 2009), passim.

2   Philip Hatfield, *The Other Feud,* 76–77.

3   Ibid., 13.

4   Hatfield and Spence, *Tale of the Devil,* 64.

5   Philip Hatfield, *The Other Feud,* 31.

6   Ibid., 35.

7   Hatfield and Spence, *Tale of the Devil,* 42.

8   Philip Hatfield, *The Other Feud,* 16.

9   Hatfield and Spence, *Tale of the Devil,* 68–69.

10   Waller, *Feud,* 159–60.

11   Robert M. Baker and Brian E. Hall, "Alphabetical Roster," The 39th Kentucky Mounted Infantry Webpage. http://reocities.com/rmbaker66/index.html.

12   This description is based on a photo at: http://reocities.com/rmbaker66/index.html.

13   Philip Hatfield, *The Other Feud,* 25–26.

14   Baker and Hall, The 39th Kentucky Mounted Infantry Webpage. http://reocities.com/rmbaker66/index.html.

15   Philip Hatfield, *The Other Feud,* 42.

16   Ibid., 38–39.

17   Hatfield and Spence, *Tale of the Devil,* 79–80.

18   Ibid., 62.

19   Philip Hatfield, *The Other Feud,* 56.

20   Hatfield and Spence, *Tale of the Devil,* 81–82.

21   Philip Hatfield, *The Other Feud,* 54.

22   Hatfield and Spence, *Tale of the Devil,* 84.

23   Ibid., 165–66.

24   Waller, *Feud,* 17.

25   McCoy, *The McCoys,* 11.

26   Philip Hatfield, *The Other Feud,* 12.

27   Rice, *Hatfields and the McCoys*, 12.

28   Baker and Hall, The 39th Kentucky Mounted Infantry Webpage. http://reocities.com/
rmbaker66/index.html.

29   Crawford, *An American Vendetta*, 49.

30   Baker and Hall, The 39th Kentucky Mounted Infantry Webpage. http://reocities.com/
rmbaker66/index.html.

31   Waller, *Feud*, 158–59.

32   "Last Will and Testament of Jacob Cline," Cline Family Association, http://
clinefamilyassociation.com/will_of_jacob_rich_jake_cline.

33   Waller, *Feud*, 160.

34   Ibid., 177.

35   Ibid., 141.

36   Ibid., 41.

37   Ibid., 97.

38   Rice, *Hatfields and the McCoys*, 31.

Chapter 4: Hog Trial

1   Jones, *Hatfields and the McCoys*, 18.

2   The reconstruction of the Hog Trial that follows is based on accounts from Jones,
Hatfields and the McCoys, 18–21; McCoy, *The McCoys*, 13–19; and Rice, *Hatfields and
the McCoys*, 14–16.

3   Waller, *Feud*, 49, 63.

4   Hatfield and Spence, *Tale of the Devil*, 108. Coleman A. Hatfield maintained that two
wayward hogs swam the Tug Fork to West Virginia, where Floyd Hatfield had already
moved, and that the trial occurred in West Virginia under the jurisdiction of Wall
Hatfield, Devil Anse's older brother, who turned the trial over to a man named Stafford.

5   Crawford, *An American Vendetta*, 31.

6   Hatfield and Spence, *Tale of the Devil*, 108.

7   McCoy, *The McCoys*, 17.

8   Hatfield and Spence, *Tale of the Devil*, 107.

9   Waller, *Feud*, 64.

10   Hatfield and Spence, *Tale of the Devil*, 109.

11   Ibid.

12   McCoy, *The McCoys*, 17.

13   Jones, *Hatfields and the McCoys*, 20.

14   McCoy, *The McCoys*, 16.

15   Waller, *Feud*, 64.

16 Hatfield and Spence, *Tale of the Devil,* 107–9. Coleman C. Hatfield suggests that Devil Anse Hatfield regarded the Hog Trial as a falling out of McCoys that had little bearing on the Hatfields, since Floyd Hatfield, Bill Staton, and Selkirk McCoy all had ties of kinship to Ranel McCoy. Although Devil Anse is himself quoted in a newspaper as stating that the feud began with the Hog Trial, Coleman C. feels the feud began with the murder of Devil Anse's brother Ellison by three of Ranel McCoy's sons in 1882. However, John Floyd, a Hatfield family friend and West Virginia state official during the feud years, claimed the feud began during the Civil War (Jones, *Hatfields and the McCoys,* 108). West Virginia governor E. Willis Wilson, a Hatfield ally after whom Devil Anse and Levicy Hatfield named a son, concurred with Floyd, maintaining that the two families had embraced different sides during the war (Jones, *Hatfields and the McCoys,* 112). Crawford (*An American Vendetta,* 18), however, maintains that the blighted love affair between Roseanna McCoy and Johnse Hatfield was the basis of the feud. So, as usual in accounts of this feud (just as during the feud itself), no one agrees on anything.

17 McCoy, *The McCoys,* 19.

18 Ibid.

19 Jones, *Hatfields and the McCoys,* 4.

20 McCoy, *The McCoys,* 141.

21 Jones, *Hatfields and the McCoys,* 21.

22 Waller, *Feud,* 65.

23 McCoy, *The McCoys,* 21.

24 Rice, *Hatfields and the McCoys,* 16.

25 Waller, *Feud,* 36.

26 This description is based on photo #038431 in the West Virginia State Archives.

27 Crawford, *An American Vendetta,* 7.

28 Waller, *Feud,* 272.

29 McCoy, *The McCoys,* 22–23.

30 Hatfield and Spence, *Tale of the Devil,* 109–10.

31 Rice, *Hatfields and the McCoys,* 17.

32 Waller, *Feud,* 66.

33 Ibid.

Chapter 5: Montagues and Capulets of the Cumberlands

1   The following reconstruction of the romance between Johnse Hatfield and Roseanna McCoy is based on accounts from Jones, *Hatfields and the McCoys,* 34–38; McCoy, *The McCoys,* 25–39; and Rice, *Hatfields and the McCoys,* 19–21.

2   McCoy, *The McCoys,* 25.

3   Jones, *Hatfields and the McCoys,* 32–33.

4   Ibid., 33.

5   McCoy, *The McCoys,* 27. But Jones, *Hatfields and the McCoys,* 35, describes Roseanna as having black hair, so who knows?

6   Based on photo #038427 from the West Virginia State Archives.

7   Crawford, *An American Vendetta,* 16.

8   G. Elliot Hatfield, *The Hatfields* (Stanville, KY: Big Sandy Valley Historical Society, 1974), 34.

9   Hatfield and Spence, *Tale of the Devil,* 111. Coleman A. Hatfield states that Devil Anse was not responsible for preventing Roseanna and Johnse's marriage, that Johnse went on to marry four times without Devil Anse's objecting, and that Devil Anse should have objected more to Johnse's marrying Nancy McCoy than Roseanna because her father Harmon McCoy was more of an enemy to Devil Anse than was Ranel, with whom, Coleman A. maintains, Devil Anse had bushwhacked during the Civil War.

10 Jones, *Hatfields and the McCoys,* 37; Rice, *Hatfields and the McCoys,* 21.

11 McCoy, *The McCoys,* 36.

12 Ibid., 37.

13 Rice, *Hatfields and the McCoys,* 21.

14 McCoy, *The McCoys,* 39.

15 Ibid., 41–42.

16 Waller, *Feud,* 71. Jones, *Hatfields and the McCoys,* 37, attributes Johnse's arrest to "many indictments." McCoy, *The McCoys,* 44, says Ranel, Jim, Tolbert, and Pharmer arrested Johnse for seduction. Rice, *Hatfields and the McCoys,* 22, maintains that Ranel, Jim, Tolbert, and Pharmer arrested Johnse for moonshining and carrying a concealed weapon.

17 West Virginia Division of Culture and History, transcript of interview with Margaret Hatfield, June 11, 1992, for the film *West Virginia,* WV History Film Project, www .wvculture.org/history/wvmemory/filmtranscripts/wvhatfield.html.

18 Jones, *Hatfields and the McCoys,* 38.

19 L. D. Hatfield, *True Story,* 37.

20 Hatfield and Spence, *Tale of the Devil,* 125.

21 Jones, *Hatfields and the McCoys,* 4.

22 Hatfield and Spence, *Tale of the Devil,* 179.

23 Waller, *Feud,* 70.

24 McCoy, *The McCoys,* 47.

25 Rice, *Hatfields and the McCoys,* 22.

26 Waller, *Feud,* 71.

27 McCoy, *The McCoys,* 50.

28 Ibid., 52. But Rice (*Hatfield and McCoys,* 23) reports that one source claimed that Roseanna succumbed to measles and had a miscarriage, whereas another claimed that the baby was a boy named Melvin. (Melvin was actually the son of Ranel's son Tolbert.)

29   Ibid., 51.

30   Ibid., 62.

31   Ibid.

32   Ibid., 66.

33   Ibid., 54–57.

34   Ibid., 58–59.

35   Ibid., 105.

36   Ibid., 60–61.

37   Rice, *Hatfields and the McCoys*, 23.

Chapter 6: Pawpaw Murders

1   Even the date of this Election Day is disputed. Coleman A. Hatfield (*Tale of the Devil*, 116) insists that it was Saturday, August 5, 1882.

2   The location is also in dispute. Hatfield and Spence (*Tale of the Devil*, 116) say that the election grounds were at Preacher Anse Hatfield's cabin. But Jones (*Hatfields and the McCoys*, 40) maintains that they were at Jerry Hatfield's cabin. Perhaps the two were neighbors?

3   Hatfield and Spence, *Tale of the Devil*, 116.

4   Ibid.

5   Jones, *Hatfields and the McCoys*, 41.

6   Waller, *Feud*, 71.

7   Hatfield and Spence, *Tale of the Devil*, 116.

8   Ibid., 135.

9   Hatfield and Spence (*Tale of the Devil*, 116) claim that Floyd McCoy was also involved in this attack on Ellison Hatfield, though it seems unlikely since he had the reputation of being timid and uninterested in fighting.

10   Ibid., 117.

11   Hatfield and Spence, *Tale of the Devil*, 116; Jones, *Hatfields and the McCoys*, 41–43; Rice, *Hatfields and the McCoys*, 24.

12   McCoy, *The McCoys*, 76.

13   Jones, *Hatfields and the McCoys*, 40.

14   Other researchers refer to this Elias Hatfield as "Bad Elias": Rice, *Hatfields and the McCoys*, 24; Jones, *Hatfields and the McCoys*, 40.

15   According to Jones (*Hatfields and the McCoys*, 40–41), Tolbert had harangued Bad Elias about this debt earlier in the day, and Preacher Anse Hatfield had persuaded the two men to let it go. Tolbert's wife had also tried to persuade him to go home with her, but he refused.

16   Waller, *Feud*, 72.

17 Ibid., 72.

18 McCoy, *The McCoys,* 74.

19 No other researcher agrees with her, but Truda McCoy insists that the third McCoy son involved in this clash was sixteen-year-old Bill instead of eighteen-year-old Bud, explaining that they looked so much alike that people often confused them. Truda's main sources of information for this episode were Sam and Jim McCoy, Bill's and Bud's brothers, and Martha McCoy, Bill's and Bud's sister-in-law. It seems likely that these three would have known which brother was involved, especially since Bud was eventually killed for Bill's supposed role in this scuffle (McCoy, *The McCoys,* 225).

20 Truda McCoy (*The McCoys,* 75) says that Devil Anse Hatfield retrieved the pistol and shot at the fleeing McCoy sons. But other researchers maintain that Devil Anse wasn't present that day (Hatfield and Spence, *Tale of the Devil,* 117).

21 Truda McCoy (*The McCoys,* 76) claims the constables were John Hatfield and Floyd Hatfield (a different Floyd from the Hog Trial). Matthew Hatfield was also one of the constables, say Jones (*Hatfields and the McCoys,* 43) and Rice (*Hatfields and the McCoys,* 24).

22 Jones, *Hatfields and the McCoys,* 44.

23 McCoy, *The McCoys,* 76. Rice (*Hatfields and the McCoys,* 26) maintains that Ranel McCoy remained with his captive sons.

24 Jones, *Hatfields and the McCoys,* 45.

25 McCoy, *The McCoys,* 77.

26 Ibid., 78.

27 Jones, *Hatfields and the McCoys,* 44.

28 Ibid.

29 Ibid.

30 Truda McCoy (*The McCoys,* 79) says that Devil Anse Hatfield accosted the party and seized the prisoners, and that Jim, Sam, and Floyd McCoy objected but were overpowered. She claims that Jim started to organize a posse, but his mother, Sarah, talked him out of it.

31 Jones, *Hatfields and the McCoys,* 45.

32 Ibid., 46.

33 Waller, *Feud,* 74.

34 Jones (*Hatfields and the McCoys,* 47) says that Ranel McCoy was still with his sons but departed on his horse for Pikeville at this point to summon help.

35 Ibid., 48.

36 Accounts of the upcoming episode are given by Rice (*Hatfields and the McCoys,* 26–28), Jones (*Hatfields and the McCoys,* 47–53), and McCoy (*The McCoys,* 81–87).

37 Jones, *Hatfields and the McCoys,* 50.

38 Jones (*Hatfields and the McCoys,* 91) states that the identity of the Hatfield male who was Ellison Mounts's father was in question and that it might have been Wall. Yet the

fact that Mounts was named Ellison would appear to support the widespread belief that Ellison Hatfield was, in fact, his father.

39 McCoy, *The McCoys*, 87.

40 Jones, *Hatfields and McCoys*, 50.

41 Crawford, *An American Vendetta*, 82: Eldean Wellman quoting Joseph Platania, "Men to Match the Mountains: Devil Anse Hatfield and Uncle Dyke Garrett," *Goldenseal* 10, no. 3: 26–32.

42 Hatfield and Spence, *Tale of the Devil*, 120.

43 Ibid., 119–20.

44 Jones, *Hatfields and the McCoys*, 52.

45 L. D. Hatfield, *True Story*, 24.

46 Hatfield and Spence, *Tale of the Devil*, 166.

47 Hatfield and Spence (*Tale of the Devil*, 115) state that the bodies were found the next morning.

48 Jones, *Hatfields and the McCoys*, 54–55.

49 Hatfield and Spence, *Tale of the Devil*, 120–21.

50 Ibid., 121.

51 Ibid., 115.

52 McCoy, p. 90.

53 Jones (*Hatfields and the McCoys*, 56) maintains that Ranel McCoy didn't return from Pikeville or learn of his sons' deaths until after their funeral.

54 McCoy, *The McCoys*, 93.

Chapter 7: Devil Anse and the Hellhounds

1 Hatfield and Spence, *Tale of the Devil*, 125.

2 Jones, *Hatfields and the McCoys*, 68.

3 Ibid., 57.

4 Ibid., 58.

5 Crawford, *An American Vendetta*, 19.

6 Jones, *Hatfields and the McCoys*, 56–57.

7 Hatfield and Spence, *Tale of the Devil*, 122.

8 Jones, *Hatfields and the McCoys*, 63–64.

9 McCoy, *The McCoys*, 95.

10 Versions of this story are told in Jones, *Hatfields and the McCoys*, 69; McCoy, *The McCoys*, 95–96; and Rice, *Hatfields and the McCoys*, 31. Also, Shirley Donnelly, *The Hatfield-McCoy Feud Reader* (Parsons, WV: McClain, 1971), 9. McCoy says that Sam McCoy was with the Scotts and that they were walking to a mill to have some corn ground.

11 McCoy, *The McCoys,* 97.

12 Jones, *Hatfields and the McCoys,* 69; Rice, *Hatfields and the McCoys,* 31.

13 Hatfield and Spence, *Tale of the Devil,* 93.

14 Based on photo #038506 in the West Virginia State Archives.

15 Crawford, *An American Vendetta,* 24–25.

16 Ibid., 31.

17 Hatfield and Spence, *Tale of the Devil,* 91.

18 Ibid., 153.

19 McCoy, *The McCoys,* 113–14.

20 Ibid., 102.

21 Jones, *Hatfields and the McCoys,* 73.

22 McCoy, *The McCoys,* 103.

23 Ibid., 105–7.

24 Ibid., 165.

25 Ibid., 114.

26 Donnelly, *Hatfield-McCoy Feud Reader,* 17.

27 Jones (*Hatfields and the McCoys,* 73) and Rice (*Hatfields and the McCoys,* 33) state that it was two unmasked men.

28 McCoy, *The McCoys,* 115.

29 Hatfield and Spence, *Tale of the Devil,* 127. However, Jones (*Hatfields and the McCoys,* 73) and Rice (*Hatfields and the McCoys,* 33) maintain that the two whipped women were Mary Daniels and her daughter.

30 Jones, *Hatfields and the McCoys,* 74; Rice, *Hatfields and the McCoys,* 33.

31 McCoy, *The McCoys,* 119.

32 Rice, *Hatfields and the McCoys,* 33–35.

33 McCoy, *The McCoys,* 119–26.

34 Ibid., 126–27.

35 Hatfield and Spence, *Tale of the Devil,* 128.

36 McCoy, *The McCoys,* 127; Rice, *Hatfields and the McCoys,* 51.

37 Rice, *Hatfields and the McCoys,* 35–36.

38 McCoy, *The McCoys,* 127.

39 Rice, *Hatfields and the McCoys,* 51.

40 Jones, *Hatfields and the McCoys,* 151; Rice, *Hatfields and the McCoys,* 51.

41 Hatfield and Spence, *Tale of the Devil,* 204.

42 *Courier-Journal* (Louisville, KY), March 17, 1888, as quoted in Rice, *Hatfields and the McCoys,* 31.

43   Rice, *Hatfields and the McCoys,* 31.

44   Hatfield and Spence, *Tale of the Devil,* 138.

45   Jones, *Hatfields and the McCoys,* 81; Rice, *Hatfields and the McCoys,* 50.

46   Rice, *Hatfields and the McCoys,* 52.

47   Waller, *Feud,* 165–67.

48   Crawford, *An American Vendetta,* Wellman endnote #18, 84.

49   Baker and Hall, 39th Kentucky Mounted Infantry Webpage, http://reocities.com/
     rmbaker66/index.html.

50   Waller, *Feud,* 160.

51   Based on sketches of Dils and his Pikeville home reproduced in Waller, 120–21.

52   Ibid., 167.

53   Jones, *Hatfields and McCoys,* 82; Rice, *Hatfields and McCoys,* 51; Waller, *Feud,* 172.

54   Waller, *Feud,* 171.

55   Jones, *Hatfields and McCoys,* 80; Donnelly, *Hatfield-McCoy Feud Reader,* 9.

56   Waller, *Feud,* 172.

57   Jones, *Hatfields and McCoys,* 83; Rice, *Hatfields and McCoys,* 52; Waller, *Feud,* 167.

58   McCoy, *The McCoys,* 129–30. Jones (*Hatfields and McCoys,* 179) says that Billy Phillips
     died in prison.

59   McCoy, *The McCoys,* 130.

60   Waller, *Feud,* 173.

61   Rice, *Hatfields and McCoys,* 53.

62   Jones, *Hatfields and McCoys,* 84.

63   Rice, *Hatfields and McCoys,* 52–53.

64   Based on photo #038533 in the West Virginia State Archives.

65   Waller, *Feud,* 173.

66   Ibid., 175.

67   Philip Hatfield, *The Other Feud,* 20.

68   Jones, *Hatfields and the McCoys,* 85; Waller, *Feud,* 175.

69   Jones, *Hatfields and the McCoys,* 84–85; Rice, *Hatfields and the McCoys,* 53–54; Waller,
     Feud, 177.

70   Jones, *Hatfields and the McCoys,* 86; Rice, *Hatfields and the McCoys,* 54–55; Waller,
     Feud, 177.

71   Waller, *Feud,* 178.

72   Ibid., 178.

73   Hatfield and Spence, *Tale of the Devil,* 140.

Chapter 8: New Year's Night Massacre

1 Ibid., 163.

2 Ibid., 167.

3 Jones, *Hatfields and the McCoys*, 94; Rice, *Hatfields and the McCoys*, 60.

4 McCoy, *The McCoys*, 138.

5 Hatfield and Spence, *Tale of the Devil*, 168.

6 Ibid., 161.

7 Waller, *Feud*, 179.

8 Hatfield and Spence, *Tale of the Devil*, 168.

9 Jones, *Hatfields and the McCoys*, 92; Rice, *Hatfields and the McCoys*, 60.

10 Waller, *Feud*, 180.

11 Jones, *Hatfields and the McCoys*, 111.

12 McCoy (*The McCoys*, 140) says there were fifteen participants.

13 Rice, *Hatfields and the McCoys*, 59.

14 Hatfield and Spence, *Tale of the Devil*, 169.

15 Ibid.

16 Jones, *Hatfields and the McCoys*, 92.

17 The reporter who also trashed Cap Hatfield described French Ellis as an especially unsavory character, with "a small, bullet head, frosty complexion, washed-out eyes, little pug nose, and great sandy mustache lining the cruel, tightly-nipped mouth" (Crawford, *An American Vendetta*, 23).

18 McCoy (*The McCoys*, 140) claims, incorrectly, that Devil Anse was with the group.

19 Accounts of the New Year's Night Massacre are given by Jones, *Hatfields and the McCoys*, 90–98; McCoy, *The McCoys*, 138–48; Rice, *Hatfields and the McCoys*, 58–64; and Hatfield and Spence, *Tale of the Devil*, 164–71.

20 Hatfield and Spence, *Tale of the Devil*, 169. Jones (*Hatfields and the McCoys*, 128), however, quotes Wall Hatfield as stating that his nephew Bob did participate in the New Year's Night Massacre.

21 Jones, *Hatfields and the McCoys*, 93.

22 Ibid., 94.

23 McCoy, *The McCoys*, 141.

24 Hatfield and Spence, *Tale of the Devil*, 169.

25 McCoy (*The McCoys*, 146) says that Ranel shot Johnse as Ranel fled the burning house.

26 Jones, *Hatfields and the McCoys*, 95; Rice, *Hatfields and the McCoys*, 61; McCoy, *The McCoys*, 142.

27 Hatfield and Spence, *Tale of the Devil*, 169.

28   McCoy, *The McCoys*, 143.

29   Ibid., 144.

30   Jones, *Hatfields and the McCoys*, 96; Rice, *Hatfields and the McCoys*, 62; Hatfield and Spence, *Tale of the Devil*, 170; Crawford, *An American Vendetta*, 12.

31   McCoy, *The McCoys*, 144, 147; Rice, *Hatfields and the McCoys*, 64. Crawford, (*An American Vendetta*, 12) quotes Charlie Gillespie as stating that Cottontop Mounts beat Sarah McCoy.

32   Jones (*Hatfields and the McCoys*, 97) and Rice (*Hatfields and the McCoys*, 63) finger Johnse Hatfield for bashing in Sarah McCoy's skull. McCoy (*The McCoys*, 145) claims that Jim Vance did this. Crawford (*An American Vendetta*, 12) says that Charlie Gillespie later stated that Cottontop Mounts was responsible.

33   McCoy, *The McCoys*, 145.

34   Hatfield and Spence, *Tale of the Devil*, 170. By Cap Hatfield, states Crawford (*An American Vendetta*, 12), citing Charlie Gillespie's confession.

35   L. D. Hatfield, *True Story*, 34; Hatfield and Spence, *Tale of the Devil*, 170.

36   Jones, *Hatfields and the McCoys*, 100; McCoy, *The McCoys*, 146; Rice, *Hatfields and the McCoys*, 64; Waller, *Feud*, 181.

37   McCoy, *The McCoys*, 146; Rice, *Hatfields and the McCoys*, 63.

38   Jones, *Hatfields and the McCoys*, 97.

39   Hatfield and Spence, *Tale of the Devil*, 170.

40   Statement by Charlie Gillespie in *Cincinnati* (OH) *Enquirer*, October 14, 1888, and *Wheeling* (WV) *Intelligencer*, Oct. 17, 1888, as quoted by Waller, 181.

41   Jones, *Hatfields and the McCoys*, 98.

42   McCoy, *The McCoys*, 146; Rice, *Hatfields and the McCoys*, 64. Jones (*Hatfields and the McCoys*, 100) says it was Sarah's hair that was frozen to the ground.

43   *Big Sandy News* (Louisa, KY), January 12, 1888, as quoted in Rice, *Hatfields and the McCoys*, 66.

44   McCoy, *The McCoys*, 146.

45   Jones, *Hatfields and the McCoys*, 98; Donnelly, *Hatfield-McCoy Feud Reader*, 11.

46   Jones, *Hatfields and the McCoys*, 99; Rice, *Hatfields and the McCoys*, 64.

47   McCoy, *The McCoys*, 149.

48   Ibid., 111.

49   Hatfield and Spence, *Tale of the Devil*, 171.

50   Ibid., 161.

51   Accounts of the murder of Jim Vance: Jones, *Hatfields and the McCoys*, 101–2; Rice, *Hatfields and the McCoys*, 68–69; McCoy, *The McCoys*, 180–85; Hatfield and Spence, *Tale of the Devil*, 172–74.

52   Hatfield and Spence, *Tale of the Devil*, 172.

53   Jones, *Hatfields and the McCoys,* 101.

54   McCoy, *The McCoys,* 183.

55   Hatfield and Spence, *Tale of the Devil,* 173; in the stomach, says Jones, *Hatfields and the McCoys,* 102. Hatfield and Spence (172) state that Bud McCoy was also shot in this skirmish, which they have probably confused with the upcoming Battle of Grapevine Creek.

56   Hatfield and Spence, *Tale of the Devil,* 173. Rice (*Hatfields and the McCoys,* 69) says Vance sent Cap away so he would be safe.

57   Hatfield and Spence, *Tale of the Devil,* 173.

58   L. D. Hatfield, *True Story,* 32.

59   Jones, *Hatfields and the McCoys,* 182; Rice, *Hatfields and the McCoys,* 70.

60   McCoy, *The McCoys,* 184. Jones (*Hatfields and the McCoys,* 105) and Waller (*Feud,* 198) place this overcoat caper after the next skirmish, the Battle of Grapevine Creek.

61   Hatfield and Spence, *Tale of the Devil,* 173.

62   Waller, *Feud,* 184; Hatfield and Spence, *Tale of the Devil,* 174.

63   Jones, *Hatfields and the McCoys,* 103.

64   Waller, *Feud,* 184.

65   Ibid., 185.

66   Hatfield and Spence, *Tale of the Devil,* 175.

67   Waller, *Feud,* 269, note #62.

68   Hatfield and Spence, *Tale of the Devil,* 177.

69   L. D. Hatfield, *True Story,* 33; Jones, *Hatfields and the McCoys,* 104. Hatfield and Spence (*Tale of the Devil,* 177) say that Bill Dempsey was a cousin of Jack Dempsey, the heavyweight boxing champion in the 1920s.

70   McCoy, *The McCoys,* 177.

71   McCoy (*The McCoys,* 172–79) places the Battle of Grapevine Creek before the murder of Jim Vance.

72   Waller, *Feud,* 186.

73   Crawford, *An American Vendetta,* 18.

74   Ibid.

75   Based on photo #038535 in the West Virginia State Archives.

76   Hatfield and Spence, *Tale of the Devil,* 178. McCoy (*The McCoys,* 175) and Jones (*Hatfields and the McCoys,* 104) state that Cap Hatfield shot Bud McCoy.

77   Hatfield and Spence, *Tale of the Devil,* 178.

Chapter 9: All Over but the Shouting

1   Ibid., 178–79.

2   Waller, *Feud,* 206–7.

3   Charles Howell, *Pittsburgh* (PA) *Times,* February 1, 1888, as quoted in Waller, *Feud,* 222.

4   Howell, *Pittsburgh Times,* as quoted in Rice (*Hatfields and the McCoys,* 73–74).

5   Howell, *Pittsburgh Times,* as quoted in Waller (*Feud,* 222).

6   Waller, *Feud,* 221.

7   Ibid., 198–99.

8   Hatfield and Spence, *Tale of the Devil,* 179.

9   Waller, *Feud,* 198–99.

10 Ibid., 201.

11 Hatfield and Spence, *Tale of the Devil,* 180–81.

12 Crawford, *An American Vendetta,* 34.

13 Rice, *Hatfields and the McCoys,* 93.

14 Jones, *Hatfields and the McCoys,* 142.

15 Accounts of these wranglings are given in Jones, *Hatfields and the McCoys,* 107–30; Hatfield and Spence, *Tale of the Devil,* 181–82; Waller, *Feud,* 207–19; McCoy, *The McCoys,* 186–95; and Rice, *Hatfields and the McCoys,* 76–91.

16 Jones, *Hatfields and the McCoys,* 124.

17 Hatfield and Spence, *Tale of the Devil,* 133.

18 Waller, *Feud,* 209–10.

19 Crawford, *An American Vendetta,* 14.

20 Rice, *Hatfields and the McCoys,* 93.

21 Waller, *Feud,* 212.

22 McCoy, *The McCoys,* 199.

23 Ibid.

24 Editorial, *New York Times,* February 18, 1888.

25 *Courier-Journal* (Louisville, KY), February 7, 1888, as quoted in Jones (*Hatfields and the McCoys,* 117).

26 Jones, *Hatfields and the McCoys,* 124.

27 *New York Times,* February 18, 1888, as quoted in Waller (*Feud,* 213).

28 Jones, *Hatfields and the McCoys,* 128.

29 McCoy, *The McCoys,* 155.

30 Waller, *Feud,* 240–41.

31 McCoy, *The McCoys,* 162–4.

32 Rice, *Hatfields and the McCoys,* 92.

33 Ibid., 94.

34 Crawford, *An American Vendetta,* 84; note 18 by Eldean Wellman.

35 Ibid., 14–15.

36 Waller, *Feud,* 222.

37 Crawford, preface to *An American Vendetta,* 1. Crawford's arrogance and temerity astonish me. I have lived in the southern Appalachians for much of my life, but even I make statements and judgments about the area with great reluctance and caution.

38 Waller, *Feud,* 221.

39 Crawford, *An American Vendetta,* 26.

40 Ibid.

41 Ibid., 25.

42 Ibid., 2.

43 Untitled editorial, *New York Times,* December 26, 1878.

44 Rice, *Hatfields and the McCoys,* 98–99.

45 Jones, *Hatfields and the McCoys,* 149–50.

46 Ibid., 150.

47 Hatfield and Davis, *Feuding Hatfields,* 48–52.

48 Rice, *Hatfields and the McCoys,* 95.

49 Jones, *Hatfields and the McCoys,*150.

50 Ibid., 151–52.

51 Ibid., 152.

52 McCoy, *The McCoys,* 224.

Chapter 10: "The Hatfields Made Me Do It!"

1   Jones, *Hatfields and the McCoys,* 153–54.

2   Accounts of the trials can be found in: Jones, *Hatfields and the McCoys,* 154–56; McCoy, *The McCoys,* 198–204; Rice, *Hatfields and the McCoys,* 101–6; and Hatfield and Spence, *Tale of the Devil,* 182–83.

3   McCoy, *The McCoys,* 198.

4   Waller, *Feud,* 229.

5   Ibid.

6   Rice, *Hatfields and the McCoys,* 101.

7   Ibid., 102.

8   Jones, *Hatfields and the McCoys,* 48.

9   Rice, *Hatfields and the McCoys,* 103–4.

10 McCoy, *The McCoys,* 199.

11 Jones, *Hatfields and the McCoys,* 182.

12 McCoy, *The McCoys,* 200.

13 Ibid., 202.

14 Ibid., 203.

15 Jones, *Hatfields and the McCoys*, 159.

16 Ibid., 158.

17 McCoy, *The McCoys*, 74. The McCoy descendants agree with Truda's assessment of Bill's role in the murder of Ellison Hatfield, because they have installed a stone marker in Hardy, Kentucky, that reads: Six of the sixteen children of Randolph and Sarah McCoy lie buried here having suffered untimely death. Three bound to paw paw trees at the mouth of Blackberry Creek in August 1882. One is believed to have died of grief because his brother had been shot in his stead. Two perished when their home was burned in January 1888. The homesite is visible across the valley above this place.

18 Ibid., 111–12.

19 Accounts of this episode can be found in: Jones, *Hatfields and the McCoys*, 161–67; Rice, *Hatfields and the McCoys*, 107–8; and Hatfield and Spence, *Tale of the Devil*, 183–87.

20 Hatfield and Spence (*Tale of the Devil*, 185) say the beverage in question was brandy.

21 L. D. Hatfield, *True Story*, 40; Rice, *Hatfields and the McCoys*, 107.

22 Jones (*Hatfields and the McCoys*, 162) says five.

23 Ibid.

24 Hatfield and Spence, *Tale of the Devil*, 187.

25 Waller, *Feud*, 232.

26 McCoy (*The McCoys*, 205) says the hanging occurred on December 3, 1889. In reality, it was delayed because of an appeal.

27 Accounts of the hanging can be found in: Jones, *Hatfields and the McCoys*, 168–74; Rice, *Hatfields and the McCoys*, 110–11; and McCoy, *The McCoys*, 205–11.

28 McCoy, *The McCoys*, 208.

29 Jones, *Hatfields and the McCoys*, 168–9.

30 Ibid., 170–71.

31 McCoy, *The McCoys*, 208–9.

32 Jones, *Hatfields and the McCoys*, 171.

33 McCoy, *The McCoys*, 209.

34 Jones, *Hatfields and the McCoys*, 172.

35 McCoy, *The McCoys*, 206–7.

36 Jones, *Hatfields and the McCoys*, 172–73. McCoy (*McCoys*, 209) says that he whispered to the sheriff that he didn't kill Alifair McCoy.

37 Jones, *Hatfields and the McCoys*, 173.

38 McCoy, *The McCoys*, 211.

39 Jones, *Hatfields and the McCoys,* 194.

40 Ibid., 184.

41 Williams, *West Virginia,* 125–26.

42 Jones, *Hatfields and the McCoys,* 182; Rice, *Hatfields and the McCoys,* 113.

43 Jones, *Hatfields and the McCoys,* 185; Donnelly, *Hatfield-McCoy Feud Reader,* 14.

44 Jones, *Hatfields and the McCoys,* 183.

45 Ibid., 185.

46 Ibid., 186.

47 Ibid., 197.

Chapter 11: Survivors

1   Ibid., 208.

2   McCoy, *The McCoys,* 214.

3   Ibid., 215.

4   Ibid.

5   Jones, *Hatfields and the McCoys,* 221.

6   Ibid., 215–16.

7   McCoy, *The McCoys,* 216.

8   Ibid., 316.

9   Waller, *Feud,* 238.

10 Ibid., 241.

11 McCoy, *The McCoys,* 229.

12 Ibid., 213–14.

13 Ibid.

14 McCoy (*The McCoys,* 219) says Johnse expected Nancy to join him there. But this seems unlikely because he had already divorced her by then, and she was having babies with Frank Phillips.

15 Hatfield and Spence, *Tale of the Devil,* 238.

16 Ibid., 243.

17 Ibid., 250–51.

18 L. D. Hatfield, *True Story,* 38.

19 Jones, *Hatfields and the McCoys,* 210–11.

20 Hatfield and Spence, *Tale of the Devil,* 296.

21 Jones, *Hatfields and the McCoys,* 217.

22 Hatfield and Spence, *Tale of the Devil,* 305.

23 Ibid., p. 235.

24 Ibid., p. 221.

25 Jones, *Hatfields and the McCoys,* 209.

26 Hatfield and Spence, *Tale of the Devil,* 252.

27 Jones, *Hatfields and the McCoys,* 209; Rice, *Hatfields and the McCoys,* 120.

28 Hatfield and Spence, *Tale of the Devil,* 253.

29 Ibid., 254–55; Jones, *Hatfields and the McCoys,* 219.

30 Hatfield and Spence, *Tale of the Devil,* 236. Eldean Wellman (Crawford, *An American Vendetta,* 85) also maintains that Rebel Bill Smith was the brother of Devil Anse Hatfield's sister Emma's husband, thus the uncle of Emma's daughter Nancy Elizabeth Smith.

31 Hatfield and Spence, *Tale of the Devil,* 223.

32 Ibid., 224.

33 Ibid., 225.

34 Ibid., 224.

35 Waller, *Feud,* 242–43.

36 Hatfield and Spence, *Tale of the Devil,* 229.

37 Ibid., 115.

38 Ibid., 228–29.

39 Waller, *Feud,* 41.

40 Hatfield and Spence, *Tale of the Devil,* 230.

41 Jones, *Hatfields and the McCoys,* 199.

42 Accounts of this episode can be found in: Rice, *Hatfields and the McCoys,* 118–19; Jones, *Hatfields and the McCoys,* 199–203; and Hatfield and Spence, *Tale of the Devil,* 230–33.

43 Hatfield and Spence, *Tale of the Devil,* 231.

44 Jones, *Hatfields and the McCoys,* 200; Rice, *Hatfields and the McCoys,* 119.

45 Jones, *Hatfields and the McCoys,* 201; Rice (*Hatfields and the McCoys,* 119) says that Joe Glenn shot this Rutherford to protect Cap.

46 Hatfield and Spence, *Tale of the Devil,* 233. The attic was that of Dan Christian, an orphan whom Devil Anse Hatfield had rescued from a westward-bound wagon train and taken into his home.

47 Ibid., 233–34.

48 Jones, *Hatfields and the McCoys,* 203; Rice, *Hatfields and the McCoys,* 119.

49 Jones, *Hatfields and the McCoys,* 206.

50 Ibid., 203.

51 Ibid., 206.

52 Hatfield and Spence, *Tale of the Devil,* 234–35.

53   L. D. Hatfield, *True Story*, 35.

54   Hatfield and Spence, *Tale of the Devil*, 221.

55   Ibid., 272.

56   Ibid.

57   Ibid., 273; Donnelly, *Hatfield-McCoy Feud Reader*, 15.

58   Hatfield and Spence, *Tale of the Devil*, 221. Aileen Hatfield died young. Severely depressed for several years, she was perhaps another case of collateral damage from the feud (Hatfield and Spence, *Tale of the Devil*, 314). The legacy of violence passed down by her great-grandfather and grandfather was, no doubt, a dispiriting one for an idealistic young person—just as the hanging of his great-grandfather Abner Vance had proved so disastrous for Devil Anse Hatfield.

59   Jones, *Hatfields and the McCoys*, 217.

60   Hatfield and Spence, *Tale of the Devil*, 246.

61   Ibid., 222.

62   Waller, *Feud*, 243.

63   Hatfield and Spence, *Tale of the Devil*, 222.

64   Jones, *Hatfields and the McCoys*, 185.

65   Waller, *Feud*, 243.

66   Donnelly, *Hatfield-McCoy Reader*, 16.

67   Hatfield and Spence, *Tale of the Devil*, 222.

68   Ibid., 265.

69   Ibid., 222.

70   Donnelly, *Hatfield-McCoy Feud Reader*, 15.

71   Ibid.

72   Hatfield and Spence, *Tale of the Devil*, 171.

73   Ibid., 14.

74   Jones, *Hatfields and the McCoys*, 173.

75   Jones (*Hatfields and the McCoys*, 216) says that Devil Anse covered the logs of his original cabin with siding and added porches, rather than building a new house.

76   Hatfield and Spence, *Tale of the Devil*, 259.

77   Ibid., 244.

78   Crawford, *An American Vendetta*, 21.

79   Jones, *Hatfields and the McCoys*, 217.

80   Hatfield and Spence, *Tale of the Devil*, 115.

81   Rice, *Hatfields and the McCoys*, 121. Jones (*Hatfields and the McCoys*, 220) says Devil Anse's conversion occurred after the shooting deaths of his sons Troy and Elias.

82   Hatfield and Spence, *Tale of the Devil*, 97.

83 Ibid., 256. Jones (*Hatfields and the McCoys,* 220) says, incorrectly, that the baptism occurred after the deaths of Troy and Elias and that Cap and Johnse were baptized with Devil Anse.

84 Hatfield and Spence, *Tale of the Devil,* 215.

85 Jones, *Hatfields and the McCoys,* 222.

86 Hatfield and Spence, *Tale of the Devil,* 121.

87 "Steel Casket Purchased by Feudist Leader at a Cost of $2000," *Intelligencer* (Williamson, WV), January 9, 1921.

88 McCoy (*The McCoys,* 218) says there were five thousand at the funeral. Rice (*Hatfields and the McCoys,* 123) says "several thousand."

89 Jones, *Hatfields and the McCoys,* 233.

90 Ibid.; Donnelly, *Hatfield-McCoy Feud Reader,* 22; Waller, *Feud,* 290, note 10.

91 L. D. Hatfield, *True Story,* 51; Donnelly, *Hatfield-McCoy Feud Reader,* 22.

92 L. D. Hatfield, *True Story,* 51.

93 Based on photo #038401 in the West Virginia State Archives.

94 Jones, *Hatfields and the McCoys,* 234.

95 Based on my own observations and photos.

96 Hatfield and Spence, *Tale of the Devil,* 154.

97 Ibid.

98 Rice, *Hatfields and the McCoys,* 124.

Chapter 12: Other Feuds

1 John Ed Pearce, *Days of Darkness: The Feuds of Eastern Kentucky* (Lexington: University Press of Kentucky, 1994). The most cogent account of the various feuds is found here. Pearce has struggled valiantly to make sense of the nonsensical.

2 Pearce, *Days of Darkness,* 133.

3 Ibid., 135.

4 Ibid., 150.

5 Ibid., 162.

6 Ibid., 165.

7 For details see Pearce, *Days of Darkness,* 187–94.

8 Pearce, *Days of Darkness,* 184.

9 Ibid., 198.

10 Ibid., 33.

11 Ibid., 36.

12 Ibid., 37–38.

13 Ibid., 41.

14 Ibid., 40.

15 Ibid., 43–44.

16 Ibid., 44.

17 Ibid., 97. Other accounts of the Rowan County Wars: Rice, *Hatfields and the McCoys,* 42–45; Fred Brown and Juanita Blair, *Days of Anger, Days of Tears: The History of the Rowan County War* (Nicholasville, KY: Wind Publications, 2007); and Lewis Franklin Johnson, excerpt from *Famous Kentucky Tragedies and Trials* on the Alexander Stewart Family of Kentucky webpage: www.kentuckystewarts.com/RowanCounty/TheolliverMartinFeud.htm.

18 Pearce, *Days of Darkness,* 98.

19 Ibid., 96.

20 Ibid., 99.

21 Ibid., 101.

22 Ibid., 102–3.

23 Ibid., 106.

24 Ibid.

25 Ibid., 107.

26 Ibid., 107–8.

27 Ibid., 109–10.

28 Ibid., 110.

29 Ibid., 110.

30 Ibid., 95.

31 The national press had a field day with the Turner-Howard feud. Reports were published in papers from Portland, Maine, to Portland, Oregon, from New York City to Los Angeles. At the height of it, in 1889, the *New York Times* published five articles about it in six weeks (September 17, October 15, October 24, October 27, and October 28). The *Atlanta (GA) Constitution* also printed articles on July, 28, 1889, and October 24, 1889.

32 Pearce, *Days of Darkness,* 15.

33 Ibid., 17.

34 Ibid., 16.

35 Ibid., 17.

36 Ibid.

37 Ibid., 18.

38 Ibid., 19.

39 Ibid., 22–23.

40 Ibid., 26–27.

41 Ibid., 76–77; "The French and Eversole War," based on Charles Mutzenburg, *Kentucky's Famous Feuds and Tragedies:* http://echandgs0.tripod.com/feuds/id1.html.

42 Pearce, *Days of Darkness,* 78–79.

43 Ibid., 79–80.

44 Ibid., 81.

45 Ibid., 81–82.

46 Ibid., 82.

47 Ibid., 85.

48 Ibid., 88–92.

49 Ibid., 111.

50 Waller, *Feud,* 221.

Chapter 13: The Corsica of America

1 Ibid., 169.

2 Elihu Jasper Sutherland, *Pioneer Recollections of Southwest Virginia* (Clintwood, VA: Mullins Printing, 1984), 174.

3 Shapiro (*Appalachia on Our Mind,* 80), quoting Ellen Churchill Semple, "The Anglo-Saxons of the Kentucky Mountains: A Study in Anthropogeography," *Geographical Journal* (London: June 1901) 17: 588–623.

4 Daniel Sharfstein, *The Invisible Line: Three American Families and the Secret Journey from Black to White* (New York: Penguin, 2011), 74.

5 Ibid., 173.

6 Brewton Berry, *Almost White* (New York: Collier Macmillan, 1969) 16.

7 Edgar Thompson, "The Little Races," *American Anthropologist* 74, no. 5 (1972): 1295–1306.

8 John S. Kessler, Donald B. Ball, and N. Brent Kennedy, *North from the Mountains: A Folk History of the Carmel Melungeon Settlement, Highland County, Ohio* (Macon, GA: Mercer University Press, 2001) 35–42.

9 McCoy, *The McCoys,* 114.

10 Caryl Lamont, "Thomas Bailey Christian and Chief Cornstalk," Christian Family Genealogy Forum: http://genforum.genealogy.com/christian/messages/2949.html.

11 McCoy, *The McCoys,* 73.

12 Jones, *Hatfields and the McCoys,* 38.

13 Crawford, *An American Vendetta,* 32.

14 Ibid., 16.

15 Ibid., 12.

16 McCoy, *The McCoys,* 3.

17   Roxanne Khamsi. "Genes Reveal West African Heritage of White Brits," NewScientist online, January 24, 2007, www.newscientist.com, DOI: 10.1038/sj.ejhg.5201771.

18   Fulvio Cruciani, Roberta La Fratta, Beniamino Trombetta, Piero Santolamazza, Daniele Sellitto, Eliane Beraud Colomb, and Jean-Michel Dugoujon, et al., "Tracing Past Human Male Movements in Northern/Eastern Africa and Western Eurasia: New Clues from Y-Chromosomal Haplogroups E-M78 and J-M12," *Molecular Biology and Evolution* 24, no. 6 (June 2007): 1300–1311, DOI: 10.

19   "Hatfield Early Origins," House of Names website: www.houseofnames.com/hatfield-family-crest.

20   McCoy, *The McCoys*, 3.

21   David Hackett Fischer, *Albion's Seed: Four British Folkways in America* (New York: Oxford University Press, 1989), 605–782.

22   Ibid., 693–94.

23   Nisbett and Cohen, *Culture of Honor*, xv.

24   Pat Solley, "Corsican Soup and Pulp Fiction" (e-SoupSong: Jan. 1, 2002): www.soupsong.com/zjan02.html.

25   Nisbett and Cohen, *Culture of Honor*, 5.

26   Ibid., 42–53.

27   Ibid., 1.

28   Ibid., 22.

29   Ibid., 9.

30   Untitled editorial, *New York Times*, December 26, 1878.

31   Nisbett and Cohen, *Culture of Honor*, 5.

32   John Shelton Reed, *One South: An Ethnic Approach to Regional Culture* (Baton Rouge: Louisiana State University Press, 1982), 147.

33   West Virginia Division of Culture and History, transcript of interview with Margaret Hatfield, June 11, 1992, for the film *West Virginia*, WV History Film Project: www.wvculture.org/history/wvmemory/filmtranscripts/wvhatfield.html.

34   Nisbett and Cohen, *Culture of Honor*, 88.

35   Crawford, *An American Vendetta*, 31.

36   Waller, *Feud*, 267, note 19.

37   "Hatfield-McCoy Feud Blamed on 'Rage' Disease," (Associated Press, Apr. 5, 2007): www.msnbc.msn.com/id/17967965/ns/health-health_care/t/hatfield-mccoy-feud-blamed-rage-disease/#.TyCB-pi4KrI.

38   Ibid.

39   Waller, *Feud*, 196–97.

40   Ibid., 70.

41   Williams, *West Virginia*, 103–4.

42 Ibid., 104.

43 Nando Pelusi, "Neanderthink: The Appeal of the Bad Boy," *Psychology Today,* January 1, 2009.

44 Hatfield and Spence, *Tale of the Devil,* 103–4.

45 Ibid., 24.

46 Ibid., 153.

47 McCoy, *The McCoys,* 81.

48 Ibid., 126.

49 Ibid., 48.

50 Blaise Pascal, *Pensees,* trans. A. J. Krailsheimer (New York: Penguin, 2003), 136.

51 Hatfield and Spence, *Tale of the Devil,* 164.

52 Mildred Haun, "Shin-Bone Rocks," in *The Hawk's Done Gone and Other Stories by Mildred Haun,* ed. Herschel Gower (Nashville, TN: Vanderbilt University Press, 1968), 183–96.

53 Henry Caudill, *Night Comes to the Cumberlands* (Boston: Atlantic Monthly Press, 1962), 79.

54 Rice, *Hatfields and the McCoys,* 7.

55 Crawford, *An American Vendetta,* 4, 40.

56 Donnelly (*Hatfield-McCoy Feud Reader,* 17). Hatfield and Spence (*Tale of the Devil,* 121) say Sarah Staton had five children when her husband was murdered, with a sixth on the way.

Chapter 14: The Inner Hillbilly

1 Howell, *Pittsburgh* (PA) *Times,* February, 1, 1888, as quoted in Waller, *Feud,* 222.

2 Pearce, *Days of Darkness,* 7.

3 Ibid., 58.

4 Crawford, *An American Vendetta,* 23.

5 Philip Hatfield, *The Other Feud,* 73–74.

6 Crawford, *An American Vendetta,* 36.

7 "'Devil Anse' Hatfield of Feud Fame Dies in Logan County," *Charleston (WV) Daily Gazette,* Jan. 8, 1921, as reproduced in L. D. Hatfield, *True Story,* 47.

8 Hatfield and Spence, *Tale of the Devil,* 244.

9 Ibid., 105–6.

10 Ibid., 261–65.

11 Ibid., 92.

12 Hatfield and Davis, *Feuding Hatfields,* 125–26.

13 Jones, *Hatfields and the McCoys,* 197.

14   Saira Shah, *The Storyteller's Daughter* (New York: Alfred A. Knopf, 2003).

15   "Devil Anse Hatfield of Feud Fame," *Charleston (WV) Gazette,* January 8, 1921, as
     reproduced in L. D. Hatfield, *True Story,* 49. But Hatfield and Spence (*Tale of the
     Devil, 259)* label this story "improbable (and eventually false)."

16   *Fort Wayne Journal-Gazette,* Jan. 9, 1916, as reproduced in K. M. Presland, "Emmett
     Dalton: His Life after the Coffreyville Raid: Destination Hollywood": www.kayempea
     .net/hollywood.shtml.

17   McCoy, *The McCoys,* 217.

18   Ibid.

19   Hatfield and Spence, *Tale of the Devil,* 258.

20   See Crawford, *An American Vendetta,* passim, and the newspaper articles at "Newspaper
     Articles": http://swansonwill.tripod.com/newspaper.htm.

21   J. W. Williamson, *Southern Mountaineers in Silent Films* (Jefferson, NC: McFarland and
     Co., Inc., 1994), 301.

22   Shapiro, *Appalachia on Our Mind,* 102.

23   William Goodell Frost, "Our Contemporary Ancestors in the Southern Mountains,"
     Atlantic Monthly 83 (March 1899), 311.

24   Williamson, *Southern Mountaineers,* 7.

25   Ibid.

26   Ibid, 9.

27   An excellent account of the industrialization of the Southern mountains is: Ronald
     Eller, *Miners, Millhands, and Mountaineers* (Knoxville: University of Tennessee Press,
     1982). See also the documentary *Mine Wars: The Coal Miners' War for Freedom,* written
     and directed by Bill Richardson (Williamson, WV: Bill Richardson Productions,
     2004).

28   Williams, *West Virginia,* 149.

29   Eller, *Miners,* 56.

30   Caudill, *Night Comes,* 65–66; Eller, *Miners,* 54–57.

31   Eller, *Miners,* 55–56; Williams, *West Virginia,* 109.

32   Richardson, *Mine Wars.*

33   Caudill, *Night Comes,* 98–100; Eller, *Miners,* 162.

34   Caudill, *Night Comes,* 114; Eller, *Miners,* 188.

35   Eller, *Miners,* 183.

36   Caudill, *Night Comes,* 103–4.

37   Richardson, *Mine Wars.*

38   Eller, *Miners,* 196–97.

39   Richardson, *Mine Wars.*

40   Eller, *Miners,* 217–18; Richardson, *Mine Wars.*

41   Eller, *Miners,* 213.

42   Eller, *Miners,* 177; Richardson, *Mine Wars.*

43   Richardson, *Mine Wars.*

44   Caudill, *Night Comes,* 118–22.

45   Richardson, *Mine Wars.*

46   Ibid.

47   Ibid.

48   John Milton Cooper Jr., *Woodrow Wilson: A Biography* (New York: Vintage, 2011). 8.

49   Richardson, *Mine Wars.*

50   Waller, *Feud,* 244.

51   Accounts of the Matewan Massacre can be found in Jones, *Hatfields and the McCoys,* 225–31; L. D. Hatfield, *True Story,* 62–66; Hatfield and Spence, *Tale of the Devil,* 274– 75; and Richardson, *Mine Wars.* See also Lon Savage, *Thunder in the Mountains: The West Virginia Mine War 1920–21.* (Pittsburgh: University of Pittsburgh Press, 1990), passim.

52   L. D. Hatfield, *True Story,* 64.

53   Jones, *Hatfields and the McCoys,* 236.

54   Richardson, *Mines Wars.*

55   Williams, *West Virginia,* 115.

56   Ibid.

57   Waller, *Feud,* 244.

58   Hatfield and Spence, *Tale of the Devil,* 275.

59   Jones, *Hatfields and the McCoys,* 237.

60   Richardson, *Mine Wars.*

61   Ibid.

62   Ibid.

63   Ibid.

64   Ibid.

65   Williams, *West Virginia,* 147.

66   Richardson, *Mine Wars.*

67   Williams, *West Virginia,* 147.

68   Richardson, *Mine Wars.*

69   Ibid.

70   Ibid.

71   Savage, *Thunder*, 161.

72   Waller, *Feud*, 228.

73   Jeffrey H. Schwartz, "Development and Progress of the Appalachian Higher Education Network: Executive Summary" (Appalachian Regional Commission, May, 2004): www .arc.gov/images/newsroom/publications/AHEN/AHENetwork.pdf.

74   M. A. Palmer et al, "Mountaintop Mining Consequences," *Science*, v.327, no. 5962 (January 2010) 148–49.

75   Kentuckians for the Commonwealth homepage, "Health Impacts Are Harmful and Costly": www.kftc.org/our-work/canary-project/campaigns/mtr/health.

76   Travis Donovan, "Mountaintop Removal Mining Birth Defects: New Study Suggests Controversial Coal Operations Linked to Adverse Health Effects," *Huffington Post*, updated Aug. 27, 2011: www.huffingtonpost.com/2011/06/27/mountaintop-removal-coal-mining-birth-defects_n_885172.html.

77   Kris Maher, "Coal-Town Puzzle: Mountain vs. Jobs," online *Wall Street Journal*, June 13, 2011: http://online.wsj.com/article_email/SB1000142405270230466590457638178 0771812772-lMyQjAxMTAxMDEwMzExNDMyWj.html

78   "Business of the Year: Alpha Natural Resources," *Tri-Cities Business Journal* (Johnson City, TN: Mountaineer Publishing, Jan., 2012) 8–12: http://www.alphanr.com/ News%20Releases/BusinessJournal_January.

79   *The Last Mountain*, written and directed by Bill Haney (Los Angeles and Boston: Uncommon Productions, 2011).

Chapter 15: Man Toys

1   Hatfield and Spence, *Tale of the Devil*, 112.

2   William Henry Reed, unpublished memoirs.

3   Annette Potter, "The Hanging of Marshall Benton Taylor," Annette Potter Family Genealogy homepage: http://yeahpot.com/taylor/hangingofredfox.html.

4   "Two More Dead in Allen Feud," *New York Times*, March 16, 1912: www .blueridgeinstitute.org/ballads/allensnews.html.

5   Sutherland, *Pioneer Recollections*, 170.

6   Marlitta Perkins, "Alf Killen, Unionist Scout and Guerrilla: A Brief History," Our Alternate Impression: Alf Killen's Unionist Home Guards website: http://geocitiessites .com/Pentagon/Fort/2754/Alf_Killen.html.

7   Anita Owens Adkins and Callie Long, "Joel D. 'Dusty Pants' Long, USA": www.oocities.org/pentagon/Quarters/1365/JLong.html.

8   Sutherland, *Pioneer Recollections*, 183.

9   Bible, Exodus 34: 6–7.

10   Waller, *Feud*, 10.

Epilogue

1   "The Reunion They Said Would Never Happen": http://genealogy.about.com/library/
    weekly/aa043000a.htm.

2   "Hatfield-McCoy Feud Goes to the Graves," (Jun. 1, 2002), Goliath website: www
    .granta.com/New-Writing/War-and-Peace-on-the-Big-Sandy-River.

3   Dean H. King, "War and Peace on the Big Sandy River," *Granta* (Sept. 3, 2011):
    http://goliath.ecnext.com/coms2/gi_0199-1800483/Hatfield-McCoy-feud-goes-to.html.

~~ SELECTED BIBLIOGRAPHY ~~

BOOKS AND ARTICLES

Berry, Brewton. *Almost White*. New York: Collier Macmillan, 1969.

Brown, Fred, and Juanita Blair. *Days of Anger, Days of Tears: The History of the Rowan County War*. Nicholasville, KY: Wind Publications, 2007.

"Business of the Year: Alpha Natural Resources." *Business Journal of Tri-Cities TN/VA* (January 2012): 8–12.

Caudill, Harry. *Night Comes to the Cumberlands*. Boston: Atlantic Monthly Press, 1962.

Cooper, John Milton, Jr. *Woodrow Wilson: A Biography*. New York: Vintage, 2011.

Crawford, T. C. *An American Vendetta: A Story of Barbarism in the United States*. Edited by Eldean Wellman. Verdunville, WV: Eldean Wellman, 2004.

Cruciani, Fulvio, Roberta La Fratta, Beniamino Trombetta, Piero Santolamazza, Daniele Sellitto, Eliane Beraud Colomb, and Jean-Michel Dugoujon, et al. "Tracing Past Human Male Movements in Northern/Eastern Africa and Western Eurasia: New Clues from Y-Chromosomal Haplogroups E-M78 and J-M12." *Molecular Biology and Evolution* 24, no. 6 (June 2007): 1300–1311, DOI: 10.

Donnelly, Shirley. *The Hatfield-McCoy Feud Reader*. Parsons, WV: McClain, 1971.

Eller, Ronald. *Miners, Millhands, and Mountaineers*. Knoxville: University of Tennessee Press, 1982.

Fischer, David Hackett. *Albion's Seed: Four British Folkways in America*. New York: Oxford University Press, 1989.

Hatfield, Coleman C., and F. Keith Davis. *The Feuding Hatfields and McCoys*. Chapmanville, WV: Woodland Press, 2008.

Hatfield, Coleman C., and Robert Y. Spence. *The Tale of the Devil: The Biography of Devil Anse Hatfield*. Chapmanville, WV: Woodland Press, 2007.

Hatfield, G. Elliot. *The Hatfields*. Stanville, KY: Big Sandy Valley Historical Society, 1974.

Hatfield, L. D. *The True Story of the Hatfield and McCoy Feud.* LaVergne, TN: Kessinger Legacy Reprints, 1945.

Hatfield, Philip. *The Other Feud: William Anderson "Devil Anse" Hatfield in the Civil War.* Lexington, KY: Philip Hatfield, 2010.

Haun, Mildred. *The Hawk's Done Gone and Other Stories by Mildred Haun.* Edited by Herschel Gower. Nashville, TN: Vanderbilt University Press, 1968.

Jones, Virgil Carrington. *The Hatfields and the McCoys.* Chapel Hill: University of North Carolina Press, 1948.

Kessler, John S., Donald B. Ball, and N. Brent Kennedy. *North from the Mountains: A Folk History of the Carmel Melungeon Settlement, Highland County, Ohio.* Macon, GA: Mercer University Press, 2001.

Khamsi, Roxanne. "Genes Reveal West African Heritage of White Brits." NewScientist online, January 24, 2007, www.newscientist.com, DOI: 10.1038/ sj.ejhg.5201771.

MacCorkle, William A. *Recollections of Fifty Years of West Virginia.* New York: G. P. Putnam, 1928.

McCoy, Truda Williams. *The McCoys: Their Story as Told to the Author by Eye Witnesses and Descendants.* Pikeville, KY: Preservation Council Press, 1976.

Nisbett, Richard E., and Dov Cohen. *Culture of Honor: The Psychology of Honor in the South.* Boulder, CO: Westview Press, 1996.

Otterbein, Keith F. "Five Feuds: An Analysis of Homicides in Eastern Kentucky in the Late Nineteenth Century." *American Anthropologist* 102, no. 2 (June 2000): 231–43.

Pascal, Blaise. *Pensees.* New York: Penguin, 1995.

Pearce, John Ed. *Days of Darkness: The Feuds of Eastern Kentucky.* Lexington: University Press of Kentucky, 1994.

Pelusi, Nando. "Neanderthink: The Appeal of the Bad Boy." *Psychology Today,* January 1, 2009.

Platania, Joseph. "Men to Match the Mountains: Devil Anse Hatfield and Uncle Dyke Garrett." *Goldenseal* 10, no. 3: 26–32.

Reed, John Shelton. *One South: An Ethnic Approach to Regional Culture.* Baton Rouge: Louisiana State University Press, 1982.

Rice, Otis K. *The Hatfields and the McCoys.* Lexington: University Press of Kentucky, 1982.

Savage, Lon. *Thunder in the Mountains: The West Virginia Mine War 1920–21.* Pittsburgh: University of Pittsburgh Press, 1990.

Shah, Saira. *The Storyteller's Daughter.* New York: Alfred A. Knopf, 2003.

Shapiro, Henry D. *Appalachia on Our Mind: The Southern Mountains and Mountaineers in the American Consciousness, 1870–1920.* Chapel Hill: University of North Carolina Press, 1978.

Sharfstein, Daniel. *The Invisible Line: Three American Families and the Secret Journey from Black to White.* New York: Penguin, 2011.

Sutherland, Daniel E. *A Savage Conflict: The Decisive Role of Guerrillas in the American Civil War.* Chapel Hill: University of North Carolina Press, 2009.

Sutherland, Elihu Jasper. *Pioneer Recollections of Southwest Virginia.* Clintwood, VA: Mullins Printing, 1984.

Thompson, Edgar. "The Little Races." *American Anthropologist* 74, no. 5 (1972): 1295–1306.

Waller, Altina L. *Feud: Hatfields, McCoys, and Social Change in Appalachia, 1860–1900.* Chapel Hill: University of North Carolina Press, 1988.

Williams, John Alexander. *Appalachia: A History.* Chapel Hill: University of North Carolina Press, 2002.

Williams, John Alexander. *West Virginia: A History.* New York: W. W. Norton and Co., 1984.

Williamson, J. W. *Southern Mountaineers in Silent Films.* Jefferson, NC: McFarland and Co., Inc., 1994.

FILMS AND DVDs

Feud (DVD). Written and directed by Bill Richardson. Williamson, WV: Bill Richardson Productions, 1998.

The Hatfields and the McCoys. Written and directed by Clyde Ware. Los Angeles: Charles Fries Productions, 1974.

Hatfields and McCoys: An American Feud (DVD). New York: A&E Biography, 1996.

Matewan. Written and directed by John Sayles. New York: Cinecom Entertainment Group, 1987.

Mine Wars (DVD). Written and directed by Bill Richardson. Williamson, WV: Bill Richardson Productions, 2004.

Roseanna McCoy. Directed by Irving Reis. Los Angeles: Samuel Goldwyn, 1949.

Secrets of the Valley: Prehistory of the Kanawha (DVD). Written by Erika Celeste. Huntington, WV: Paradise Film Institute, 2010.

CDs

Hatfield-McCoy: Historic Feud Sites Audio Driving Tour. Produced by Randy Jones. East KY Broadcasting, 2005.

The Hatfields and the McCoys: The Great Vendetta. Composed and sung by Jimmy Wolford. Wolf Records, 1998.

Newspapers (various issues)

Atlanta Constitution

Big Sandy News (Louisa, KY)

Burlington (VT) *Free Press*

Cincinnati (OH) *Enquirer*

Courier-Journal (Louisville, KY)

Intelligencer (Wheeling, WV)

Kingsport (TN) *Times News*

New York Times

Pittsburgh Times

❧ Index ❧